The Use of Algorithms in Criminal Law

This edited collection provides the reader with a comprehensive knowledge of automated decision-making, artificial intelligence (AI), and algorithms, and how they can be used in criminal proceedings. Focusing on the experience in Central and Eastern European countries, the book offers a clear overview of the advantages and disadvantages of new technologies in criminal law.

After a primer on how AI can be used in law enforcement to enhance operational effectiveness and improve public safety, chapters offer a comprehensive look at the current status of the use of new technologies in the criminal law of the Central and Eastern European countries. When appropriate, contributors formulate concrete postulates for the change of the current legal regulations as well as offer advice on how to use such technologies to one's advantage or how to defend against their abuse by public authorities.

Navigating the intersection of technology and criminal justice, this book is invaluable for anyone with an interest in whether and how computers will shape the fate of criminal suspects and the operation of criminal justice systems. It is essential reading for scholars and students of comparative criminal justice, criminology, sociology, politics, and socio-legal studies.

Konrad Burdziak is attorney at law, assoc. prof., PhD in legal sciences (dr. habil.), certified suicidologist and a long-time employee of scientific and research institutions (University of Szczecin; Institute of Justice). He completed a three-month research internship at the University of Tallinn (Estonia), where he carried out a research project funded by the Polish National Science Centre, and a two-week query in the UK, where he carried out a research project funded by VisegradGrants. He is author or co-author of several dozen scientific publications (including eight scientific monographs) and more than 40 papers at national and international scientific conferences and participated in Polish and international research projects (e.g. Polish-Hungarian Research Platform or the Algorithms used in the field of criminal sciences project financed by VisegradGrants). He is an expert at the Centre for Advanced Research on Integrity, Rights and

Inclusion of the Child (Estonia). He specialises in criminal law, constitutional law, and theory and philosophy of law. He collaborates with specialists from Poland and abroad.

István Ambrus is an assoc. prof., PhD in legal sciences (dr. habil.) and a Hungarian lawyer specialising in criminal law and criminology. He currently serves as the head of the Department of Criminology at the Faculty of Law at Eötvös Loránd University (ELTE) in Budapest and is also a lecturer in the Department of Criminal Law at the same institution. In 2022, he was awarded the title of "Promising Researcher of ELTE" for his scientific achievements. His research focuses on the responses of criminal law to modern technological challenges, such as artificial intelligence and cybercrime. In 2021, he published a monograph titled "Digitalization and Criminal Law," summarising his research in this field. In addition to his academic work, István Ambrus actively participates in international research projects. In 2022–2023, he led a project titled "Algorithms used in the field of criminal sciences" funded by the Visegrad Fund. His dedication to studying the impact of modern technologies on criminal law makes him one of the leading experts in this field in Hungary.

Routledge Frontiers of Criminal Justice

Rational Anger
An International Comparison of Legal Systems
Stina Bergman Blix and Nina Törnqvist

The Quest for Reparations for Indian Residential School Abuse
Confronting the Legacy of the Independent Assessment Process
Konstantin Petoukhov

The Role of Food in Resettlement and Rehabilitation
Good Food and Good Lives
Edited by Julie Parsons and Kevin Wong

Overseeing Rights in Prison
The Irish Experience of Human Rights Protection in Prisons
Sophie van der Valk

Crime Prevention and Treatment Policies
A Biopsychosocial Approach
Anthony Walsh

Education in Youth Detention Homes
An Ethnographic Study of Schooling Against the Odds
David Wästerfors

The Use of Algorithms in Criminal Law
A Central European Perspective
Edited by Konrad Burdziak and István Ambrus

For more information about this series, please visit: www.routledge.com/Routledge-Frontiers-of-Criminal-Justice/book-series/RFCJ

The Use of Algorithms in Criminal Law

A Central European Perspective

Edited by Konrad Burdziak and István Ambrus

Routledge
Taylor & Francis Group
NEW YORK AND LONDON

First published 2026
by Routledge
605 Third Avenue, New York, NY 10158

and by Routledge
4 Park Square, Milton Park, Abingdon, Oxon, OX14 4RN

Routledge is an imprint of the Taylor & Francis Group, an informa business

ISBN: 9781032871837 (hbk)
ISBN: 9781032872186 (pbk)
ISBN: 9781003531500 (ebk)

DOI: 10.4324/9781003531500

Typeset in Sabon
by KnowledgeWorks Global Ltd.

Contents

Contributors

Assoc. prof. István Ambrus, PhD DSc

István Ambrus is a Hungarian lawyer specialising in criminal law and criminology. He currently serves as the head of the Department of Criminology at the Faculty of Law at Eötvös Loránd University (ELTE) in Budapest and is also a lecturer in the Department of Criminal Law at the same institution. In 2022, he was awarded the title of "Promising Researcher of ELTE" for his scientific achievements. His research focuses on the responses of criminal law to modern technological challenges, such as artificial intelligence and cybercrime. In 2021, he published a monograph titled "Digitalization and Criminal Law," summarising his research in this field. In addition to his academic work, István Ambrus actively participates in international research projects. In 2022–2023, he led a project titled "Algorithms Applied in the Field of Forensic Sciences," funded by the Visegrad Fund. His dedication to studying the impact of modern technologies on criminal law makes him one of the leading experts in this field in Hungary.

Assoc. prof. JUDr. Radovan Blažek, PhD

SCOPUS: 57200332785

Blažek graduated at the Faculty of Law of the Comenius University in Bratislava (2005), where he also completed a PhD in criminal law (2008) and received the title of associate professor (2019). He also completed his studies at the Institute of International Relations of Comenius University, Faculty of Law (2007). He currently works at the Department of Criminal Law, Criminology and Criminalistics focusing on procedural criminal law and criminalistics. He is the author of several scientific publications and regularly participates on international and domestic scientific conferences. During his professional career, he completed several educational stays abroad (Belgium, Canada, Lithuania, Latvia, Luxembourg, Germany, Poland, Portugal, Austria, Russia, Italy, and Spain) focused on criminal law and European affairs. He also completed a five-month internship in the German parliament (2009). From September 2015 he also worked at the Malacky District Prosecutor's Office, from June 15 to December 15, 2023 at the Bratislava Regional Prosecutor's Office, international department, from December 16, 2023 to June 15, 2024 he worked at the General Prosecutor's Office, department of legislation and constitutional law. In 2022, he completed a six-month internship at the European Court of Human Rights in Strasbourg. In total, he was the researcher of ten national projects of APVV, VEGA, and KEGA and another two international projects and he is currently principal researcher of project APVV – "Optimizing the sanctioning mechanism in the area of environmental protection and increasing its efficiency" started on July 1, 2024.

Assoc. prof. JUDr. Lukáš Bohuslav, PhD

SCOPUS: 58651754700

Bohuslav graduated at the Faculty of Law of Charles University (2009), where he also completed a PhD in criminal law (2013) and received the title of associate professor (2023; Plea Bargain). He currently works at the Department of Criminal Law, Criminology and Criminalistics focusing on substantive and procedural criminal law and criminalistics. He is the author of dozens of topics and textbooks and two monographs (Criminal Corporate Liability and Plea Bargain). He completed educational stays abroad (Belgium, Spain, Switzerland, the US, and the UK). He has been a member of more than ten grants at the Faculty of Law (CUNI), National Recovery Plan or V4 Grant. He is attorney at law, Member of the Criminal Law Commission of the Legislative Council of the Government, Member of the Working Group on Criminal Policy (Ministry of Justice of the Czech Republic), Member of the CBA Legal Privilege Committee, Member of the Union of Advocates and its Arbitration Committee. He is a member of the editorial board of the journal Criminal Law (Czech Republic), Acta Facultatis Iuridicae Universitatis Comenianae (Slovakia). He is a prospective evaluator of Czech research, development, and innovation.

Assoc. prof. Konrad Burdziak, PhD DSc

Burdziak is attorney at law, PhD, DSc in legal sciences (dr. habil.), certified suicidologist, and a long-time employee of scientific and research institutions (University of Szczecin; Institute of Justice), he completed a three-month research internship at the University of Tallinn (Estonia), where he carried out a research project funded by the Polish National Science Centre, and a two-week query in the UK, where he carried out a research project funded by VisegradGrants. He is author or co-author of several dozen scientific publications (including eight scientific monographs) and more than 40 papers at national and international scientific conferences and participated in Polish and international research projects (e.g. Polish-Hungarian Research Platform or the Algorithms used in the field of criminal sciences project financed by VisegradGrants). He is an expert at the Centre for Advanced Research on Integrity, Rights and Inclusion of the Child (Estonia), an expert-consultant at the meetings of the European Institute for Gender Equality (EU), former member of the Interdisciplinary Team for Prevention of Suicidal Behaviour (Poland); former member of the Team and Working Group for the Implementation of the International Classification of Crime for Statistical Purposes into the Polish System of Public Statistics, which is an auxiliary body of the Polish Council of Ministers. He is a graduate of the 21st Specialization Course in International Criminal Law for Young Penalists (organised by the Siracusa International Institute for Criminal Justice and Human Rights in cooperation with the International Association of Penal Law, the Irish Centre for Human Rights, the National University of Ireland Galway, the Middlesex University Department of Law). He specialises in criminal law, constitutional law, and theory and philosophy of law. He collaborates with specialists from Poland and abroad.

JUDr. Radka Čihulková

Radka Čihulková graduated from the Faculty of Law, Charles University in Prague (2024), where she also obtained her JUDr. degree in criminal law (2024) and is currently pursuing a PhD in the same field. In 2022, she completed the Diploma in English Law and Legal Skills at the British Law Centre, affiliated with the University of Cambridge, Faculty of Law. She is currently working at Bříza & Trubač, s.r.o., attorneys at law, specialising in economic crime, with a particular focus on tax offenses from the perspective of the defense. Her research interests include criminal law and forensic sciences, and she has authored several scholarly publications in both international and domestic academic journals. During her studies, she has been actively involved in research projects in the field of criminal law, including the SVV project "Criminal Procedure Code de lege lata and de lege ferenda in the constitutional law context" and "Electronic Evidence in Criminal Proceedings."

Professor Melissa Hamilton, JD, PhD

Professor Hamilton is a Professor of Law & Criminal Justice at the University of Surrey and an AI Fellow with the Surrey Institute for People-Centred AI. She earned a Juris Doctorate in Law and PhD in Criminology. Prof. Hamilton holds memberships in the American Psychological Association, Royal Statistical Society, Association of Threat Assessment

Professionals, International Corrections and Prisons Association, and the State Bar of Texas. Research interests include the application of data sciences, forensic sciences, and AI technologies to informing relevant legal issues and improving criminal justice practices. She has served as an expert witness in the US and the UK in civil and criminal cases and in class action lawsuits on various criminal justice issues.

Dr. jur. Máté Hodula

Hodula graduated at the Faculty of Law of the Eötvös Loránd University in Budapest with summa cum laude (2018), where he also started a PhD in criminal law (2020). He was also a member of the Bibó István College for Advanced Studies during his university years, later as an assistant teacher until 2022. Currently he is a PhD student at the Department of Criminal Law at the Eötvös Loránd University, where he is expected to finish his studies in 2025. His supervisor is dr. habil. István Ambrus, PhD. After graduating, he worked at the Hungarian Helsinki Committee, then as an attorney at the Kemenes Law Firm in Budapest. He completed his bar exam in 2023.

Assoc. prof. Noémi Komporday-Orosz, PhD

Noémi Komporday-Orosz is a Hungarian legal scholar specialising in criminal law. She serves as an assistant professor at the Department of Criminal Law at Eötvös Loránd University (ELTE) Faculty of Law in Budapest. Additionally, she holds the position of judge at the Pest Central District Court, focusing on criminal cases, including those involving juveniles.

Assoc. prof. JUDr. hab. Magdalena Kowalewska-Łukuć, PhD

Kowalewska-Łukuć graduated at the Faculty of Law of the Adam Mickiewicz University in Poznan (2011), where she also completed a PhD in criminal law (2014). She also completed her master studies at the Institute of Psychology on Adam Mickiewicz University, Faculty of Social Sciences (2011). She currently works at Faculty of Law and Administration on University of Szczecin focusing on substantial criminal law and criminology. She is the author of several scientific publications and regularly participates on international and domestic scientific conferences. In 2023 she received postdoctoral degree (doctor habilitatus) in legal sciences.

Assoc. prof. Kitti Mezei, PhD

Kitti Mezei is a Hungarian lawyer specialising in criminal law, cybercrime, and the impact of new technologies on legal systems. She currently serves as an assistant professor at the Institute for Legal Studies of the Hungarian Centre for Social Sciences (TK JTI). **Research Interests:** Criminal law and disruptive technologies, Cybercrime, Economic criminal law.

JUDr. Lenka Miklóssyová

Miklóssyová completed her bachelor's degree in the combined program of "Economics and Law" at the Faculty of National Economy of the University of Economics in Bratislava and the Faculty of Law of Comenius University in Bratislava ("FLAW UK") in 2019. She continued her studies at the master's level in "Law" at FLAW UK, graduating with honors in 2021. Currently, she serves as a doctoral candidate at the Department of Criminal Law, Criminology, and Criminalistics at FLAW UK and as a specialist staff member in the project "Chance to Return" under the General Directorate of the Prison and Judicial Guard Corps of the Slovak Republic. Her professional focus is primarily on drug-related criminal activity, recidivism among offenders, and the efficiency of criminal proceedings. During her time at the faculty, she has been actively involved in teaching criminal procedural law and other, mainly practical subjects within clinical legal education.

Daniel Oborák

He is a law graduate currently studying PhD programme at the Department of Criminal Law, Faculty of Law, Charles University. His doctoral research is primarily focused on cybercrime, specifically the issue of cybergrooming of children, due to his primary interest in the technological aspects of criminal law and criminal investigation in his academic career. He has published an article on the criminal investigation methodology of cybergrooming, in which he focused on the use of modern technologies during the criminal investigation process. Additionally, he has been conducting research on the utilisation of artificial intelligence in criminal proceedings and crime prevention.

Dominika Skoczylas, PhD

Graduate of the Faculty of Law and Administration at the University of Szczecin (2016). In 2021, she obtained her doctoral degree in the field of social sciences in the discipline of legal sciences on the basis of the defence of her dissertation entitled "National cybersecurity system." She is currently an assistant professor at the Faculty of Law and Administration of the University of Szczecin and a member of the Research Team of Administrative Law of New Technologies and Space Law at the Faculty of Law and Administration of the University of Szczecin. She specialises primarily in administrative law and new technology law. She is the author of numerous publications on cybersecurity, electronic communications law, artificial intelligence, new technologies, administrative law and space law, including the author of a scientific monograph, entitled "National cybersecurity system" and participant of Staff mobility for teaching (STA, programme Erasmus+) in Universita Degli Studi Di Foggia, Italy, topic: "Cybersecurity as a determinant of global socio-economic development – a legal and social perspective" (2022) and in Univerza v Mariboru, Slovenia, topic: "Digital transformation in the age of cyberpandemics, cyberwar and cyberthreats. Legal and technological conditions for ensuring a high common level of cybersecurity in the European Union and beyond" (2023).

Ass. prof. JUDr. Lucia Vasilik, PhD

Vasilik graduated from the Faculty of Law of the Comenius University in Bratislava in 2015. In 2024 she successfully completed her doctoral studies in criminal law at the Department of Criminal Law, Criminology and Criminalistics, Faculty of Law of the Comenius University in Bratislava, where she currently works as an assistant professor and teaches courses in criminal procedural law and criminalistics and carries out scientific research. Since December 2022 she has been working at the General Directorate of the Corps of Prison and Court Guard in the section of the National Project Chance for Reentry. In her publications, she mainly deals with the following topics: effectiveness of criminal proceedings, crime prevention, artificial intelligence, restorative justice, resocialisation of convicts, and actively participates in and co-organises domestic and international scientific conferences.

Part I

Foreword

Foreword

Konrad Burdziak and István Ambrus

Modern technologies are entering our lives in a significant manner. Mobile phones, computers, and the Internet are a permanent part of our everyday life, regardless of our age or profession. We encounter them throughout the day, sometimes even in a way that we are not fully aware of (see, e.g., facial recognition systems based on artificial intelligence (AI) or advertisements adapted to our preferences based on constant listening to us).

Modern technologies have also become an everyday reality and an excellent tool not only for law-abiding citizens but (unfortunately) also for perpetrators of crimes. Computer fraud and forgery, grooming, hacking, cyberstalking, skimming – these are just examples of crimes that law enforcement agencies must fight today, and for which modern technologies, especially the Internet, are used.

It is no wonder, considering the above, that modern technologies are also starting to be used in counteracting crime, including in the justice system. Although new technologies are not entering the scene of combatting crime quickly enough and are not used widely, more and more often we see the use of, among others, algorithm-based tools in the legal systems of various countries, which objectify, simplify, and accelerate the decision-making process, while reducing costs in this regard. According to international literature, today it is no longer about whether algorithms and tools based on them are present in law enforcement, but about: (1) to what extent decisions in criminal law can be automated; (2) to what extent the results of using algorithm-based tools can be used in criminal law; (3) what are the advantages and disadvantages of automating criminal law?

In the scope of criminal law, the use of algorithms can be extremely helpful, for example in the context of the issue of conditional early release of a convict from serving the rest of the prison sentence or, in other words, in the context of a situation in which after the convict has served part of the sentence, the court decides to release them from penal institution. Currently, in Central European countries, tools using modern technologies are not used, even though such tools can provide an objective and extremely

DOI: 10.4324/9781003531500-2

detailed assessment of the convict and their potential risk of relapse to crime. As a result, court decisions are often poorly justified (this is the conclusion from the research conducted by K. Burdziak et al. in Poland[1]) and may raise doubts from the perspective of the need to ensure the safety of society. Tools of this type are successfully used in other countries, including Great Britain, where the OASys system, i.e. Offender Assessment System, operates, and at the same time – as R. Moore points out – "A separate tool is used for young offenders aged 10–17 known as Asset (Baker, 2004; Wilson and Hinks, 2011), while other tools are used for specific types of offending, e.g., Risk Matrix 2000 (RM2000) for sexual offending (Thornton, 2007) and the Spousal Assault Risk Assessment Guide (SARA) for domestic violence (Kropp et al., 1995). For adult offenders who are not assessed through OASys, a second generation tool is available – the Offender Group Recon – viction Scale v.3 (OGRS3). This tool predicts proven reoffending with one and two years using age at sentence, gender, number of previous sanctions, age at first sanction and current offence (Howard et al., 2009)".[2]

This monograph focuses on the analysis of the possibilities of using tools based on algorithms and AI in the countries of Central and Eastern Europe and presents the results of the findings of researchers involved in the research project financed by Visegrad Grants, Visegrad Fund, entitled Algorithms used in the field of criminal sciences. The presented results of the findings of researchers from four countries (Poland, Hungary, the Czech Republic, and Slovakia) are crucial from the perspective of the mentioned region due to the fact that new technologies have not been used there even to a small extent. All chapters that make up this monograph present, on the one hand, a concise description of the legal systems in force in Poland, Hungary, the Czech Republic, and Slovakia, their needs and systemic gaps in the criminal law in a broad sense, and on the other hand, they present specific possibilities of using individual tools in a way that allows for increasing the effectiveness of law enforcement agencies and the justice system. However, individual authors do not limit themselves to analysing practical issues, as most chapters also contain findings of a highly abstract nature, strictly theoretical in nature, which can also be used by those interested outside the region of the interest of this monograph.

The monograph covers basically all key issues from the perspective of countries considering introducing algorithm-based tools into their legal systems. For example, Konrad Burdziak, in his text, analyses the possibility or lack thereof of autonomous and uncontrolled by human decision-making by algorithm-based tools during sentencing in criminal proceedings, analysing the above from the perspective of fundamental human freedoms and rights, including the right to fair treatment and, above all, dignity. In the author's opinion, the use of algorithms and tools based on them can bring many benefits, including in particular reducing political pressure on law enforcement bodies and minimising the risk of transferring political sympathies to decisions made in criminal cases. This is particularly relevant in Poland and – as it seems – in other "young" democracies, in which the temptation to bother a person with different political views, even if not realised by the people involved in criminal proceedings (including judges), can be very high. Conversely, giving algorithm-based tools the freedom to make decisions on criminal law issues (even trivial ones) can lead to extremely tragic consequences.

Mate Hodula examines the issue of criminal liability for the malfunctioning of algorithm- and AI-based tools, indicating that liability for the "actions" of AI will become an increasingly pressing issue in the near future. Although the indicated author considers a certain degree of fragmentation of judgments in upcoming criminal proceedings as a real and inevitable possibility, it is extremely important to summarise the basic doctrinal principles so a "responsibility limbo" can be avoided. Referring to the findings of Istvan Ambrus, M. Hodula states, among other things, that when it comes to the mens rea element behind the actions regulated by algorithms, it can be divided into direct liability, latent liability (where a latent offender is a person who incites the commission of an intentional crime, using a person who cannot be prosecuted due to being underage or insane, due to acting under the unlawful influence of coercion or coercion or mistaken belief), criminal liability similar for senior officers and management staff, and liability for breaching the duty of care. The autonomy of the algorithm and the complexity of the problem are directly proportional – the more an individual influences its operation, the easier it is to establish responsibility for their actions.

Daniel Oborak examines the use of algorithms in the automation of criminal proceedings, with a special focus on the decision-making process. The author presents a critical perspective on the integration of computer-driven algorithms into the decision-making process, proposing that the human factor, based on the recognition of personal experiences rather than a purely statistical approach, is a fundamental pillar of the criminal justice system. The author identifies the main challenges associated with the use of contemporary AI tools in criminal proceedings worldwide. This is illustrated by a case study of the risk assessment tool "COMPAS", which has been adopted by many jurisdictions in the US to estimate the risk of relapsing to crime for a given defendant, and assumes that these tools face a serious challenge due to the ambiguity of the algorithmic process. In addition, the author addresses the issue of the potential amplification of bias by software tools. This can occur when statistically significant discriminatory elements from previous decisions are treated by the algorithm uncritically, as if they were a regular part of the given data set. Finally, the author addresses the potential use of algorithmic decision-making in the context of Czech criminal law, given that it has not yet been implemented in any form in Czech criminal proceedings.

Radka Cihulkova points out that the development and application of algorithms are a promising way to increase the efficiency and reliability of collecting, analysing and presenting electronic evidence in criminal investigations. As she points out, although law enforcement agencies have been working with electronic evidence for a relatively long time, many practical challenges related to the use of electronic evidence can still be identified. The chapter by the indicated author sheds light on the definition and legal regulations of securing electronic evidence, mainly, but not only, in the Czech Republic, the methods of securing electronic evidence in practice and the method of accessing digital data. The author points out the difficulties and threats related to the current methods of securing electronic evidence, consisting in the possibility of changing or destroying electronic evidence and ensuring its integrity during criminal proceedings. Simultaneously, these threats often reduce the evidentiary value of electronic evidence and facilitate its questioning. And it is precisely these threats that could be eliminated by the use of algorithms in securing electronic evidence. The main goal of this chapter is, in the author's assumption, to describe potentially useful algorithms for securing electronic evidence and to propose possible solutions by using algorithms in proceedings in order to obtain evidence that is lawful and justified.

Radovan Blazek discusses the possibility of using AI and algorithms in criminal proceedings in Slovakia based on good examples from other countries. The chapter first presents the roots and sources of algorithms in criminal proceedings around the world. Then the author analyses individual parts of criminal proceedings in Slovakia and describes possible tools, means and stages of criminal proceedings, where algorithms could be suitable. Finally, possible shortcuts and problems that may arise when introducing algorithms into criminal proceedings in Slovakia are also analysed.

Dominka Skoczylas draws attention to the context of cybersecurity of systems based on algorithms and AI. The chapter presents arguments and counterarguments for the use of AI algorithms on a macro scale. The aspect of cybersecurity requires discussion, because, on the one hand, algorithms can be useful, but, on the other hand, they can disrupt the proper functioning of networks and ICT systems. Due to the application of the EU Act on AI and the national cybersecurity system, the discussed issues were analysed in the context of opportunities and challenges for the socio-economic development of Poland. The author also asked another question, namely whether algorithms can contribute to the increase in cyber threats, considering that they can have a significant impact on the number and effectiveness of cyberattacks, which negatively affects socio-economic development.

Lucia Vasilik, in turn, draws attention to the risk assessment tools developed in the Slovak Republic by the Prison and Court Guard Corps, indicating that they have been digitalised, but are not yet supported by AI systems. According to the author, this situation persists for several reasons. The first is the lack of technological support in the conditions of the Zbor väzenskej a justičnej stráže (ZVJS). The second is the problematic provisions of the General Data Protection Regulation(GDPR) and the Police Directive in the area of protecting the fundamental rights of data subjects in relation to the use of automated systems for making individual decisions and protecting personal data. However, this topic remains open for the future, especially in the context of increasing the efficiency and accuracy of individual predictions generated by the tools. However, according to Lucia Vasilik, any introduction of AI must take place only after due consideration, testing, and verification of the reliability and impartiality of the AI system. According to the author, even in such a case, individual predictions in the field of imprisonment should not be left exclusively to AI, but must be under the control and interaction of human evaluators.

As shown above, the thematic scope of the monograph is very broad, and the topics discussed have not yet found in-depth development in the literature on the subject. The authors therefore hope that everyone will find something for themselves here, and the monograph itself will be an important voice in the global debate on algorithms and AI and their use in the legal systems of individual countries.

Notes

1 BURDZIAK, Konrad, NIKOŁAJEW, Jerzy, JANKOWSKI, Michał, KOWALEWSKA-ŁUKUĆ, Magdalena. Diagnostyka sądowo-kryminalna w orzekaniu i wykonywaniu warunkowego przedterminowego zwolnienia w teorii i praktyce sądowej – raport z badania, Prawo w Działaniu, 39, 2019. https://doi.org/10.32041/pwd.3901, pp. 9–68.

2 MOORE, Robin. The Offender Assessment System (OASys) and the 2009–2013 research projects. In: MOORE, Robin (ed.). A compendium of research and analysis on the Offender Assessment System (OASys) 2009–2013, Ministry of Justice Analytical Series 2015, https://assets.publishing.service.gov.uk/government/uploads/system/uploads/attachment_data/file/449357/research-analysis-offender-assessment-system.pdf, p. 2 (accessed 6 November 24).

Part II

Introduction

Violence risk assessment algorithms in criminal justice

Melissa Hamilton

0.1 Introduction

Algorithmic risk assessment is now firmly embedded within the criminal justice system.[1] Predictions of which individuals are likely to commit violent offenses are driving decisions from police making arrests to judges in sentencing and then on the back-end release on parole.[2] These decisions have significant consequences to the individuals who may be incarcerated and for long periods as a result. Preventing harm to the public is likewise of interest.

It is important for algorithmic justice to be meted out competently and fairly.[3] While risk assessment algorithms continue to be improved, there are many aspects of the process that are not adequately addressed. This essay will explore the field in terms of various dimensions of the risk of violence: probability, type of harm, severity, imminence, frequency, duration, and setting. Artificial intelligence (AI) presents as a promising avenue to deepen the risk assessment work into those dimensions. To set the stage, next is a summary of the violence risk algorithm scheme in criminal justice.

0.2 Background to violence risk algorithms

Risk assessment has long been a part of criminal justice decision-making because of a legitimate goal of protecting the public while most efficiently using scarce resources.[4] At its basic level, risk assessment in criminal justice is about predicting the potential to offend in the future.[5] Historically, risk predictions were generally based on the gut instinct or personal perception of the official responsible for making the relevant decision.[6] A recognized flaw in such a practice is that human estimates of risk are replete with explicit and implicit biases.[7] Risk estimates by humans (e.g., judges and probation officers) are prone to significant error rates.[8] Officials have therefore sought to replace human judgments with risk assessment tools that quantitatively evaluate risk.[9]

DOI: 10.4324/9781003531500-4

More specifically, contemporary risk tools use algorithms to sort individuals into categories based on their likelihood for failure.[10] An algorithm is simply an equation in which inputs are received and processed to produce a quantitatively derived output.[11] Regarding risk assessment, the inputs are predictors and the output is the estimated likelihood of reoffending. This new wave of algorithmic risk assessment is part of the evidence-based practices movement that relies upon science to identify strong predictors of offending (i.e., the inputs).[12] The evidence base here refers to scientific studies that track offenders to statistically identify factors which correlate with recidivism.[13]

In the more traditional model, tool developers package the correlated factors and weight them according to their predictive strength, which then becomes the algorithm.[14] Common predictive factors with heavier weights are criminal history, age, and educational attainment. The tools tend to output summary scores based on their algorithms. In turn, the scores are often combined into a small number of groupings to form ordinal buckets, often with terminologies applied such as low, medium, and high risk.[15]

Overall, this ideology of algorithmic justice is trending in the criminal legal system as a means to be smarter on crime.[16] Proponents cite to a variety of benefits from the algorithmic risk era in criminal justice. Broadly speaking, "[d]ata-driven algorithmic decision making may enhance overall government efficiency and public service delivery, by optimizing bureaucratic processes, providing real-time feedback and predicting outcomes."[17] The algorithmic risk assessment model presents as a transparent, consistent, and logical method of classification.[18] The mathematical character of risk assessment suggests the ability to quantify the future and transport it into the present.[19]

With an algorithmic tool in hand, criminal justice officials can more consistently input relevant data and receive software-produced risk classifications.[20] This form of algorithmic justice and governance[21] has become popular for driving how officials triage their populations to manage them accordingly.[22] Algorithmic risk assessments inform decisions about custodial release, sentencing, institutional placements, supervision levels, and programming assignments.[23] Indeed, risk assessment can follow an individual at various stages in their life span through the criminal justice system.[24]

Risk tools are often compared as superior to the human predictions they are meant to replace.[25] The risk algorithms are lauded for reducing the arbitrariness of,[26] and errors produced by, subjective human judgments.[27] Predictions by mortals may vary for reasons that computer programs do not, such as by simply being tired, hungry, or distracted.[28] Algorithmic risk prediction is also thought to exceed a human brain's ability to efficiently and rationally process numerous data points simultaneously.[29] Algorithmic modeling is just better at identifying personal and social correlations within individuals and across people that pertain to human behavior.[30]

Algorithmic tools are perceived as reducing the potential for more blatant human corruption.[31] Humans can disregard rules through creative machinations while algorithms (unless driven by unsupervised machine learning techniques) cannot reject any strict rules embedded therein.[32] Moreover, algorithms may produce more just and fair outcomes in terms of sociodemographic circumstances.[33] Accordingly, "[v]endors promote these models to the public and to the agencies that use them as the answer to human bias, arguing that computers cannot harbor personal animus or individual prejudice based on race, gender, or any other legally protected characteristic."[34]

As the twenty-first century moves forward, the potential for meaningful innovations offered by AI is infiltrating algorithmic risk tools. AI-driven processes can find elaborate patterns in behavior that tool developers who are human may not be capable of cognitively detecting.[35] AI can even illuminate predictive factors that are atheoretical or otherwise appear counterintuitive.[36] It could be, for example, that committing more serious crimes such as homicide may not correlate with a higher risk of serious reoffending. Given sufficient data and computing capacity, AI can create predictive algorithms with greater complexity and power.[37] This new form of computational criminology "is an interdisciplinary science that uses computational methods and computer models to improve understanding of non-obvious connections and complex problems, and to develop effective solutions in the field of criminal justice."[38] Machine learning advantages include combining predictive factors synergistically in unique ways.[39] Machine learning could detect nonlinear relationships and intricate interactions between variables.[40] Then when AI is fed new data and allowed to recalibrate its forecasting methods accordingly likely increases in accuracy rates will follow.[41]

The background just given applies to risk assessment in criminal justice regarding any type of reoffending. This article is more specifically interested in algorithmic tools that assess violent offending. Policymakers, stakeholders, and the public often express a heightened fear and revulsion toward violent crime.[42] Dozens of algorithmic risk assessment tools that are designed to focus on violent recidivism are now available.[43] Yet these tools are far from perfect. The next section discusses issues and concerns that policymakers, practitioners, and developers ought to further consider to potentially overhaul the violence risk algorithmic scheme to better suit the needs for which the tools are intended to serve.

0.3 The dimensions of violence risk

Algorithmic tools for the risk of violence are heterogeneous. The tools vary in the developmental methodologies deployed in their creation, intended population on which they are designed to be used, setting in which to be deployed, policy purpose meant to serve, conceptualization of what violence exactly entails, and defining attributes of risk.[44] Thus, a best practice is to apply a risk tool that is most suitable to the intended population and the goals to be achieved.[45] In other words, a legal question to be addressed is whether the tool is fit for purpose in terms of providing risk information that is most relevant to the legal question at issue.

Several examples of the idea of fitness set the stage. If the question is in sentencing as to whether to assign a life sentence, whether *de jure* or a *de facto* (i.e., a prison term exceeding the individual's natural lifespan), a tool may not appear very informative if it commingles predictions of very minor offending (e.g., low level threat) with extreme crimes (e.g., murder) – meaning the tool cannot differentiate whether the estimated outcome such as high risk is prone toward predicting the low level threat. A tool that predicts violent acts decades into the future might not be a good fit when the context is deciding if the individual should be released pretrial and therefore the temporal interest is of a more immediate risk. If the interest is in selectively assigning significant rehabilitative resources to those likely to repeatedly commit violent acts if released, a tool might not be suitable if it cannot differentiate the persistent transgressor from the single act offender.

As a further illustration, if the purpose for adopting a tool is to assist in assigning a new prisoner to the most appropriate security classification in a penal institution, then presumably a significant interest is their risk of violence within prison as opposed to violence in the community. These may not be synonymous as there are context and environmental factors that differ between institutionalization and freedom. Thus, a tool that was only developed for individuals free in the community could be a poor fit for the suggested in-prison security classification question.

Another issue of fitness regards the legal threshold of proof. If the relevant threshold, for instance, is a balance of probabilities, then a violence risk tool is arguably not well befitting the task if the tool is unable to isolate to a group with a more than 50% chance of violently reoffending.

This section explores these and related dimensions of risk that are pertinent to selecting and implementing an algorithmic risk tool within a criminal law regime. In scientific terms, the subject is how to operationalize the concepts of risk and recidivism. Possible dimensions discussed herein include probability, type of harm, severity, imminence, frequency, duration, and setting. Most violence risk tools to date, and the underlying risk assessment literature, provide little to no information on many of these features of risk.[46] The result is that the tools arguably are over- or underestimating the risk of the outcome that is of greatest interest to the decisionmakers and stakeholders. Even so, encouraging advancements from the deployment of AI into risk tool development offer hope in expending into these domains to progress the algorithmic risk regime to better meet the needs of criminal law.

0.3.1 *Probability*

Risk assessment is generally not meant to be a dichotomous exercise (i.e., yes/no) in terms of determining whether a person will or will not violently reoffend. Instead, a common communication method is a proportional estimate of the likelihood of a new violent offence (theoretically ranging from 0% to 100%).[47] A popular violence risk tool (VRAG-R) as an illustration exhibits nine different risk groupings with associated violent recidivism rates for a five-year follow-up period ranging from 9% to 76%.[48]

Most violence risk assessment algorithms in use today offer a proportional statistic with its outcome. AI designs are not necessarily essential to create models that produce probability estimates. Still, it is conceivable that AI could improve upon the estimates' accuracy and within a narrower confidence interval indicating the estimated value's relative stability.[49] Promising work has begun with evidence that machine learning outperforms non-AI models in estimating the proportional likelihood of groups for violent reoffending.[50]

The proportional statistic may be helpful to the decisionmaker to get some sense of the magnitude of likelihood for violence. For many decisions, a further connection to the criminal law is between probability and the relevant standard of proof for the legal question at issue. Substantive criminal procedure rules may dictate the threshold of evidence required to justify a legal outcome. The "more likely than not" standard, or called "balance of probabilities" in some jurisdictions, is often applicable (e.g., pretrial or parole release). Where the consequences are greater, such as whether to detain a defendant pretrial based on a threat to the community, the law may apply a "clear and convincing" evidence standard.[51] The typical trial standard is "proof beyond a reasonable doubt." The relevant numerical predictive probability along with each such standard of proof is posited in Figure 0.1.[52]

The more likely than not threshold arguably is equivalent to a greater than 50% likelihood of reoffending. The clear and convincing standard is greater, such as at the 75% level. Proof beyond a reasonable doubt is stronger still with a suggestion of 90%.

Standard of Proof	*Probability Threshold*
More likely than not	> 50%
Clear and convincing	75%
Proof beyond a reasonable doubt	90%

Figure 0.1 Probability Table with Standards of Proof

A statistician would likely muddy the waters with such a simplistic perspective, arguing that probability estimates are error laden. It is more appropriate – statistically speaking – to consider confidence intervals to account for such errors.[53] With a typical 95% confidence interval, this would require that the lower end of the interval meets or exceeds the relevant probability threshold at any given standard of proof.[54] Assume a probability estimate of 54% with a confidence interval from 48% to 60%. This would not meet the more likely than not burden of proof as the low end of 48% does not exceed the requisite 50% bar.

These linkages between probability and the standard of proof are to date largely theoretical. There is a little evidence that they have been applied in real-world settings. One reason is that the standards of proof are often more generic. The preponderance and the clear and convincing standards most typically orient toward whether to accept prior objective "facts" offered. Arguably, it is difficult to conceive of risk assessment outcomes in the same factual sense given that they entail predictions of *future* behavior, the criminal law assumes individuals have free will, and the algorithms are not claimed to be causal in nature. It is also the case that the beyond a reasonable doubt baseline may rarely be applicable as there is no real suggestion that algorithmic risk should play an important role in the adjudicative stage of a criminal trial. Still, the pairings are offered here as a potential means to more systematically and concretely drive the use of algorithmic outcomes in terms of the decisions they serve.

0.3.2 *Type of harm*

In criminal law, offending is often categorized into various types, such as those involving violent crime, property crime, fraud, environmental crime, or public order offenses. This Article has already circumscribed the idea of type of harm by expressly centering on violence. A simplistic view would be that, having chosen violence as the outcome predicted, nothing further needs to be said on this aspect of risk.

Actually, the concept of "violence" is indeterminate. Violence constitutes a broad abstraction in itself due to its heterogeneity.[55] Violent crimes are further disjointed with invariant definitions across jurisdictions.[56] Accordingly, the idea of violence in the algorithmic risk world is indefinite and leads to open questions that have yet to be resolved or to achieve any form of consensus in the forensic science world or in criminal law.

Some jurisdictions include in their category of violence a number of crimes that others would not necessarily associate with actual violent behavior, such as the possession of a gun or other weapon.[57] Carrying a firearm or weapon, even where it is illegal, is not necessarily indicative of a proactive intention to use it against another person or to commit a crime.

The carrier may be transporting the item to engage in target practice, to hunt game, or to deliver it to a shop for cleaning or repair. Even if the possession by itself constitutes a criminal offense in the relevant jurisdiction, it could be that the carrier lives in, or travels through, crime-ridden areas where self-defensive actions might suddenly feel needed to save one's life if aggressively attacked. Is it clear that this should be defined as a violent offense simply by virtue of the possession without use or threat?

This leads to another relevant question: Is violence as the predicted outcome to be conceptualized only in terms of *criminal* acts of violence? Or does violence for purposes of an algorithmic risk tool include lawful acts that threaten or cause physical harm to others, such as legitimate uses of force (policemaking a valid arrest, acting in self-defense, physically disciplining a child-in jurisdictions where legal), contact sports, medical procedures involving bodily contact, or accidents causing physical harm to others?[58]

Parsing these categories is not merely a theoretical exercise. One study evaluating multiple scales from two popular violence risk tools found their predictive performances varied when researchers separately looked at (a) physical violence, (b) threatening behavior, (c) criminal violence (which could include acts within the physical violence category), and (d) all violence (a composite of the prior three).[59] In most of the scales, though not all, the most accurate performances were with the criminal violence subgrouping.

Violence is an act of aggression, but aggression does not always threaten physical harm to another human.[60] In that respect then, should violence include all forms of aggression whether involving physical, emotional, or psychological harms?[61] Some commentators would answer in the affirmative, conceiving violence as "acts that cause or have the potential to cause bodily harm" and in turn defining bodily harm to mean "physical or psychological (mental, emotional, or social) harm that is more than incidental or fleeting."[62] Acts would thereby be included if they happened to cause another such anguish regardless of the offender's mental state (e.g., purpose, knowing, or recklessness) with respect to such harm. This yields a wider scope in the types of offenses that would be swept up into the idea of violence. Consider the potential psychological impacts to victims of fraud, theft, vandalism, indecent exposure, lewd phone calls, harassment, or environmental crimes. Without diminishing that victims of these offenses can suffer long-term emotional consequences, the potential result expands the concept violence itself dramatically. The expansion also increases the numbers, from violence counted as a rather rare event to a much larger multiple. Without a proper adjustment, the risk tool would then assign a greater number of individuals to the high-risk category, which has repercussions to the triaging process and assignment of scare resources (e.g., prison beds, rehabilitative programs).

A conceptualization might assume all sex offenses to qualify as violent crimes. This would mean including statutory rape (sexual acts that are otherwise consensual but for a criminal law distinction based on the relative age difference of the parties) and prostitution-based crimes that do not include a clear element of coercion or force.[63] This assumption could be overinclusive as well by including non-contact crimes, such as indecent exposure, voyeurism (e.g., peeping tom-type offending), or downloading indecent images of children,

Expanding further, a number of criminal law jurisdictions merge certain property offenses expressly into their definition of violence. In the United States, statutes exist that define a "crime of violence" to include "physical force against the person *or property* of another."[64] In those cases, a violent offense might include a rather insignificant amount of damage done to a trivial object and without requiring there exist even a minimal risk of bodily injury. Behavior directed at property, but that has the potential to harm persons, is thereby redefined as violent in nature.[65]

One of the downsides to an algorithmic tool in adopting one of those broader definitions of violence is that there will be quite different base rates for the various forms lumped together.[66] Disaggregating would yield unequal probability rates, such as for acts intended to cause physical harm to a person versus harm mean to cause psychological injury versus harm directed at property. Without distinguishing, the overall proportional likelihood statistic given is rather generic as predicting any one of the myriad acts within the bucket. Plus, the overall statistic is larger than if the probability numbers of the constituent categories because the number of recidivist events is additive in this scenario (e.g., bodily harm events plus (+) psychological harm events plus (+) property damage events).

The better perspective for purposes of the criminal law and to allow algorithmic tools to offer more informative assessments would be to ratchet back the definition. Thus, experts propose limiting violence to a more conservative definition to involve actual or attempted malicious physical contact:

> [W]hile this is helpful to the researcher, the expanded definition of violence weakens the strength of the empirical findings that are made in the threat assessment and violence risk assessment scientific literature, as the testing is not being done on the common thought criteria of future physical violence, but on a more diluted definition that can obscure how helpful the research is in differentiating between those in the sample that will or will not commit physical violence in the future. We think the primary goal of this work, first and foremost, should be stopping direct physical harm, with secondary goals being to reduce emotional and psychological harm.[67]

Indeed, some algorithms exist that move in the opposite direction to parse violence involving physical bodily harm more discretely. Specialized tools focus on distinct forms of violence.[68] These include instruments that predict more specific acts, such as arson,[69] stalking,[70] firearm violence,[71] and child abuse.[72] AI designs are likely to assist in both distinguishing a more refined definition of violence as involving physical bodily injury and in further breaking it down into more specific categories. The goals of the use of the algorithm should dictate these choices. For example, a criminal justice reform that is designed to target reducing grievous domestic abuse could usefully select a tool capable of predicting relevant events, such as one that designed to predict lethal intimate partner abuse.[73] Science supports this whereby research indicates that some of the most salient predictive factors for domestic abuse are unique to it (as compared to those for violence outside the domestic context).[74] The benefits to limiting violence risk tools to acts posing a threat to the physical body are relevant to the next topic of severity of crime.

0.3.3 Severity

The severity of potential offending is often an influential consideration in the criminal law. Philosophical justice goals such as retribution and incapacitation often aim toward greater degrees of seriousness.[75] Proportionality and public safety threat are likewise relevant concerns.

In some sense, the type of harm as discussed in the prior subsection provides some indication of contrasts in severity of that harm. For example, violent crime involving bodily injury is often perceived as categorically a more serious offense than property crime. However, such a perception presents an overgeneralization, and one that could undermine some of the intentions behind deploying an algorithmic justice scheme. To illustrate, it does not seem that proportionality is served to base the degree or type of punishment on a high probability of a minor outcome (e.g., petty offending).[76] Further, decisions to foster public safety do not seem well served when the crime avoided is relatively inconsequential. Hence, risk tools that lump together crimes of varying degrees of seriousness really are only offering a likelihood of committing the most minor offenses that come within the definitional scope. These tools thus arguably provide little information to the important decisions being made.

Even when limited to offenses involving physical bodily injury, violence risk algorithms often include minor threats or assaults within their predicted outcomes.[77] Indeed, a recognized limitation is that most violence risk tools fail to distinguish gradations of offending.[78] For instance, certain of the violence risk algorithms count felony and misdemeanor acts the same and thus might not be a good fit for a decisionmaker interested in the potential for grievous injury.[79] It is not evident that the public (or criminal justice official) would view minor acts of a violent nature to automatically constitute a greater severity than a number of forms of property crime, such as burglary of an occupied home, drug trafficking, large-scale fraud involving numerous victims, or significant environmental crimes. The consequence of this observation is that the assessment of risk most appropriately considers at the very least both the type of harm and its severity. Proxy measures such as assuming all violent crimes are serious in nature are thus insufficient.

Another issue here is that there may be different predictors for more versus less serious forms of violence.[80] For example, mania is associated with minor violence but not with severe violence or homicide.[81] Relatedly, regarding intimate partner violence risk tools that are broad enough to count a loud argument as abuse, commenters argued that this led to heterogenous outcomes which can skew estimates because a risk factor salient in predicting that argument may not be important for the more serious act of assault causing injuries.[82]

Good practice identifies the relevant base point of severity appropriate to the decision the risk assessment tool is designed to inform. One simplistic option to differentiating severity would distinguish felony versus misdemeanor violence.[83] There is some evidence that algorithmic models perform quite differently when studying performance statistics on felonies versus misdemeanors.[84] Another option would be to distinguish violence resulting in bodily contact from threats of violence.[85] Still, such proxies are likely inadequate. A felony is a rather low hurdle and would sweep in far too many crimes that many would judge as relatively inconsequential. Besides, jurisdictions vary widely on the crimes to which they assign felony status and thus such a defining characteristic would differ simply by geography. As for the physical violence versus threat option, it is not always clear that the physical violence would be more serious. For example, the threat of lethal harm might be perceived as more egregious than a slap making contact with the arm of another person. Indeed, any simple dichotomy as in serious versus nonserious appears questionable.

An alternative could be to create a severity score as an index to more nuanced classifications based on typologies of harm. Researchers have been working on ways to create more sophisticated severity scales for violent offending that include various measures regarding characteristics of the offense, harm caused, harm intended, offender, and victim.[86]

Stakeholders could benefit from some disaggregation in understanding whether the likelihood statistic is tied to the more or less serious offense.[87] More refined accuracy rates are also relevant. An example is that a sentencing judge might wish to know whether an algorithmic prediction of a serious violent offense is more accurate than one that is geared to a minor offense.[88] Presumably, the judge would place a different level of confidence on the risk tool accordingly.

A challenge to be addressed is the argument that the more one distinguishes increasingly serious offenses, the more inaccurate a tool will be.[89] It is harder to accurately predict more severe and uncommon forms of violence (e.g., homicide) because their rarity means there is less data from which the algorithm can learn.[90] From a data science perspective, "[t]raditional statistical procedures underestimate the probability of rare events because maximum likelihood estimation of the logistic model is limited due by small-sample bias."[91] One commentator's analysis is bleak: "for homicide, at least, the incident rate is so low that prediction is impossible."[92]

This limitation may no longer be fully justified. AI designs, such as those using machine learning and deep learning technologies, have the potential to significantly improve the ability to assess rare events, including severe forms of violence.[93] Non-AI models typically only include a relatively small number of predictors with strong associations to the outcome of interest. AI forecasting instead can incorporate numerous (even hundreds of) factors, many of which have weak associations individually yet in the aggregate create more accurate outcomes.[94] As an illustration, a machine learning technique was deployed on a dataset of individuals on probation in a large eastern city in the United States.[95] The intent was to predict either perpetrators or victims of homicide (or attempts) among a population of probationers. The base rate of the outcome of interest in the group studied was quite low – 2%. Nonetheless, the machine learning classifier achieved a 77% prediction accuracy rate for the completed and attempted homicides.

Researchers tested machine learning algorithms on another low base rate event (5%) of intimate partner violence involving injury.[96] Through a series of complicated AI applications, the simulation was able to isolate a very high-risk group for violence with injury with a mean reoffense rate of 72%, albeit using a synthetic dataset. Another effort has used machine learning to identify predictors for a sexual assault turning lethal.[97] In further examples, machine learning algorithms have been tested to predict serious violent crimes (defined as murder, attempted murder, rape, aggravated assault, and arson),[98] or more distinct categories, such as fatal violence,[99] high-harm offending by outlaw motorcycle gangs,[100] and gun violence.[101]

0.3.4 Imminence

Depending on the nature of the decision being made and other goals, the immediacy of the threat being predicted might be a pertinent data point. Officials often have a greater sense of urgency to intervene or deter when a threat of severe violent action is imminent.[102] Though there may be situations where longer-term forecasts are more relevant. Thus, applications may range from an interest in quite short periods, more intermediate time frames, or long-term projections.[103]

Unfortunately, most violence algorithms offer distant future predictions, often five years or so into the future.[104] This is likely because the oldest and most commonly used violence algorithms were originally developed for use in forensic psychiatric settings in which medical professionals are interested in possibilities for the patients in the mid- and distant futures.[105]

An algorithm is created on a fixed follow-up period or if its underlying data used various time frames, will have a maximum time frame. In either case, the risk estimate should be tied to the relevant time frame or else that estimate loses its validity.[106] This means that a long-term prognostication cannot be easily refitted into a prediction for a shorter period. One reason is that the likelihood of a new violent offence declines steadily as time passes without any violent behavior.[107]

Notably, an available statistical model that provides information on imminence is the hazard ratio. This statistic is a measure of the time-to-event. Here, this would indicate whether one or more predictors are associated with violent reoffending at various periods of time. A slightly different measure is survival time, which could be a more discrete tracking of time to failure (meaning the number of days to commission of the recidivist event at interest). As an illustration, researchers found variations in the association of certain predictors to sexual reoffending based on the time lag between release and the new sexual crime.[108]

Promising research is emerging in which researchers are creating algorithms that can better predict imminent violence.[109] Focusing more on dynamic predictors (factors that are changeable and impact on likelihood of violence) rather than on static predictors (characteristics that are stable over time) may be relevant.[110] More specifically, incorporating those dynamic factors that are more temporally proximate to violent acts into the algorithms may be even more helpful.[111] Also relevant would be to include acute risk factors (as compared to those which tend to change more slowly) and violence triggers, which may overlap with the temporally proximate dynamic factors.[112] A study using machine learning techniques was able to identify dynamic factors that were proximal factors for death during sexual assault.[113] Other work is using machine learning to identify factors that indicate an escalation toward near-term violence.[114] On the other hand, some work suggests that incorporating protective factors can help tools' ability to assess decreasing risk of imminent recidivism.[115]

0.3.5 Frequency

Frequency of committing serious violent offenses is relevant at times for decisionmakers.[116] Certain crimes by their nature often involve repeated acts of violence or threats against the same victim, such as stalking and child abuse (e.g., abandonment and neglect), and thus frequency may be particularly salient to them.[117] Evidence of an escalation in frequency of violent behavior may be informative at some decision points. Here, the idea is not retrospective in nature in terms of the career offender *per se* or one with a lengthy past criminal history. In contrast, this frequency is concerned with those who are likely to commit numerous serious offenses in the future. Arguably, the reciprocal is likewise relevant, being the relevance of predicting the potential for desistence (i.e., the state of being crime-free for an extended period of time).[118] The person who would repeatedly and violently reoffend clearly poses a greater threat to the community than the one who would desist after a single violent act.

Frequency should not be confused with severity. A high recidivism rate does not necessarily imply a high rate of committing serious offenses.[119] Though these constructs might for policy reasons be used together when the concern is about the group that are repeat *and* serious offenders. Identifying that group and focusing intensive treatment could maximize crime reduction.[120]

The idea of frequency alludes to the notion of persistence,[121] which may suggest undeterrability. Another reason to focus on frequency is derived from observations that relatively few offenders are responsible for the majority of violent crimes.[122] A jurisdiction might then wish to use algorithms in a focused deterrence strategy to slow the revolving door in and out of the justice system for those most prolific violent offenders.[123] As an illustration, a study of the population in Sweden found that 1% of the population accounted for 63% of violent crimes, with a subset of 0.1% of the population being the high-persistence offenders having 11 or more violent crime convictions.[124] As another example, a study found that 3% of intimate partner violence offenders in its sample accounted for 90% of total intimate partner abuse crime by intimate perpetrators; further, researchers observed a general increase in frequency among that 3%.[125]

Current algorithms for violent offending have not generally been honed toward outcomes that differentiate one versus multiple recidivist outcomes. It is not evident why this is the case. Recidivism studies outside of the algorithmic risk paradigm have collected data on the likelihood of one reoffense and additionally included the number of new offenses.[126] At least one project has been cognizant of the potential for looking at whether the risk of reoffending in domestic violence cases is cumulative in terms of increasing with each subsequent incident.[127] It is conceivable that AI could be deployed to learn on longitudinal datasets of offenders with multiple violence what attributes distinguish the repeat cases and those with increasingly greater numbers of violent acts.

0.3.6 Duration

Duration adds a layer of context into the understanding of risk in that it might be useful to distinguish the individual who commits a flurry of violence in a very short time frame and then desists from the one who persists over a longer period. Duration can interact with frequency. For instance, a repeat offender whose frequency is declining over time may suggest a transition to a state of desistance.[128]

A major flaw in the common reliance in risk assessment algorithms upon a dichotomous outcome of having violently reoffended or not is that it ignores the weight of data science evidence that most violent offenders will age-out even without significant intervention.[129] The well-established age-crime curve means that most violent acts are committed at a young age, with the rate of violence falling in a rather linear fashion after the teenage years.[130]

To date, risk assessment algorithms typically do not include a measure for the duration of repeat future offending. Once individuals are observed to commit a new violence offense, the tools typically assign them a static position of violent recidivist.

However, risk assessment practices could incorporate this dimension of duration. One rather crude way is to reassess the individual at various times to account for fluctuations in risk levels. An algorithmic approach to duration is at least present in work accomplished on desistence. This orientation focuses on identifying and including protective factors (i.e., those that correlate with not violently reoffending) into algorithmic models.[131] Another way of incorporating this dimension is based on findings that a longer time of remaining violence free is associated with a decline in the rate of violent offending, particularly for those initially rated as high risk.[132] One attempt has shown, evidently without needing machine learning tools, that adding a recidivism-free measure improved results above the predictive ability of a popular dynamic risk algorithmic tool.[133]

AI technologies conceivably could use longitudinal datasets to learn the predictors for prospective violent criminal careers. Work on psychological correlates to a criminal thinking style and the dimensions underlying a criminal lifestyle could be useful.[134]

0.3.7 Setting

There can be a significant difference in risk for an individual as to whether they are then currently residing in an institutional setting (e.g., prison or hospital) versus being in the community. Notably, characteristics of the institution increase and decrease at the same time the likelihood of violent offending. In terms of increasing known offending, an institutionalized individuals are more likely to be monitored by staff and thus have a greater risk of detection, and more likely to be held accountable for rules violations regarding aggression (thus more likely being recorded as reoffending behaviors) because of the greater attention to safety and the orderly running of the facilities.[135] On the other hand, the institutional setting may reduce certain risk factors for violent offending, such as more limited access to alcohol, drugs, weapons, and medications to ameliorate mental health symptoms.

Many violence risk tools are validated on individuals free in the community. Others are more focused on institutional settings. Examples are violence risk tools designed to predict aggression by youth in the hospital,[136] violence in acute medical care settings,[137] and violence in prison.[138] AI holds promise for further refinements on predictive models best suitable for specific settings considering risk relevant differences.

0.4 Conclusion

The deployment of algorithmic risk assessment in criminal justice allows officials a scientific method to distinguish those who posing different levels of dangerousness. The focus herein was on violence. While algorithmic tools often utilize quite broad definitions of violence, at least in some instances a more curtailed focus on chronic offender who is at risk of committing serious acts involving threat or injury to physical human bodies would be more suitable. Relevant dimensions to the risk would include those relating to likelihood, seriousness, immediacy, repetitiveness, length of criminal career, and environmental context for violence. Algorithmic modeling, including the use of AI methodologies, could usefully progress risk assessment tools into those dimensions, as relevant to the decision at issue and population to be assessed.

Notes

1 TRAVAINI, G. et al.: Machine Learning and Criminal Justice: A Systematic Review of Advanced Methodology for Recidivism Risk Prediction. *International Journal of Environmental Research and Public Health*. Volume 19, 2022, pp. 10594.

2 BLUMSTEIN, A. Some Perspectives on Quantitative Criminology Pre-JQC: And then Some. *Journal of Quantitative Criminology*. Volume 26, 2010, pp. 549–561.

3 BIDDLE, J.B.: On Predicting Recidivism: Epistemic Risk, Tradeoffs, and Values in Machine Learning. *Canadian Journal of Philosophy*. Volume 52, Issue 3, 2022, pp. 321–341.

4 HYATT, J.M., CHANENSON, S.L., and BERGSTROM, M.H.: Reform in Motion: The Promise and Perils of Incorporating Risk Assessments and Cost-Benefit Analysis into Pennsylvania Sentencing. *Duquesne Law Review*. Volume 49, Issue 4, 2011, pp. 707–749.

5 HAMILTON, M.: Risk and Needs Assessment: Constitutional and Ethical Challenges. *American Criminal Law Review*. Volume 52, 2015, pp. 231–291.
6 KLINGELE, C.: The Promises and Perils of Evidence-Based Corrections. *Notre Dame Law Review*. Volume 91, Issue 2, 2015, pp. 537–584.
7 ECKHOUSE, L., LUM, K., and CICCOLINI, J.: Layers of Bias: A Unified Approach for Understanding Problems with Risk Assessment. *Criminal Justice and Behavior*. Volume 46, Issue 2, 2019, pp. 185–209.
8 GIPSON RANKIN, S.M.: Technological Tethereds: Potential Impact of Untrustworthy Artificial Intelligence in Criminal Justice Risk Assessment Instruments. *Washington and Lee Law Review*. Volume 78, Issue 2, 2021, pp. 647–724.
9 COFONE, I.: Algorithmic Discrimination is an Information Problem. *Hastings Law Journal*. Volume 70, Issue 6, 2019, pp. 1389–1443.
10 RISTROPH, R.: Criminal Law as Public Ordering. *University of Toronto Law Journal*. Volume 70, Issue supplement 1, 2020, pp. 64–83.
11 BINNS, R.: Algorithmic Accountability and Public Reason. *Philosophy & Technology*. Volume 31, 2018, pp. 543–556.
12 HAMILTON, M.: Debating Algorithmic Fairness. *UC Davis Law Review Online*. Volume 52, 2019, pp. 261–296.
13 GREENE, T. et al.: Forks Over Knives: Predictive Inconsistency in Criminal Justice Algorithmic Risk Assessment Tools. *Journal of the Royal Statistical Society Series A*. Volume 195, 2022, pp. S165–S789.
14 ECKHOUSE, LUM, and CICCOLINI: Layers of Bias, pp. 185–209.
15 BIDDLE: On Predicting Recidivism, pp. 321–341.
16 BERK, R.: Accuracy and Fairness for Juvenile Justice Risk Assessments. *Journal of Empirical Legal Studies*. Volume 16, Issue 1, 2019, pp. 175–194.
17 LEPRI, B. et al., Fair, Transparent, and Accountable Algorithmic Decision-Making Processes. *Philosophy and Technology*. Volume 31, 2018, pp. 611–627 (at 612)
18 HYATT, CHANENSON, and BERGSTROM: Reform in Motion, pp. 707–749.
19 ROFFEY, M. and KALISKI, S.Z.: To Predict or not to Predict – That is the Question. *African Journal of Psychiatry*. Volume 15, Issue 4, 2012, pp. 227–233.
20 WORMITH, J.S.: Automated Offender Risk Assessment. *Criminology & Public Policy*. Volume 16, Issue 1, 2017, pp. 281–303.
21 HANNAH-MOFFAT, K., Algorithmic Risk Governance: Big Data Analytics, Race and Information Activism in Criminal Justice Debates. *Theoretical Criminology*. Volume 23, Issue 4, 2019, pp. 453–577.
22 MONAHAN, J.: Preface: Recidivism Risk Assessment in the 21st Century. In *Handbook of recidivism risk/needs assessment tools* (SINGH, J.P. et al. eds.). Hoboken, NJ: John Wiley & Sons, 2018, 315 pp., ISBN 9781119184294.
23 HAMILTON, Z., KIGERL, A., and KOWALSKI, M.: Prediction is Local: The Benefits of Risk Assessment Optimization. *Justice Quarterly*. Volume 39, Issue 4, 2022, pp. 722–744.
24 EAGLIN, J.M.: Constructing Recidivism Risk. *Emory Law Journal*. Volume 67, Issue 1, 2018, pp. 59–122.
25 BLUMSTEIN: Some Perspectives on Quantitative Criminology Pre-JQC, pp. 549–561.
26 ZALNIERIUTE, M. et al.: From Rule of Law to Statute Drafting: Legal Issues for Algorithms in Government Decision-Making. In *Cambridge handbook on the law of algorithms* (BARFIELD, W. ed. 2020). Cambridge: Cambridge University Press, 2020, 780 pp., ISBN 9781108680844.

27 SINGER, J.C. et al.: A Convergent Approach to Sex Offender Risk Assessment. In *The Wiley-Blackwell handbook of legal and ethical aspects of sex offender treatment and management* (HARRISON, K. and RAINEY, B. eds.). Oxford: John Wiley & Sons, 2013, 520 pp., ISBN 978-1-119-94555-0.
28 RUBACK, R.B. et al.: Communicating Risk Information at Criminal Sentencing in Pennsylvania: An Experimental Analysis. *Federal Probation*. Volume 80, Issue 2, 2016, pp. 47–56.
29 CHRISTIN, A. et al.: *Courts and Predictive Algorithms* 1 [Internet] 2015, http://www.datacivilrights.org/pubs/2015-1027/Courts_and_Predictive_Algorithms.pdf.
30 WILLIAMS, B.A., BROOKS, C.F., and SHMARGAD, Y.: How Algorithms Discriminate Based on Data They Lack. *Journal of Information Policy*. Volume 8, Issue 1, 2018, pp. 78–115.
31 ZALNIERIUTE et al.: From Rule of Law to Statute Drafting, 780 pp., ISBN 9781108680844.
32 ZALNIERIUTE et al.: From Rule of Law to Statute Drafting, 780 pp., ISBN 9781108680844.
33 GHASEMI, M. et al.: The Application of Machine Learning to a General Risk-Need Assessment Instrument in the Prediction of Criminal Recidivism. *Criminal Justice and Behavior*. Volume 48, Issue 4, 2021, pp. 518–538.
34 ECKHOUSE, LUM, and CICCOLINI: Layers of Bias, pp. 185–209.
35 GHASEMI et al.: The Application of Machine Learning to a General Risk-Need Assessment Instrument in the Prediction of Criminal Recidivism, pp. 518–538.
36 FAGAN, F. and LEVMORE, S.: The Impact of Artificial Intelligence on Rules, Standards, and Judicial Discretion. *Southern California Law Review*. Volume 93, 2019, pp. 1–35.
37 HOGAN, N.R., DAVIDGE, E.Q., and CORABIAN, G.: On the Ethics and Practicalities of Artificial Intelligence, Risk Assessment, and Race. *Journal of the American Academy of Psychiatry and Law*. Volume 49, 2021, pp. 326–334.
38 KOVALCHUK, O. et al.: Associative Rule Mining for the Assessment of the Risk of Recidivism. IntelITSIS: 4nd International Workshop on Intelligent Information Technologies and Systems of Information Security. 2023 <https://ceur-ws.org/Vol-3373/paper24.pdf>.
39 MAYNARD, B.R. et al.: Towards More Accurate Classification of Risk of Arrest among Offenders on Community Supervision: An Application of Machine Learning Versus Logistic Regression. *Criminal Behaviour and Mental Health*. Volume 33, Issue 3, 2023, pp. 156–171.
40 ETZLER, S. et al.: Machine Learning and Risk Assessment: Random Forest Does not Outperform Logistic Regression in the Prediction of Sexual Recidivism. *Assessment*. 2023 <https://journals-sagepub-com.surrey.idm.oclc.org/doi/epub/10.1177/10731911231164624>.
41 SPIVAK, B.L. and SHEPHERD, S.M.: Ethics, Artificial Intelligence, and Risk Assessment. *Journal of the American Academy of Psychiatry and Law*. Volume 49, 2021, pp. 335–337.
42 O'HEAR, M. and WHEELOCK, D.: Violent Crime and Punitiveness: An Empirical Study of Public Opinion. *Marquette Law Review*. Volume 103, Issue 3, 2020, pp. 1035–1071.
43 DOUGLAS, T. et al.: Risk Assessment Tools in Criminal Justice and Forensic Psychiatry: The Need for Better Data. *European Psychiatry*. Volume 42, 2017, pp. 134–137.

44 HEILBRUN, K. et al.: Approaches to Violence Risk Assessment. In *Handbook of violence risk assessment*. 2nd ed. (DOUGLAS, K.S. and OTTO, R.K. eds.). New York: Routledge, 2021, 494 pp., ISBN 978-1-135-51837-4
45 VILJOEN, J.L. and VINCENT, G.M.: Risk Assessments and Reoffending: Implementation and Impact on Risk Management. *Clinical Psychology: Science and Practice*. 2020, e12378.
46 GOEL, S. et al.: The Accuracy, Equity, and Jurisprudence of Criminal Risk Assessment. In *Research handbook on big data law* (VOGL, R. ed.). Northampton, MA: Elgar, 2021, 544 pp., ISBN 9781788972826.
47 STEVENSON, M.: Assessing Risk Assessment in Action. *Minnesota Law Review*. Volume 103, 2018, pp. 303–384.
48 HARRIS, G.T., RICE, M.E., QUINSEY, V.L., and CORMIER, C.A.: *Violent offenders: Appraising and managing risk*. 3rd ed. Washington, DC: American Psychological Association, 2015, 470 pp., ISBN 978-1-4338-1901-8.
49 GHASEMI et al. The Application of Machine Learning to a General Risk-Need Assessment Instrument in the Prediction of Criminal Recidivism, pp. 518–538.
50 SALO, B. LAAKSONEN, T., and SANTTILA, P.: Predictive Power of Dynamic (vs. Static) Risk Factors in the Finnish Risk and Needs Assessment Form. *Criminal Justice and Behavior*. Volume 46, Issue 7, 2019, pp. 939–960.
51 United States v. Salerno, 481 U.S. 739 (1987).
52 VARS, F.E.: Delineating Sexual Dangerousness. *Houston Law Review*. Volume 50, 2013, pp. 855–898.
53 IMREY, P.B. and DAWID, P.: A Commentary on Statistical Assessment of Violence Recidivism Risk. *Statistics and Public Policy*. Volume 2, Issue 1, 2015, pp. 1–18.
54 HAMILTON, M.: Judicial Gatekeeping on Scientific Validity with Risk Assessment Tools. *Behavioral Sciences & the Law*. Volume 38, Issue 3, 2020, pp. 226–245.
55 CONNORS, M.H. and LARGE, M.M.: Calibrating Violence Risk Assessments for Uncertainty. *General Psychiatry*. Volume 36, Issue 2, 2023, pp. e100921–e100921.
56 STAHLY-BUTTS, M. and AKBAR, A.A.: Reforms for Radicals? An Abolitionist Framework. *U.C.L.A. Law Review*. Volume 68, 2022, pp. 1544–1583.
57 MCLEOD, A.M.: Prison Abolition and Grounded Justice. *U.C.L.A. Law Review*. Volume 62, 2015, pp. 1156–1239.
58 MELOY, J.R. et al.: Threat Assessment and Threat Management. In *International handbook of threat assessment*. 2nd ed. (MELOY, J.R. and HOFFMAN, J. eds.). New York: Oxford University Press, 2021, 760 pp., ISBN 9780190940188.
59 DOUGLAS, K.S. et al.: Assessing Risk for Violence among Psychiatric Patients. *Journal of Consulting and Clinical Psychology*. Volume 67, Issue 6, 1999, pp. 917–930.
60 WORMITH, J.S. et al.: An Overview of Violent Behaviour from Aggression to Homicide. In *The Wiley handbook of what works in violence risk management* (WORMITH, J.S., CRAIG, L.A., and HOGUE, T.E. eds.). Hoboken, NJ: Wiley, 2020, 608 pp., ISBN 9781119315971.
61 WORMITH et al.: An Overview of Violent Behaviour from Aggression to Homicide, 608 pp.
62 HART, S.D. and DOUGLAS, K.S.: *Violence risk assessment and management: The Oxford handbook of psychology and law* (DEMATTEO, D. and

SCHERR, J.C. eds.). New York: Oxford University Press, 2023, 824 pp., ISBN 9780197649152.
63 PHILLIPS, H.K. et al.: Risk Assessment in Offenders with Mental Disorders. *Journal of Interpersonal Violence*. Volume 20, Issue 10, 2005, pp. 833–847.
64 18 U.S.C. § 3156(a)(4) and 18 U.S.C. § 924(c)(3)(A) (emphasis added).
65 HEILBRUN et al.: Approaches to Violence Risk Assessment, 494 pp.
66 CONNORS and LARGE: Calibrating Violence Risk Assessments for Uncertainty, pp. e100921–e100921.
67 CAWOOD, J.S. and CORCORAN, M.H.: *Violence assessment and intervention: The practitioner's handbook*. 3rd ed. New York: Routledge, 2020, 490 pp., ISBN 978-0-429-34436-7.
68 WORMITH et al.: An Overview of Violent Behaviour from Aggression to Homicide, 608 pp.
69 WATT, B.D. and ONG, S.: Current Directions of Risk Assessment in Deliberate Firesetters. In *The Psychology of Arson: A Practical Guide to Understanding and Managing Deliberate Firesetters* (DOLEY, R., DICKENS, G., and GANNON, T. eds.). New York: Routledge, 2016, 334 pp., ISBN 978-1-315-68596-0.
70 MCEWAN, T.E. et al.: The Reliability and Predictive Validity of the Stalking Risk Profile. *Assessment*. Volume 25, Issue 2, 2018, pp. 259–276.
71 GOLDSTICK, J.E. et al.: Development of the SaFETy Score: A Clinical Screening Tool for Predicting Future Firearm Violence Risk. *Annals of Internal Medicine*. Volume 166, Issue 10, 2017, pp. 707–714.
72 VAN DER PUT, C.E. et al.: Predicting Child Maltreatment: A Meta-Analysis of the Predictive Validity of Risk Assessment Instruments. *Child Abuse & Neglect*. Volume 73, 2017, 71–88.
73 GRAHAM, L.M. et al.: The Validity and Reliability of Available Intimate Partner Homicide and Reassault Risk Assessment Tools. *Trauma, Violence, & Abuse*. Volume 22, Issue 1, 2019, 18–40.
74 HILTON, N.Z.: *Domestic violence risk assessment: Tools for effective prediction and management*. Toronto: American Psychological Association, 2021, 349 pp., ISBN 9781433833229.
75 WASIK, M.: Crime Seriousness and the Offender-Victim Relationship in Sentencing. In *Fundamentals of sentencing theory* (ASHWORTH, A. and WASIK, M. eds.). New York: Oxford University Press, 2004, 300 pp., ISBN 0-19-826256-6.
76 HESTER, R.: Risk Assessment at Sentencing: The Pennsylvania Experience. In *Predictive sentencing: normative and empirical perspectives* (DE KEIJSER, J.W. et al. eds.). Oxford: Hart, 2019, 304 pp., ISBN 9781509921430
77 BRENNAN, T. and DIETERICH, W.: Correctional Offender Management Profiles for Alternative Sanctions (COMPAS). In *Handbook of recidivism risk/needs assessment tools* (SINGH, J.P. et al. eds.). Hoboken, NJ: John Wiley & Sons, 2018, 352 pp., ISBN 9781119184294.
78 FAZEL, S. and BJØKLY, S.: Methodological Considerations in Risk Assessment Research. In *International perspectives on violence risk assessment* (SINGH, J.P. et al. eds.). New York: Oxford, 2016, 418 pp., ISBN 9780199386307.
79 BRENNAN and DIETERICH: Correctional Offender Management Profiles for Alternative Sanctions (COMPAS), 352 pp., ISBN 9781119184294.
80 DOUGLAS, K.S. and OGLOFF, J.R.P.: Multiple Facets of Risk for Violence: The Impact of Judgmental Specificity on Structured Decisions about Violence Risk. *International Journal of Forensic Mental Health*. Volume 2, Issue 1, 2003, pp. 19–34.

81 CONNORS and LARGE: Calibrating Violence Risk Assessments for Uncertainty, pp. e100921–e100921.
82 BERK, R.A. and SORENSON, S.B.: Algorithmic Approach to Forecasting Rare Violent Events. *Criminology and Public Policy*. Volume 19, 2020, pp. 213–233.
83 DUWE, G. and KIDEUK, K.: Sacrificing Accuracy for Transparency in Recidivism Risk Assessment. *Corrections*. Volume 1, Issue 3, 2016, pp. 155–176.
84 WANG, C., HAN, B., PATEL, B., and RUDIN, R. In Pursuit of Interpretable, Fair, and Accurate Machine Learning for Criminal Recidivism Prediction. *Journal of Quantitative Criminology*. Volume 39, Issue 2, 2022, pp. 519–581.
85 DOUGLAS et al.: Assessing Risk for Violence among Psychiatric Patients, pp. 917–930.
86 LOEWENSTEIN, K.M., HARINAM, V., and ARIEL, B.: Intimate Partner Violence in Denmark: A Study of Offending Patterns Based on Official Statistics. *European Journal of Crime, Criminal Law and Criminal Justice*. Volume 30, 2022, pp. 288–308.
87 GARRETT, B.L. and STEVENSON, M. Open Risk Assessment. *Behavioral Sciences & the Law*. Volume 38, 2020, pp. 279–286.
88 BERK, R. and HYATT, J.: Machine Learning Forecasts of Risk to Inform Sentencing Decisions. *Federal Sentencing Reporter*. Volume 27, Issue 4, 2015, pp. 222–228.
89 OGLOFF, J.R.P. and DAVIS, M.R.: From Predicting Dangerousness to Assessing and Managing Risk for Violence. In *The Wiley handbook of what works in violence risk management* (WORMITH, J.S., CRAIG, L.A., and HOGUE, T.E. eds.). Hoboken, NJ: Wiley, 2020, 576 pp., ISBN 978111931597.
90 GARRETT, B.L. and MONAHAN, J.: Judging Risk. *California Law Review*. Volume 48, 2020, pp. 439–493.
91 REID, J.A. and BEAUREGARD, E.: Exploring a Machine Learning Approach: Predicting Death in Sexual Assault. *Journal of Criminal Justice*. Volume 71, 2020, pp. 101741–101741.
92 DUTTON, D.G.: Caveat assessor: Potential pitfalls for generic assessment for intimate partner violence. intimate partner violence prevention and intervention. In *Intimate partner violence prevention and intervention* (BALDRY, A.C. et al. eds.). New York: Nova Science, 2008, 224 pp., ISBN 978-1-60021-858-3.
93 COCKERILL, R.G.: Ethics Implications of the Use of Artificial Intelligence in Violence Risk Assessment. *Journal of the American Academy of Psychiatry and Law*. Volume 48, 2020, pp. 345–349.
94 BERK and HYATT: Machine Learning Forecasts of Risk to Inform Sentencing Decisions, pp. 222–228.
95 BERK, R.: *Machine learning risk assessments in criminal justice settings*. Switzerland: Springer Nature, 2019, 178 pp., ISBN 978-3-030-02272-3.
96 BERK and SORENSON: Algorithmic Approach to Forecasting Rare Violent Events, pp. 213–233.
97 REID and BEAUREGARD: Exploring a Machine Learning Approach, pp. 101741–101741.
98 BERK, R.A. and BLEICH, J.: Statistical Procedures for Forecasting Criminal Behavior. *Criminology and Public Policy*. Volume 12, Issue 3, 2013, pp. 513–544.
99 ZENG, J., USTUN, B., and RUDIN, C.: Interpretable Classification Models for Recidivism Prediction. *Journal of the Royal Statistical Society Series A*. Volume 180, Part 3, 2017, 689–722.

100 MORGAN, A. and CUBIT, T.: Predicting High-Harm Offending Using Machine Learning: An Application to Outlaw Motorcycle Gangs. *Trends and Issues in Crime and Criminal Justice*. Issue 646, 2022, pp. 1–18.
101 WHEELER, A.P., WORDEN, R.E., and SILVER, J.R.: The Accuracy of the Violent Offender Identification Directive Tool to Predict Future Gun Violence. *Criminal Justice and Behavior*. Volume 36, Issue 5, 2019, pp. 770–788.
102 HEILBRUN. et al.: Approaches to Violence Risk Assessment, 494 pp.
103 HEILBRUN et al.: Approaches to Violence Risk Assessment, 494 pp.
104 GREENE et al.: Forks Over Knives, pp. S165–S789.
105 HARRIS, RICE, QUINSEY, and CORMIER: *Violent offenders: Appraising and managing risk*, 470 pp.
106 SCURICH, N.: An Introduction to the Assessment of Violence Risk. *International perspectives on violence risk assessment* (SINGH, J.P. et al. eds.). New York: Oxford, 2016, 418 pp., ISBN 9780199386307.
107 HELMUS, L.M. and QUINSEY, V.L.: Predicting Violent Reoffending with the VRAG-R. 119–141. In *The Wiley handbook of what works in violence risk management* (WORMITH, J.S., CRAIG, L.A., and HOGUE, T.E. eds.). Hoboken, NJ: Wiley, 2020, 608 pp., ISBN 9781119315971.
108 DE LA CRUZ, R., FUENTES, C., and PADILLA, O.: A Bayesian Mixture Cure Rate Model for Estimating Short-Term and Long-Term Recidivism. *Entropy*. Volume 25, Issue 1, 2023, pp. 56.
109 LOCKERTSEN, Ø et al.: Risk Assessment of Imminent Violence in Acute Psychiatry: A Step Towards an Extended Model. *The Journal of Forensic Psychiatry & Psychology*. Volume 31, Issue 1, 2020, pp. 41–63.
110 PARMIGIANI, G. et al.: The Impact of Machine Learning in Predicting Risk of Violence. *Frontiers in Psychiatry*. Volume 13, 2022, pp. 1015914.
111 PENNEY, S.R.: Innovations in Violence Risk Assessment: What Aviation Can Teach Us About Assessing and Managing Risk for Rare and Serious Outcomes. *International Journal of Law and Psychiatry*. Volume 77, 2021, pp. 101710.
112 STONE, A.G., LLOYD, C.D., and SERIN, R.C.: Dynamic Risk Factors Reassessed Regularly after Release from Incarceration Predict Imminent Violent Recidivism. *Law and Human Behavior*. Volume 45, Issue 6, 2021, pp. 512–523.
113 REID, J.A. and BEAUREGARD, E.: Exploring a Machine Learning Approach, pp. 101741–101741.
114 CHAIMOWITZ, G., MAMAK, M., and MOULDEN, H.: Using Artificial Intelligence to Improve Prediction and Prevention of Violence. *Research Outreach*. [Online] 2021.
115 DAVIES, S.T., LLOYD, C.D., and POLASCHEK, D.L.L.: Does Reassessment Enhance the Prediction of Imminent Criminal Recidivism? *Assessment*. Volume 29, Issue 5, 2022, pp. 962–980.
116 DUFF, R.A.: Dangerousness and Citizenship. In *Fundamentals of sentencing theory* (ASHWORTH, A. and WASIK, M. eds.). New York: Oxford University Press, 1998, 310 pp., ISBN 9780198262565.
117 HEILBRUN et al.: Approaches to Violence Risk Assessment, 494 pp.
118 FOX, K.J.: Desistance Frameworks. *Aggression and Violent Behavior*. Volume 63, 2022, pp. 101684.
119 BRAME, R. Static Risk Factors and Criminal Recidivism. In *Handbook on risk and needs assessment* (TAXMAN, F. ed.). New York: Routledge, 2017, 492 pp., ISBN 978-1-138-92776-6.

120 SKEEM, J.L. and POLASCHEK, D.L.L.: High Risk, Not Hopeless: Correctional Intervention for People at Risk of Violence. *Marquette Law Review.* Volume 103, Issue 3, 2020, pp. 1129–1148.
121 DIMOCK, S. Criminalizing Dangerousness: How to Preventively Detain Dangerous Offenders. *Criminal Law and Philosophy*, Volume 9, 2015, pp. 537–560.
122 For a list of studies, see PIQUERO, A.R., JENNINGS, W.G., and BARNES, J.C.: Violence in Criminal Careers: A Review of the Literature from a Developmental Life-Course Perspective. *Aggression and Violent Behavior.* Volume 17, 2012, pp. 171–179.
123 SCHNOBRICH-DAVIS, J., SWATT, M., and WAGNER, D.: Focused Deterred: Effective Crime Reduction Strategy for Chronic Offenders? *Crime Prevention and Community Safety.* Volume 23, Issue 3, 2021, pp. 302–318.
124 FALK, Ö et al.: The 1% of the Population Accountable for 63% of all Violent Crime Convictions. *Social Psychiatry and Psychiatric Epidemiology.* Vol 49, 2014, pp. 559–571.
125 BARNHAM, L., BARNES, G.C., and SHERMAN, L.W.: Targeting Escalation of Intimate Partner Violence. *Cambridge Journal of Evidence Based Policing.* Volume 1, Issue 2–3, 2017, pp. 116–142.
126 UK Ministry of Justice, Proven reoffending statistics collection, <https://www.gov.uk/government/collections/proven-reoffending-statistics>, accessed 17 June 2023.
127 MORGAN, A., BOXALL, H., and BROWN, R.: Targeting Repeat Domestic Violence: Assessing Short-Term Risk of Reoffending. *Trends & Issues in Crime and Criminal Justice.* Issue 552, 2018, pp. 1–16.
128 BRAME, R. Static Risk Factors and Criminal Recidivism. In *Handbook on risk and needs assessment* (TAXMAN, F. ed.). New York: Routledge, 2017, 492 pp., ISBN 978-1-138-92776-6.
129 GOTTFREDSON, M. and HIRSCHI, T.: The True Value of Lambda Would Appear to be Zero: An Essay on Career Criminals, Criminal Careers, Selective Incapacitation, Cohort Studies, and Related Topics. *Criminology.* Volume 24, Issue 2, 1986, pp. 213–234.
130 SAMPSON. R.J. and LAUB, J.H.: Life-Course Desisters? Trajectories of Crime among Delinquent Boys Followed to Age 70. *Criminology.* Volume 41, Issue 3, 2003, pp. 301–339.
131 YOON, D. et al.: Factors Predicting Desistance from Reoffending: A Validation Study of the SAPROF in Sexual Offenders. *International Journal of Offender Therapy and Comparative Criminology.* Volume 62, Issue 3, 2018, pp. 697–716.
132 HARRIS, R.K. et al.: High-Risk Sex Offenders May Not Be High Risk Forever. *Journal of Interpersonal Violence.* Volume 29, Issue 14, 2014, pp. 2792–2813.
133 FRISCH-SCOTT, N.E. and NAKAMURA, K.: Time for a Change: Examining the Relationships between Recidivism-Free Time, Recidivism Risk, and Risk Assessment. *Justice Quarterly.* Volume 39, Issue 6, pp. 1156–1179.
134 WALTERS, G.D.: *Crime in a psychological context: from career criminals to criminal careers.* Thousand Oaks, CA: Sage, 2012, 273 pp., ISBN 978-1-4129-9608-2.
135 HEILBRUN et al.: Approaches to Violence Risk Assessment, 494 pp.
136 BARZMAN, D. et al.: Automated Risk Assessment for School Violence. *Psychiatric Quarterly.* Volume 89, 2018, pp. 817–828.

137 GHOSH, M. et al.: The Validity and Utility of Violence Risk Assessment Tools to Predict Patient Violence in Acute Care Settings. *International Journal of Mental Health Nursing*, Volume 28, 2019, pp. 1248–1267.

138 ANDRÉS-PUEYO, A., ARBACH-LUCIONI, K., and REDONDO, S.: The RisCanvi: A New Tool for Assessing Risk for Violence in Prison and Recidivism (SINGH, J.P. et al. eds.). Hoboken, NJ: John Wiley & Sons, 2018, 315 pp., ISBN 9781119184294.

Part III

The Polish perspective

Chapter 1

Sentencing with the use of algorithms in Polish criminal proceedings

An analysis from the perspective of the basic principles of sentencing

Konrad Burdziak

1.1 Research objective

The objective of this work and the research on Polish law and criminal procedure that forms its basis is to answer the questions: (a) Is there a need to use algorithm-based tools in the sentencing process during criminal proceedings? If so, then: (b) is there a possibility to use algorithm-based tools in the sentencing process during criminal proceedings? (c) Is there a possibility for algorithm-based tools to make decisions autonomously and without human control during sentencing in criminal proceedings?

The justification for posing the above-mentioned questions was the following circumstances: (1) the continuous development of tools based on algorithms, also for the purposes of making decisions in criminal proceedings, and relatively satisfactory results achieved by them, as well as the need to achieve equally satisfactory results in criminal proceedings conducted in Poland; (2) the slowness of adjudication by Polish courts, also in criminal law cases, even though one of the key conditions for the effectiveness of a penalty is its imposition immediately after the commission of a prohibited act, and the need to change it; (3) the need to stabilise the judicial practice in criminal cases, including avoiding serious discrepancies in the scope of penalties imposed in similar situations by individual criminal courts; (4) the need (in terms of the effectiveness of the measures imposed in individual cases) for a criminal law response to the fact of committing a crime, especially in the scope of minimising the risk of recidivism; (5) the need to adjudicate criminal law measures in response to the fact of committing a crime in a manner based on objective criteria (empirical data) and scientific research, and not only on the better or worse justified predictions of individual persons (including judges); (6) unjustified abuse of individual institutions by judges adjudicating in Poland and the need to change the situation in this respect; and finally (7) doubts that currently arise in Poland and that may arise in the future regarding the status of individual

DOI: 10.4324/9781003531500-6

persons appointed to judicial positions and the need to find criteria that could exclude possible political pressure or political motives in the process of making decisions by judges in criminal proceedings.

The preliminary analysis of issues related to the potential use of algorithm-based tools in criminal proceedings, based on the findings made by the authors from countries where algorithms are commonly used, seems to suggest that the use of algorithms in the decision-making process by bodies conducting criminal proceedings in Poland may be an answer to at least some of the above-mentioned needs. algorithm-based tools, as – by definition – based on the results of empirical research and using strictly objective criteria, and not only referring to the opinion of an individual person or persons, and at the same time automated to some extent and therefore simple and quick to use, allow – at the very least – for faster examination of cases, without any need to involve a large number of people in the decision-making process, systematisation and stabilisation of judicial practice, and ensuring apolitical approach in the solutions adopted in the final analysis.

However, the question arises whether the potential use of algorithm-based tools in Polish criminal proceedings would actually constitute an answer to all the problems of these proceedings and whether it would not generate new problems that would have to be dealt with, especially to the extent that algorithm-based tools would be entrusted with autonomous and uncontrolled decision-making on key issues from the perspective of human and civil freedoms and rights.

1.2 Research method

The (general) method used in this work is the contextual method due to two circumstances: (1) it allows for a multilateral approach to the studied phenomena; (2) it aims to define all relevant contexts: genetic, historical, functional, logical, axiological, and others.[1] As R. Tokarczyk points out: "contextualism leads to obtaining (...) rich (...) analytical material (...). It aims to (...) take into account not only the internal content of the legal phenomena under study, but also the circumstances of their creation, development and end, personality traits of legislators and creators of legal ideas, connections between laws and legal views with other social phenomena. Contextualism makes it possible to achieve (...) well-established and (...) scientifically valuable (...) results of cognitive processes".[2]

The detailed research method used in the publication is (primarily) the dogmatic and legal method.[3] The study of the issue of the use of algorithm-based tools in criminal proceedings was therefore (primarily) carried out through a comprehensive analysis of the normative material relating to all the issues raised. This analysis was carried out – which is worth adding –

primarily with the use of the derivational concept of interpretation of law by M. Zieliński.[4]

1.3 Considerations

1.3.1 Is there a need to use algorithm-based tools in the sentencing process during criminal proceedings?

The answer to the question of whether there is a need to use algorithm-based tools in Poland in the sentencing process during criminal proceedings is obvious – yes, there is. The above is caused by the circumstances already indicated in the introduction to this work, i.e. circumstances and needs in the form of: (1) the circumstances of slow adjudication by Polish courts, also in criminal law cases, despite the fact that one of the key conditions for the effectiveness of a penalty is its imposition immediately after the commission of a prohibited act, and the need to change this type of situation; (2) the need to stabilise the judicial practice in criminal cases, including avoiding serious discrepancies in the scope of penalties imposed in similar situations by individual criminal courts; (3) the need to ensure the effectiveness of criminal law response measures imposed in individual cases to the fact of committing a crime, especially in the scope of minimising the risk of recidivism; (4) the need to ensure that criminal law measures are adjudicated in response to the fact of committing a crime in a manner based on objective criteria (empirical data), and not only on the more or less justified predictions of individual persons (including judges); (5) the circumstances of unjustified abuse of individual institutions by judges adjudicating in Poland and the need to change the situation in this respect; and finally (6) the doubts that currently arise in Poland and that may arise in the future regarding the status of individual persons appointed to judicial positions and the need to find criteria that could exclude possible political pressure or political motives in the process of judges making decisions in criminal proceedings.

Psychological research proves that one of the key conditions for the effectiveness of a penalty is its imposition immediately after the prohibited act has been committed. As indicated by Bogdan Wojciszke: "(…) the severity of the punishment is not decisive for the effectiveness of its deterrent function. Instead, the decisive factor is the inevitability of punishment, the conviction of the potential aggressor that he will be punished for his aggression. (…) The requirement for effective punishment is (at the same time - KB) to deprive aggression of its instrumental value - the most effective are immediate punishments, which do not allow the aggression to finish and to derive benefits from it, but which are sometimes difficult to implement in practice".[5] Meanwhile, as the Polish Ministry of Justice claims: "The average duration of criminal cases in regional courts was 8.7 months. This is 1.6 months shorter than in 2015. In these courts, judgments in criminal procedural cases in the second instance were issued more quickly. These proceedings were almost 12% shorter than in 2020. On the other hand, in district courts, criminal cases regarding petty offences accelerated in 2021 compared to 2020 by 3.2%, and family cases by 5.4%".[6] This means that criminal proceedings in the jurisdictional phase (before the court) in Poland last on average almost nine months, and to this must be added the period of conducting preparatory proceedings and the period between the initiation of preparatory proceedings and the commission of the prohibited act. Such a long time elapsed between the commission of the prohibited act and the conviction and penalty may significantly worsen the effectiveness of the imposed penalty. The use of algorithm-based tools can shorten this time, especially when algorithms are the only "entity" adjudicating (e.g. in trivial cases, including petty offences) and making a decision immediately after the preparatory proceedings have been conducted.

The positive impact of algorithm-based tools could also be observed in the context of the stabilisation of criminal judicial practice. The algorithm used in individual criminal cases would be the same, applicable to the entire country, would be based on the same, extensive database, and would most likely give similar results in similar cases. This would be all the more possible because, along with the creation of a tool based on algorithms and the decision to implement it in criminal proceedings, it would also be necessary to create and implement a manual for the bodies using the algorithm, inter alia, to ensure the proper adequacy of the entered data and a similar method of collecting and entering it into the tool. This was done, for example, in Estonia, when the Estonian version of the OASys system was introduced; the Estonian manual indicated the understanding of individual terms used in the tool, specified the established risk factors, discussed the process of using the tool in an accessible way, etc.[7] Such a solution would also be necessary in Poland.

In order to illustrate the remaining of the above-mentioned circumstances and needs, i.e. (1) the need to ensure that criminal law measures are adjudicated in response to the fact of committing a crime in a manner based on objective criteria (empirical data), and not only on the better or worse justified predictions of individual persons (including judges); (2) the circumstances of unjustified abuse of individual institutions by judges adjudicating in Poland and the need to change the situation in this respect; and (3) the circumstances of justified doubts as to the status of individual persons appointed to judicial positions and the need to find criteria that could exclude possible political pressure or political motives in the process of making decisions by judges in criminal proceedings, one can refer to cases related to adjudicating pre-trial detention, i.e. a preventive measure consisting in (relatively) short-term deprivation of personal liberty of the accused person; especially those cases in which the adjudicating body includes persons appointed under a procedure before the National Council of the Judiciary in which persons not recognised by some lawyers participated. In cases of this type (in cases related to the application and extension of pre-trial detention), we are dealing with the necessity for the adjudicating body to refer to exceptionally vague criteria in the form of: (1) a justified fear that the accused will escape or go into hiding; (2) a justified fear that the accused will induce false testimony or explanations or in some other unlawful way obstruct the criminal proceedings; (3) a severe penalty that the accused is facing; (4) a justified fear that the accused, charged with committing a crime or intentional misdemeanour, will commit a crime against life, health, or public safety, especially if they threatened to commit such a crime. In the context of criteria formulated in this way, the following questions can be posed immediately: (1) What is a justified fear of obstructing the proceedings or committing another crime? (2) What should this justification be based on? (3) Are Polish judges prepared to anticipate potential scenarios of the accused's conduct in the future? (4) Are Polish judges able to separate their political sympathies from decisions made in matters of pre-trial detention? (5) Is it at all possible to find circumstances that would justify, to a greater or lesser extent, that the accused would behave in a particular way if pre-trial detention were not applied? Of the above questions, it seems that the easiest answer would be for the last question (indirectly related to questions [1]–[3]). It seems that only the creation and implementation of an algorithm-based tool and having a strong substantive basis in previously conducted empirical scientific research can allow decisions in the discussed cases to be based on objective criteria, and not only on the intuition of a given person (judge), and at the same time criteria that allow, with a high degree of probability (based on the findings resulting from adequate statistical data), to indicate the most probable course of action of the accused in the event of not applying pre-trial detention to them. However, the use of such a tool would allow for something else, namely, it would allow for the exclusion (or at least limitation) of the direct influence of personal political sympathies on the decision of the decision-making body, which in the context of the current Polish situation is an exceptionally important issue. It is enough to mention in this respect the example of a decision taken in the context of the pre-trial detention of the former Polish Minister of Justice and current Member of the Sejm of the Republic of Poland – Marcin Romanowski. The randomly selected adjudicating panel consisted of three judges, two of whom were associated with the previous government (Law and Justice party [Prawo i Sprawiedliwość]). One of the two judges themselves filed a motion to be excluded from the bench, while the other was excluded from the bench "ex officio" by a judge sympathetic to the current ruling party (Civic Coalition [Koalicja Obywatelska], Civic Platform [Platforma Obywatelska]), which action was met with a negative reaction from the chairwoman of the National Council of the Judiciary (according to some, sympathetic to Law and Justice), who stated that: "Judge K. Chmielewski was appointed to exclude judge Rusin-Batko. He had no right to exclude judge Dziwański. If he did so, he violated the law (USP) that specifies how cases are assigned to judges".[8] Unfortunately, such political scuffles have recently become an everyday occurrence in Poland, even though they are extremely undesirable situations that undermine citizens' trust in the judiciary, and could be avoided, at least partially, by using the algorithm-based tools. Unfortunately, such political scuffles have recently become an everyday occurrence in Poland, even though they are extremely undesirable situations that undermine citizens' trust in the judiciary, and could be avoided, at least partially, by using tools based on algorithms.

The use of algorithm-based tools would also – perhaps – allow for stopping the disturbing trend in Poland of applying pre-trial detention whenever it is requested by the prosecutor, and extending its application until the conclusion of criminal proceedings. As empirical research shows: "it should be noted that there is no criticism of prosecutors' applications to apply or extend the application of detention. Courts very rarely contest the prosecutor's theses, somewhat automatically adopting their position. Such a thesis is supported by the content of the justifications, which focus on discussing the circumstances that are unfavourable to the suspect. Consequently, the prosecutor is the real 'host' of the proceedings on the application of detention, not bearing any responsibility for the content of the decision. As a rule, courts agree to apply detention for the period of preparatory proceedings, regardless of what actions the prosecutor plans to conduct during these proceedings. Thus, they do not introduce any limits for this stage of the proceedings, although they have the instruments to do so".[9] This type of situation is unacceptable, and the only way to overcome it seems to be to use algorithm-based tools, which would force judges to reflect and take a serious, substantive approach to the cases they are considering, especially if the prosecutor's office's conviction about the necessity of applying detention were at odds with the result of using the algorithm, or whether the court's opinion about the necessity or lack thereof of applying pre-trial detention were at odds with the result of using such a tool.

1.3.2 Is there a possibility to use algorithm-based tools in the sentencing process during criminal proceedings?[10]

In response to the question of whether there is a possibility to use algorithm-based tools in the sentencing process during criminal proceedings, it should be stated that it is of course possible and we have examples of countries (e.g. the US with COMPAS (Correctional Offender Management Profiling for Alternative Sanctions) or GB with OASys (Offender Assessment System)) where such tools are used. However, introducing such a solution in Poland would require a fairly time-consuming and cost-intensive process, which would involve the need to carry out measures of different natures, depending on whether it was decided to create an entirely new tool or to transfer a tool designed abroad "only" to Poland and adapt it to the Polish reality.

Assuming that the solution indicated in the second part of the above-mentioned alternative were adopted, i.e. transferring the selected system from abroad to Poland was considered, first a political decision would have to be made at the level of the executive power, so politicians (members of the government) interested in transferring specific solutions to Poland should establish contact with their counterparts in the country from which the transfer would take place and agree on the most important issues in this regard. After making agreements at the political level, it would be necessary to establish an interdisciplinary team in Poland that could co-ordinate the implementation of the system. The team should include not only academic theorists representing various scientific disciplines (lawyers, criminologists, sociologists, psychologists, statisticians, etc.) but also practitioners, including in particular all those entities that would or could have contact with the system or at least with its results. They would have to be judges, prosecutors, officials of the State Prison Service, probation officers, etc. The team's task would be primarily to prepare the methodological assumptions of the Polish version of the transferred system.

In addition to work on the methodology for conducting risk assessment in Poland, as part of the actions related to transferring a given tool to Poland, risk assessment training and random risk assessment of convicts should begin. Training should be conducted throughout the period of introducing and operating the system (and quite often) to lead to a situation in which assessments are conducted in the most adequate manner possible.

Finally, the most important stage in the procedure of introducing a given tool to Poland would be to make appropriate legislative changes. Changes that are necessary, considering the perspective of the nature of algorithm-based tools and their potential interference with human freedoms and rights, including, inter alia, the right to privacy. It should be recalled that in accordance with Article 31 section 3 of the Constitution of the Republic of Poland.[11] "Any limitation upon the exercise of constitutional freedoms and rights may be imposed only by statute, and only when necessary in a democratic state for the protection of its security or public order, or to protect the natural environment, health or public morals, or the freedoms and rights of other persons. Such limitations shall not violate the essence of freedoms and rights".

1.3.3 Is there a possibility for algorithm-based tools to make decisions autonomously and without human supervision during sentencing in criminal proceedings?

Answering the question of whether there is a possibility in Poland to make decisions autonomously and without human control using algorithm-based tools during sentencing in criminal proceedings is not a simple task. There are a number of arguments in favour of this type of solution. These include in particular: (1) the objectivity of algorithm-based tools; (2) basing these tools on scientific evidence; (3) the simplicity and speed of using these tools and obtaining the results of their use; and (4) avoiding the direct influence of political factors on the decisions made.[12]

However, the question should be asked whether the use of algorithm-based tools (and only these tools) in the decision-making process in criminal proceedings would be sufficient and acceptable from the perspective of the fundamental and overarching objective of criminal law (and law in general), which is to ensure justice. Law is, after all, the art of goodness and equity (Ius est ars boni et aequi), and not just a tool for the pragmatic and effective application of individual regulations in order to achieve some specific, short- or long-term goal, e.g. in the form of painful retribution for the perpetrators of crimes for what they have done or in the form of reducing the risk of the perpetrators relapsing into criminal behaviour or reducing crime in genere. It is impossible to achieve goodness and equity in criminal law without justice; justice understood, for example, as the outstanding philosopher of law, J. Hervada, does in his works – and which the author of this work fully accepts – i.e. as giving to each his own, and in this sense being secondary in relation to the law, or in principle in relation to the act of attributing something to someone, which the law creates.[13] "The law – in its twofold meaning: as a law (lex), or conceived as the just thing – does not have its origin in the virtue of justice, nor this virtue is prior to or higher than it. The virtue of justice presupposes the right; in this sense it is always something subsequent to the right. Every act of justice presupposes a right established in advance; that is why it is a second act".[14]

The formula of justice, i.e. the formula "giving to each his own", should be understood broadly. It should be read as encompassing all behaviours (actions and omissions) necessary for a thing to fall within the realm of the rightful person's actual possession. The rightful person, i.e. every person (and in principle every natural or legal person) who, on the basis of positive or natural law, is entitled to something; without discrimination, without insight into circumstances that are not objective in relation to a given right. However, this does not mean the necessity of giving everyone the same, equally.[15]

The phrase "his own" should also be interpreted as broadly as the phrases "giving" and "to each". This refers to a human right, a thing that belongs to a person, which – as J. Hervada points out – "can mean a good or an evil (for example, penalty due to a crime), they can be physical or non-physical things (for example, a good reputation or a function), it may be a person (for example, one's child), a human activity (work, management, etc.), it could be an animal or group of animals, or it may be a thing in the strict sense. The terms encompass everything regarding which man can say *mine*, *yours*, *his*, provided that it can be the object or content of inter-human relations - in other words, relations of otherness or intersubjectivity – and therefore law can be predicated on it".[16]

Justice in the context of law and criminal proceedings can and should be interpreted in several ways; it should be viewed from all possible and important perspectives, not only from the perspective of "goods" that should be provided to society and the injured party during the proceedings (the perspective of retribution and ensuring safety, the perspective of repairing the damage caused by the crime and compensating for the harm suffered) but also from the perspective of "goods" and "discomforts" that should be provided to the perpetrator in a fair manner during the same proceedings. The perpetrator of a crime can therefore expect (and on the basis of just criminal procedure has the full right to do so!), for example, to be treated in a humane way, i.e. focused on themselves and not on some secondary object (the principle of respect for human dignity), adapted to them and the situation they were in at the time of committing the prohibited act and is in at the time of sentencing, and finally – in a way that is adequate to their guilt and needs (justice from the perspective of the perpetrator of the crime).

The above is confirmed by key Polish legal acts; it is enough to mention in this respect: (a) Article 30 of the Constitution of the Republic of Poland: "The inherent and inalienable dignity of the person shall constitute a source of freedoms and rights of persons and citizens. It shall be inviolable. The respect and protection thereof shall be the obligation of public authorities"; (b) Article 45 section 1 of the Constitution of the Republic of Poland: "Everyone shall have the right to a fair and public hearing of his case, without undue delay, before a competent, impartial and independent court"; or c) Article 53 § 1 of the Polish Criminal Code: "The court passes a sentence at its own discretion, within the limits prescribed by law, taking into account the degree of social consequences, mitigating or aggravating circumstances, objectives of the penalty in terms of its social effect, and preventive objectives that it should achieve in relation to the convicted person. The severity of the penalty may not exceed the degree of guilt". The last regulation in particular draws attention to the multi-justice rite of Polish criminal law: the penalty must not only be adequate to what the perpetrator did and how they did it (social harmfulness), and how it should have a far-reaching impact on society and the perpetrator themselves (social effect and preventive objectives); it should also be adequate to the degree of guilt that can be attributed to the perpetrator, and therefore it should also take into account strictly subjective factors concerning their intellectual and psychological attitude to the act and their ability to recognise the significance of this act both in the ontological and socio-legal aspects and to direct their conduct. Only when all these factors are taken into account will it be possible to make the penalty, and previously the conviction, fair both for society and the injured party, as well as for the perpetrator of the crime. Analogous conclusions result from the principle of protecting human dignity, which – of course – can be understood differently (depending on our religious, political, moral, etc. views), but due to the fact that it is also a legal concept, it should be understood in a way that is acceptable to everyone (or at least to the majority). Such an approach is to understand human dignity in the way proposed by I. Kant, i.e. as the necessity of treating a person as an end (in itself), and not as a way to achieve some other end in the form of, for example, protection of specific social goods other than the good of that person.[17] In this context, it is difficult to accept the conclusion that within the framework of criminal proceedings it would be possible to strive to achieve objectives that coincide only with the needs of people or groups other than the perpetrator, omitting the perpetrator's personal needs and expectations. On the contrary, the needs and expectations of the perpetrator, and later the convicted person, should be the priority, in the sense that criminal proceedings should aim primarily at changing the convicted person, removing the causes of their improper behaviour and enabling them to function peacefully in society, and not at fulfilling certain individual or collective needs of third parties or groups unrelated to the convicted person.

Considering the above, the question arises whether algorithm-based tools and their use as exclusive decision-making entities would allow for achieving justice characterised in this way in criminal proceedings. On the one hand, it could be said that it would. One could create an adjudicating algorithm that would allow for taking into account all factors that are important from the perspective of adjudication. An algorithm that would not only take into account all these factors, but would also give them appropriate weight depending on whether at a given moment the adjudication concerned conviction, sentencing, or another measure of criminal law response to the fact of committing a crime; weight – it should be added – that could be and would probably be differentiated also in terms of the justice perspective that would be discussed at a given moment, e.g. higher weight for the subjective side (the perpetrator's intellectual and volitional attitude to the act) in the case of deciding on the penalty appropriate from the perspective of a just verdict for the perpetrator, and lower in the case of deciding on the penalty appropriate from the perspective of satisfying the social sense of justice.

If one was to present such an algorithm (to the extent that it would decide on the penalty imposed) in a simplified version of the list of steps, it could be worded as follows:

1 Deciding on a just penalty from the perspective of the perpetrator:
   - 1a Consider factors X and give them a weight of 00.
   - 1b Consider factors Y and give them a weight of 11.
   - 1c Add the result of the actions from points 1a and 1b.

2 Deciding on a just penalty from the perspective of society:
   - 2a Consider factors X and give them a weight of 33.
   - 2b Consider factors Y and give them a weight of 44.
   - 2c Add the result of the actions from points 2a and 2b.

3 Deciding on a just penalty from the perspective of the injured party:
   - 3a Consider factors X and give them a weight of 55.
   - 3b Consider factors Y and give them a weight of 66.
   - 3c Add the result of the actions from points 3a and 3b.

4 Deciding on a just penalty from all perspectives:
   - 4a Add the result of the actions from points 1c, 2c, and 3c.

5 Deciding on the final sentence:
   - 5a Indicate the penalty that is adequate to the result of the actions from point 4a.

Conversely, the question arises whether the use of such an algorithm would be sufficient and would allow for an adequate assessment of a given factual situation in all its perspectives and shades. Could such a simplified procedure, devoid of human emotions and intuition, really lead to adequate results? In the opinion of the author of this work – no, such a solution could not ensure multi-justice, which was mentioned earlier. Issues concerning the causes and situational context of the perpetrator's committing a prohibited act, as well as the perpetrator's intellectual and psychological attitude to the act and their ability to recognise the significance of this act both in the ontological and socio-legal aspects, and to direct their conduct, are too complex to be included in the simple framework of numerical values and their weights. The very issue of the subjective aspect of a prohibited act, with its entire range of potential forms and shades, and with the entire range of potential ways of assessing them in terms of their significance for evaluating a given event, makes it impossible to talk about the possibility of limiting oneself solely to tools based on algorithms. How can we reduce to numerical values and their weights the distinction between direct intent, i.e. a situation in which the perpetrator wants to commit a prohibited act, and eventual intent, i.e. a situation in which the perpetrator accepts (is indifferent to) committing this act? How can we distinguish in this way the issue of conscious and unconscious lack of intent, i.e. a situation in which the perpetrator foresees the possibility of committing a prohibited act but wants not to commit it, and a situation in which the perpetrator does not foresee the possibility of committing it (the prohibited act) at all? How can we distinguish between situations in which the perpetrator's direct intent takes the form of a specific direct intent (the perpetrator acts with a precisely defined purpose) and ordinary direct intent? How can we distinguish between situations in which the direct intent takes the form of a planned direct intent (undertaken by the perpetrator in advance) and situations in which the direct intent takes the form of a sudden direct intent (undertaken by the perpetrator at the moment of committing the act, without further thought)? How can we distinguish between and give weight to the various shades of possible direct intents, conscious and unconscious lack of intent? Should the above-mentioned issues be treated in the same way in the context of all crimes, or should they be differentiated?

All of the above questions are rhetorical in nature, as it is impossible to answer them beyond doubt and in an unambiguous manner. Creating an algorithm that takes into account subjective factors and systematises these factors in terms of their importance for individual cases is basically impossible (or at least very difficult), and in the absence of the possibility of its verification and correction by an external entity in the form of a living person, it is downright dangerous, because in a given specific situation it may constitute an unacceptable outcome of the proceedings from a justice perspective.[18] It is enough to imagine a situation in which a 17-year-old repeatedly engages in (fully intentionally and planned) sexual intercourse with his 14-year-old partner, as a result of which she becomes pregnant. This type of conduct is prohibited in Poland due to the wording of Article 200 § 1 of the Polish Criminal Code, which prohibits sexual intercourse with a minor under the age of 15, and for committing it provides for up to 15 years of imprisonment. Considering the fact that the perpetrator would act in the situation described above with planned direct intent and would commit the prohibited act multiple times, an algorithm that was not properly calibrated and prepared for such situations could propose imposing a sentence of up to 10–15 years of imprisonment on the minor perpetrator (especially if the characteristics of the act itself included the perpetrator's extensive criminal history); however, the tool would not necessarily be prepared to take into account, for example, such circumstances as the fact that the perpetrator and the injured party were in a permanent relationship, loved each other, the perpetrator expressed a desire to support and care for the injured party and the child, etc. These circumstances could only be taken into account by a court in the form of a specific person – a judge, who would check the result of using the algorithm and modify the proposed penalty. Similar problems could also appear in the context of other prohibited acts, including those threatened with very high penalties, hence either the (physically impossible) need to adapt the tool based on algorithms to all potential crimes and problems related to them, or the need for additional verification of the results of using the tool by a human.

It should be emphasised that justice does not exist in nature; justice is an assessment made by a human in the context of a given factual situation and cannot exist without a human who would make such an assessment, and at the same time it is dependent on a number of factors: both objective and subjective, including cognitive abilities, personality traits or moods and emotions of the entity making the assessment. Only a human is able to "feel" (it is hard to find a better phrase) in connection with what in a given specific case could be considered acceptable (and just) for all interested parties, would be able to sense the moods, emotions, and expectations accompanying the assessment, would be able to select means of criminal law response that is not only pragmatic and potentially capable of achieving the long-term objective of ensuring the safety of society and the change of the perpetrator, but also means adequate from the perspective of the sense of justice of all entities participating in the proceedings.

The above does not mean, of course, that the use of algorithm-based tools is not possible or necessary. The above only means that these tools should be used only as an aid, among other things, to speed up criminal proceedings and ensure their highest possible objectivity, as well as to reduce concerns about politically manipulated sentencing results. However, introducing such a solution to the Polish legal system (but also to the legal systems of other countries) would require a number of legal changes, including those concerning the highest-ranking legal acts. Tools based on algorithms, as interfering with human rights and freedoms and participating in sentencing, like courts, would have to find a basis for their functioning even in the Constitution of the Republic of Poland, and a potential constitutional regulation could take the following form – already proposed elsewhere by the author of this work – "Article X. Section 1. Algorithms and tools based on them may be used in criminal proceedings only when the possibility of their use is expressly provided for by the law and only when their use is necessary in a democratic state. Section 2. Algorithms and tools based on them cannot be the sole basis for a decision taken in criminal proceedings. Section 3. The use of algorithms may not lead to a violation of the essence of freedom and human rights. Section 4. Full characteristics of algorithms and tools based on them used in criminal proceedings constitute public information".

1.4 Conclusions

Summing up all the considerations, it should be stated that there is no possibility in Poland (or in any other democratic state) of autonomous and uncontrolled human decision-making by algorithm-based tools during sentencing in criminal proceedings.[19] The above would be a violation of basic human rights, including their right to fair treatment and, above all, their dignity. However, this does not mean that algorithms and tools based on them cannot and should not be used in the course of criminal proceedings. On the contrary – their use can bring many benefits, including, in particular, the reduction of political pressure on the bodies applying the law and the minimisation of the risk of transferring political sympathies to the decisions made in criminal cases. This is especially true in Poland and, it seems, in other "young" democracies, where the temptation to annoy a person with different political views, even if unconsciously by those involved in criminal proceedings (including judges), can be very high.

Notes

1 See TOKARCZYK, Roman. Komparatystyka prawnicza, Warsaw, 2008, p. 74.
2 TOKARCZYK. Komparatystyka prawnicza, p. 74.
3 See CROSS, Frank. The Theory and Practice of Statutory Interpretation, Stanford, 2009; CROSS, Rupert, BELL, John, ENGLE, George. Cross: Statutory Interpretation, London, 1995; WALTON, Douglas, MACAGNO, Fabrizio, SARTOR, Giovanni. Statutory Interpretation: Pragmatics and Argumentation, Cambridge, 2020. https://doi.org/10.1017/9781108554572; YULE, Kim. Statutory Interpretation: General Principles and Recent Trends, New York, 2009.
4 See BOGUCKI, Olgierd. The Derivational Theory of Legal Interpretation in Polish Legal Theory, International Journal for the Semiotics of Law – Revue internationale de Sémiotique juridique, 33, 2020, pp. 617–636. https://doi.org/10.1007/s11196-019-09628-1.
5 WOJCISZKE, Bogdan, Psychologia społeczna, Warsaw, 2020, pp. 395–396.
6 https://www.gov.pl/web/sprawiedliwosc/sady-pracuja-szybciej (accessed 20 August 2024); https://rm.coe.int/cepej-report-2020-22-e-web/1680a86279 (accessed 20 August 2024).
7 Zob. np. BURDZIAK, Konrad, RÜÜTEL, Erik. Prognoza kryminologiczna. Porównanie rozwiązań estońskich i polskich, Lublin, 2022, p. 62.
8 https://www.rp.pl/sady-i-trybunaly/art40957781-sedzia-bezprawnie-wylaczony-ze-sprawy-romanowskiego-sprawa-wniosku-o-areszt-dla-posla (accessed 20 August 2024).
9 ZAJĄC, Dominik, KAJFASZ, Jolanta. 12. Wnioski. In: KARLIK, Piotr, PILITOWSKI, Bartosz (eds.). Stosowanie tymczasowego aresztowania. Analiza prak-

tyczna, Warsaw, 2022. https://sip.lex.pl/#/monogra. ph/369526652/429904?keyword=tymczasowe%20aresztowanie&tocHit=1&cm=SREST (accessed 20 August 2024)

10 The considerations in this subsection are based on: BURDZIAK, Konrad, RÜÜTEL, Erik. Prognoza, pp. 78–80.

11 Constitution of the Republic of Poland of April 2, 1997 (Journal of Laws No. 78, item 483, as amended).

12 Zob. np. BURDZIAK, Konrad, RÜÜTEL, Erik. Prognoza, p. 124.

13 See HERVADA, Javier. Critical introduction to natural law, Montréal, QC, 2006, p. 10.

14 HERVADA. Critical introduction, p. 13.

15 HERVADA. Critical introduction, pp. 17–27.

16 HERVADA. Critical introduction, pp. 25–26.

17 Zob. BURDZIAK, Konrad. Osoba niepoczytalna a prawnokarna norma sankcjonowana. Rozważania na tle polskiego Kodeksu karnego, Warsaw, 2021, pp. 53–56.

18 Although leaving a person full discretion in sentencing may also be questionable. Hence, most likely, the introduction in the Polish Criminal Code of the regulations of Article 53 § 2a and 2b, indicating the aggravating and mitigating circumstances of criminal responsibility, which the court must always take into account ex officio, and which are determined by the legislator, i.e. an entity that is by definition objective and rational.

19 Similarly, TAYLOR, Isaac. Justice by Algorithm: The Limits of AI in Criminal Sentencing. Criminal Justice Ethics, 42(3), 2023, pp. 193–213. https://doi.org/10.1080/0731129X.2023.2275967.

Chapter 2

Using algorithms in Polish criminal law

Useful tools or risk of bias

Magdalena Kowalewska-Łukuć

2.1 Research objective

The use of algorithms in criminal law, in sentencing, the application of probation measures, the prediction of recidivism or the risk of offending in general, is becoming a reality of criminal policy in many countries and a matter of the near future in others, including Poland. Parallel to the enthusiasm surrounding the use of algorithms, or artificial intelligence (AI) in general, in criminal law, however, are concerns about their reliability and fairness. This chapter will outline the use of algorithms in criminal law against the context of the objections raised to their use and, more specifically, the biases potentially nested within them. It will also address problematic issues related to the decision-making by judges, excluding the use of algorithms, including the potential guidance of heuristics, biases or stereotypes. Against this background, the article will attempt to answer the question of how algorithms in Polish criminal law should be constructed and used to be as free of bias as possible.

The text remains grounded in the Polish legal system. However, the considerations it contains can be successfully generalised to the use of algorithms in the criminal law in general, not only in Polish criminal law and criminal proceedings.

2.2 Research method

The method used is predominantly contextual method, as it enables a multifaceted approach to the issues under investigation. Next there are socio-legal, psycho-legal and to a very limited extent dogmatic-legal.

2.3 Considerations

2.3.1 Algorithms in criminal law in general

Forecasting, or even estimating probability, is inevitably present in the justice system. This is absolutely no different in criminal law. Perhaps the most

DOI: 10.4324/9781003531500-7

prominent example of estimating probability is the formulation of a criminological prognosis. In Polish criminal law, such a prognosis is a premise for the court's decision as to whether to apply a given probationary measure. According to Article 66 § 1 of the Polish Criminal Code, when deciding on the conditional discontinuance of criminal proceedings, the court must base its decision on the assumption that, despite the discontinuance of proceedings, the offender will comply with the legal order, and, in particular will not commit a crime. This presumption, then, is built on the assessment of the offender's attitude, his/her personal qualities and conditions and his/her way of life to the present. In the case of the second of the probationary measures known to the Polish law – conditional suspension of the execution of a sentence, the criminological prognosis of the offender is formulated on the basis of similar factors – the offender's attitude, personal qualities and conditions, his or her way of life and behaviour after committing the offence. In the criminological prognosis accompanying conditional early release, the attitude, characteristics and personal conditions of the offender, the circumstances in which the offence was committed and the behaviour after the offence was committed and while serving the sentence are crucial. The assessment of these circumstances is intended to lead the court to believe that the convicted person will, upon release, comply with the penal or protective measure imposed and respect the order of the law, and, in particular will not commit the offence again.

The criminological prognosis accompanying the court in deciding on a probationary measure is not only the domain of Polish criminal law.[1] Nor does it only accompany decisions on probationary measures. For example, in Polish criminal law, in the case of a decision on the application of preventive measures, the court predicts the likelihood of the offender committing a crime again, i.e. simply criminological recidivism (Article 93b § 1 of the Polish Criminal Code). Also, still at the stage of criminal proceedings prior to the final verdict, the court or prosecutor, when deciding on the selection of appropriate preventive measures – such as bail or pre-trial detention, has to assess which of them, taking into account various data related to the offender and the alleged act, will be sufficient to secure the proper course of criminal proceedings.

AI, or more specifically algorithms in Polish criminal law, are not yet applied at present. However, this is probably a matter of time, as we have to agree, with the statement that "In this technological era, Artificial Intelligence (AI), although still in its infancy, is slowly being introduced across all jurisdictions". This is reflected in attempts to apply AI tools, including algorithms in criminal law in other countries. The pioneer is the USA. It was in the USA that one of the more popular algorithms used in criminal cases was developed in 1998 – COMPAS (Correctional Offender Management Profiling for Alternative Sanctions). In its basic version, COMPAS

Core, this tool consists of two scales – risk scale and criminogenic needs. The results obtained on the risk scale allow for a 12-month prognosis in several areas – pretrial release risk, general recidivism, violent recidivism. Furthermore the scale of criminogenic needs allows not only to estimate the risk of recidivism but also to achieve the goals of the so-called fourth generation tools, i.e. appropriate therapy and effective supervision of a given offender.[2] The scale in question is based on information on many areas of the offender's behaviour – both static, of a historical nature (e.g. conflicts with the law that previously occurred in the offender's family, his previous criminal record), as well as of a dynamic nature (e.g. residence, leisure activities, financial problems, abuse of psychoactive substances).[3]

A second example of an algorithm used quite widely in the USA is the PSA (Public Safety Assessment). The PSA is intended as a decision-making tool for pretrial release. The PSA aims to provide an objective assessment of the risk that the defendant may pose to the community and the risk that they will not appear at trial if released before trial. The goals of creating and implementing the PSA are identified as reducing the number of people in pre-trial detention, improving public safety and promoting fairness in the criminal justice system. Unlike COMPAS, PSA is based only on an analysis of static data such as the age of the defendant at the time of arrest, past offences, violent offences, past convictions and the number of convictions, number and frequency of absences from court in the past, appeals against a previous conviction and current charge of a violent offence. Based on these criteria, the PSA calculates three risk indicators: committing a new offence, committing a new violent offence, and failing to appear at trial.[4] According to the PSA developers, the algorithm was created using the largest and most diverse set of pretrial records ever assembled. It was developed based on approximately 750,000 cases from around 300 jurisdictions across the USA.[5]

2.3.2 *Objections and concerns about algorithms in criminal law*

Concerns and objections to the use of algorithms in criminal law, in addition to those raised against AI and machine learning in general, mainly focus on the argument concerning the anchoring of prejudices and stereotypes, primarily of a racial nature. A report prepared in 2016 by the investigative journalists who make up the ProPublica group has become widely known. According to this report, black defendants are far more likely than white defendants to be incorrectly judged to be at a higher risk of recidivism, while white defendants are more likely than black defendants to be incorrectly flagged as low risk.[6] The second factor of a stereotypical nature is gender – male gender is automatically associated with a higher risk of recidivism and aggressive behavior. Automatically, the degree of risk of recidivism according to the algorithms is influenced by having/not having work, the level of education or the age of the offender. For example, in Missouri's Information-Based Discretionary Sentencing System (MIBSS), with the same parameters in the other items of this tool, an unemployed offender who has not graduated from high school automatically receives 3 points less on a 16-point scale than a high school graduate with a job.[7] Lack of cultural sensitivity or insufficient cultural sensitivity of the algorithms is identified as another potentially stereotyping factor. For example, the Supreme Court of Western Australia, considering the case of the Director of Public Prosecutions for Western Australia v. Mangolamara, concluded that the prediction tools used – Sexual Violence Risk-20 (SVR-20) and the Risk for Sexual Violence Protocol (RSVP) – were not devised for and do not necessarily take account of the social circumstances of indigenous Australians in remote communities.[8]

Finally, it is argued that some algorithms in use do not have significantly higher accuracy in estimating the risk of recidivism than a human being, and one without legal or sentencing training and experience. In a study conducted in this suburb, randomly selected individuals, without any training at all, were expected to estimate the recidivism risk of individual offenders at a similar level as COMPAS.[9]

2.3.3 *Judicial assessment of the perpetrator and his/her risks*

With a high degree of probability, it can be assumed that, if judges were AI tools, the adjudications and procedural decisions made would be the same, for identical facts and legal situations and the person of the offender, regardless of which judge ruled on the case.[10] Meanwhile, because judges are only (and as much as) human beings and not machines, there are often divergent rulings on identical cases.[11] Differences in sentences imposed may result from factors such as a different assessment of the acts in relation to a given directive (e.g. in Polish criminal law in relation to the degree of social harm *in concreto*),[12] or the different decision weights assigned to the various directives, individual differences among judges in the cognitive transformation of a given weight into the level of punishment.[13] At the same time, it is possible to identify a certain group of factors that are common to judges in measuring the amount of a given punishment. This group includes factors such as the defendant's gender, family situation, employment or social status.[14] It seems to sound familiar – analogous factors were, after all, to be unfairly taken into account by algorithms when determining the risk of reoffending.

It should be noted here that judges, despite their level of education, experience or preparation for office in general, are not free from the use of cognitive schemes, including the use of heuristics. Heuristics, as certain simplified methods of inference, can in principle be useful, providing us with a certain cognitive and decision-making "economy". At the same time, however, they can lead to cognitive errors, i.e. not necessarily rational or logical conclusions and decisions. The heuristic that can potentially occur most frequently in the decision-making process of judgements is the anchoring heuristic. It involves relying, in making a decision, or formulating a judgement, on an initial baseline value/information (known as an anchor) that becomes a certain reference point. This anchor may result in additional information being ignored or not sufficiently taken into account.[15]

Translating the construct of anchoring heuristics and the experiment of D. Kahneman and A. Tversky to decision-making in a criminal proceedings, it can be assumed that the amount of punishment demanded by the prosecution provides a certain anchor and can influence the court's decision on its final level. This is also confirmed by studies carried out on this issue.[16]

In addition to the influence of cognitive schemas on judges' decisions, it is also worth noting the often unavoidable influence of their emotions. The vision of a judge devoid of emotion is most simply implausible.[17] The situation of making or forming a judgement, which is undoubtedly the case in a criminal proceeding, is inevitably accompanied by moral emotions, often unconscious.[18]

The jurisprudential practice in Poland concerning the granting of conditional early release from serving the remainder of the prison sentence can serve as an example of not necessarily rational and adequate court decisions. According to research conducted in 2019 for the Polish Justice Institute, court decisions on granting conditional early release are often made in disregard of the analysis of factors that are supposed to shape a positive criminological prognosis, i.e. the attitude, characteristics and personal conditions of the offender, the circumstances of committing the offence and behaviour after committing the offence and during serving the sentence.[19] In some cases, based on a reading of the justifications for these judgments, we may even get the impression that the decision was taken purely by chance, intuition or against the factors indicated in the Criminal Code.[20] Some cases from the practice of pre-trial detention in Polish criminal proceedings seem to present a similar picture. It can therefore be concluded that the decisions of judges cannot always be regarded as rational, free from personal convictions or even in some way justified.[21]

2.3.4 *Revision of functions and requirements for algorithms*

As indicated above, judges' decisions are not free from cognitive errors, irrationality or personal beliefs or dispositions not necessarily related to the merits of the case. It is therefore worth not dismissing the possibility of supporting judges' adjudicatory decisions with various AI tools, including algorithms. As regards the objections to algorithms, briefly sketched above, it can be concluded that an algorithm is as biased or prejudiced as its creator made it. This is vividly captured in the phrase garbage in – garbage out[22] summarising the effective creation of machine learning in general. Indeed, it is rightly pointed out that "The reliance on data in machine learning means that the accuracy and reliability of the outputs generated will depend on the integrity and appropriateness of the training data that is used. If, for example, data collection was patchy so that it was systemically skewed, then the system will learn the same skew".[23] One example is Amazon's attempts to use algorithms in its recruitment process. The system used by this company, built on data about its existing, largely male workforce, has "learned" to reject applications from women.[24] It is clear that AI, including any algorithm, relies on the data provided to it previously. Data trains the system and data calibrates the system.[25] It is therefore clear that the quality of the data, including the absence of bias, determines the good, in the sense of accurate, functioning of the algorithm.

The above signalled issue has not only been recognised in the academic field of AI and law, but is also present in the political and social debate in the USA or Canada. It can therefore be argued that the question of whether to use algorithms in criminal law should rather be reformulated as a question of how to use them, so that they can actually meet the objectives set for them, i.e. to relieve the courts of assessing the risk of recidivism and to objectify the decisions made in this regard.[26] In response to such a reformulated question, it has already been possible to formulate a number of recommendations or so-called good practices that could potentially allow for at least partial elimination of problems related to biases anchored in algorithms. Among these, improving the collection, accuracy, reliability and disclosure of algorithmic data and statutory prohibitions on the use of certain factors in algorithmic decision-making, including race or potential proxy factors, such as education, employment, geography and mandatory education on the racial effects of algorithmic risk assessments.[27]

The FATE model is also worth noting here. It defines the basic features that should characterise every system using AI – Fairness, Accountability, Transparency and Ethics. Fairness refers to treating people impartially, fairly and without discrimination. Accountability means taking responsibility for the actions taken. In the case of the use of predictive tools in judicial practice, accountability for the decision made with the help of AI remains inherently linked to the court. This is because it is the court and not the algorithm that makes the ruling. Indeed, the algorithm is only a tool and its function should only be subsidiary. Transparency means making the mechanism of the tool as transparent as possible, manifested, for example, in the publication of the weights used by the algorithms, the scoring guidelines or the limitations and ethical challenges that its developers have had to face in order to improve the transparency of their models. Ultimately, the role of ethics is to decide whether given variables can be predictive.[28]

2.4 Conclusions

Concluding the above considerations and trying to answer the question posed in the title, it should be stated that algorithms can be an effective tool in the administration of justice, including in criminal law. Effective, i.e. supporting the work of the judge and improving his/her decision-making processes. This does not mean, however, that we should unconditionally and unreflectively reform, for example, Polish criminal proceedings and make their use a statutory decree. We may take the risk of stating that the use of algorithms in criminal law, particularly outside North America, is still in *statu nascendi*. It therefore requires the development of a rational framework, assumptions and good practices. Especially since, as tried to demonstrate above, at this moment, the use of algorithms in criminal law may carry some risks, such as the anchoring of biases. At the same time, however, as also tried to signal above, judicial decisions are not free of such risks either. In each case, however, this risk can be reduced by a conscious and adequate selection of data.

In conclusion, it can therefore be pointed out that algorithms, not only are, but can be a useful tool in criminal law. However, it is up to us humans – lawyers, engineers – to ensure that, in supporting the work of the judge and the judiciary, these algorithms are as free of bias and injustice as possible.

Notes

1 See KOWALEWSKA-ŁUKUĆ Magdalena, BURDZIAK, Konrad, The use of AI in formulating a criminological prognosis of an offender, Technium Social Sciences, 25, 2021, pp. 115–116.
2 KOWALEWSKA-ŁUKUĆ Magdalena, BURDZIAK, Konrad, The use of AI in formulating a criminological prognosis of an offender, p. 121.
3 KOWALEWSKA-ŁUKUĆ Magdalena, BURDZIAK, Konrad, The use of AI in formulating a criminological prognosis of an offender, p. 121.
4 OKIDEGBE, Ngozi, The Democratizing Potential of Algorithms? Connecticut Law Review, 739, 2022, p. 18.
5 Law Commission of Ontario, The Rise and Fall of AI and Algorithms in American Criminal Justice: Lessons for Canada, Toronto 2020, p. 15.
6 LARSON, Jeff, MATTU, Surya, KIRCHNER, Lauren, ANGWIN, Julia, How We Analyzed the COMPAS Recidivism Algorithm, 2016, https://www.propublica.org/article/how-we-analyzed-the-compas-recidivism-algorithm, access: 9 December 2024.
7 STARR, Sonja Evidence-Based Sentencing and the Scientific Rationalization of Discrimination, Stanford Law Review, 4, 2014, p. 813.

8 ANDERSON, Caoimhe, The Impact of Algorithms in Criminal Sentencing on Due Process Rights, Doctoral Thesis 2019, p. 36. https://pureadmin.qub.ac.uk/ws/portalfiles/portal/236355240/The_Impact_of_Algorithms_in_Criminal_Sentencing_on_Due_Process_Rights_Master_Copy_Final_6_.pdf, accessed 9 December 2024.

9 See DRESSEL, Julia, FARID, Hany, The accuracy, fairness, and limits of predicting recidivism, Science Advances, 4, 2018, https://doi.org/10.1126/sciadv.aao5580, https://www.ncbi.nlm.nih.gov/pmc/articles/PMC5777393/#R13, accessed 9 December 2024.

10 See MARKIEWICZ, Łukasz, MARKIEWICZ-ŻUCHOWSKA, Agnieszka, Skłonności poznawcze sędziego wpływające na wysokość wymierzonej kary, Decyzje, 18, 2012, p. 51.

11 Ł. Markiewicz i A. Markiewicz-Żuchowska cite in their article the example of a case in which a second-instance court, on the basis of the same findings of fact and law, changed the sentence imposed on the accused by the first-instance court from seven years to five years and six months – MARKIEWICZ, Łukasz, MARKIEWICZ-ŻUCHOWSKA, Agnieszka, Skłonności poznawcze sędziego wpływające na wysokość wymierzonej kary, p. 50. It should be noted that this is not an isolated case.

12 In accordance with Article 53 of the Polish Criminal Code, the court, in imposing a sentence, should take into account the degree of social harmfulness of the act and taking into consideration preventive and educational aims it is to achieve with regard to the sentenced person, as well as the need to develop legal awareness of the society.

13 MARKIEWICZ, Łukasz, MARKIEWICZ-ŻUCHOWSKA, Agnieszka, Skłonności poznawcze sędziego wpływające na wysokość wymierzonej kary, p. 55.

14 As an aside, it may be added that it is impossible to exclude the influence on the court's decisions of factors such as the gender, religious or political views of the judge himself or herself, or even whether he or she has had a meal while working – see MARKIEWICZ, Łukasz, MARKIEWICZ-ŻUCHOWSKA, Agnieszka, Skłonności poznawcze sędziego wpływające na wysokość wymierzonej kary, pp. 61, 62.

15 The authors of the concept of heuristics D. Kahneman and A. Tversky, in an experiment they conducted, asked participants to indicate the percentage of African countries in the UN. Before giving a specific number, the participants were asked to spin a "wheel of fortune", on which either the number 10 or 65 could fall. The participants who drew the number 10 gave a significantly lower percentage of African member states than the participants in the second study group who drew the number 65 and treated it, presumably unconsciously, as an anchor.

16 MARKIEWICZ, Łukasz, MARKIEWICZ-ŻUCHOWSKA, Agnieszka, Skłonności poznawcze sędziego wpływające na wysokość wymierzonej kary, pp. 69–71. A similar mechanism is, moreover, observed in civil cases for compensation or damages, where the anchor becomes the amount indicated by the claimant in the claim.

17 See PARTYK, Aleksandra, Czy sędziowie mają intuicję? Przyczynek do rozważań o sędziowskich mechanizmach decyzyjnych, Sosnowiec 2023, p. 83.

18 See CHIRKOWSKA-SMOLAK, Teresa, SMOLAK, Marek, Oceny moralne w rozumowaniu sędziowskim, Ruch Prawniczy, Ekonomiczny i Socjologiczny, 2, 2017, p. 45 i BROŻEK, Bartosz, Umysł Prawniczy, Kraków 2018, pp. 74–75.

19 KOWALEWSKA-ŁUKUĆ Magdalena, BURDZIAK, Konrad, The use of AI in formulating a criminological prognosis of an offender, p. 119.

20 For example, in one of the examined cases, in the justification of the issued decision, the court clearly indicated that the convicted person is a member of a criminal subculture and adheres to its values, however, taking into account the fact that he has behaved properly in prison, it is necessary to give him a chance. Consequently, the court granted conditional early release based essentially on only one of the factors indicated by the Code for shaping a positive criminological prognosis, i.e. the convicted person's behaviour while serving his sentence, which, moreover, could have been assessed differently taking into account his membership of the prison subculture – see KOWALEWSKA-ŁUKUĆ Magdalena, BURDZIAK, Konrad, The use of AI in formulating a criminological prognosis of an offender, p. 119.

21 See PILITOWSKI, Bartosz, Aktualna praktyk stosowania tymczasowego aresztowania w Polsce. Raport z badań empirycznych, Toruń 2019, https://courtwatch.pl/wp-content/uploads/2019/12/tymczasowe_aresztowania_FCWP.pdf, accessed 9 December 2024.

22 This phrase can be rephrased as "bias in – bias out".

23 BELL, Felicity, MOSES, Lyria, LEGG, Michael, SILOVE, Jake, ZALNIERIUTE, Monika, AI Decision-Making and the Courts: A Guide for Judges, Tribunal Members and Court Administrators, Australasian Institute of Judicial Administration, 2023, p. 13.

24 BELL, Felicity, MOSES, Lyria, LEGG, Michael, SILOVE, Jake, ZALNIERIUTE, Monika, AI Decision-Making and the Courts, p. 13.

25 See Law Commission of Ontario, The Rise and Fall of AI and Algorithms in American Criminal Justice, p. 20 and ZAVRŠNIK, Aleš, Algorithmic justice: Algorithms and big data in criminal justice settings, European Journal of Criminology, 18, 2021, p. 630.

26 KOWALEWSKA-ŁUKUĆ Magdalena, BURDZIAK, Konrad, Technium Social Sciences, 25, 2021, p. 122.

27 Law Commission of Ontario, The Rise and Fall of AI and Algorithms In American Criminal Justice, p. 33.

28 See KOWALEWSKA-ŁUKUĆ Magdalena, BURDZIAK, Konrad, The use of AI in formulating a criminological prognosis of an offender, p. 123 and EGIDO, Cibrian, Artificial intelligence in criminal justice settings, 2020, p. 30, https://addi.ehu.es/bitstream/handle/10810/48983/TFG_%20Cibrian%20Egido.pdf?sequence=2&isAllowed=y, accessed 9 December 2024.

Chapter 3

Artificial intelligence algorithms in the context of cybersecurity

AI Act and the national cybersecurity system – opportunities and challenges for social and economic development in the Republic of Poland

Dominika Skoczylas

3.1 Research objective

It can be argued that the development of information and communication technologies has contributed to the modernisation of the traditional way of doing things and providing services. In the light of the above statement, it should be pointed out that changes have occurred in both the public and private sectors. There is no doubt that the greatest of these have occurred in the activities undertaken by the public administration and that computerisation has resulted in the creation of electronic administration, so-called e-government. The performance of public tasks at a distance required the introduction of specific procedures for electronic management, thus technological and organisational interaction, the development and maintenance of Infrastructure in Information and Communication Technologies (ICT)infrastructure and the growth of digital competence of network and system users were necessary. The success of computerisation depended (and still depends) on defining the rules of interaction between technological and human resources, de facto "the two systems have to be rationalised together, in the sense of development of machinery and software, training and qualification of human resources in order to keep pace with modern technologies".[1] Of course, the commitment of administrative actors in the area of digital transformation should be evaluated positively, due to, among other things, the speed and simplicity of getting things done, the availability (universality) of public information, the interoperability, personalisation and cross-border nature of e-service provision and the automation of procedures. E-government realises the right to good administration and "has a governance, democratic and social aspect".[2] However, it should not be forgotten that the determinant of proper civilisational

DOI: 10.4324/9781003531500-8

development is not only technological issues but also (and perhaps even primarily) organisational and legal conditions.

According to the principle of legalism contained in the Constitution of the Republic of Poland,[3] public authorities act on the basis and within the limits of the law. In other words, a natural effect of the digital transformation will be changes in the scope of universally applicable law. Following Iwona Niżnik-Dobosz, it should be confirmed that "for the law cannot be indifferent to the achievements and development of civilisation, as it is itself a product of civilisation and at the same time acts for the future".[4] It is therefore clear that electronic means of communication have revolutionised the hitherto classic way of providing e-services. Moreover, new challenges are emerging in the matter of efficient, effective and, above all, secure management of public affairs. A similar problem also applies to the private sector (competitiveness versus security of e-services). Ensuring maximum socio-economic development through the use of new technologies is becoming increasingly important, especially in Europe, including the Republic of Poland. The above correlates with the concern regarding the use of artificial intelligence (AI) algorithms in the context of ensuring cybersecurity. Among other things, the matter of the processing of personal data (including sensitive data) and the security of administrative procedures has become a serious problem.[5] Undoubtedly, AI algorithms can strengthen the cybersecurity of ICT networks and systems, on the other hand, they can lead to a weakening of resilience against cyberthreats and even violate basic human rights (welfare). The above depends on who is using the AI tools and for what purpose. Nevertheless, referring to the case of the Republic of Poland, there is no doubt that AI algorithms represent an opportunity for the country's socio-economic development.

The aim of the chapter will be to present arguments and counter-arguments regarding the use of AI algorithms on a macro scale. Cybersecurity aspects in the context of the implementation of AI algorithms will also be discussed. Due to the implementation of the EU AI Act[6] and the validity of the Act on the National Cybersecurity System,[7] the issues in question will be analysed in the context of opportunities and challenges for socio-economic development in the Republic of Poland.

3.2 Research method

Research methods include the analysis of basic legal acts using the literature on the subject. The study refers to fundamental legal acts, both EU law and national law. Acts of EU law such as the AI Act and the Cybersecurity Act[8] deserve special attention. In turn, in the case of national regulations, the basic legal act is the Act on the National Cybersecurity System. The issues discussed in the cited legal acts refer to the use of AI systems and cybersecurity. The work also uses domestic and foreign publications that refer to the subject of the article.

3.3 Considerations

3.3.1 *Use of artificial intelligence algorithms – arguments for and against*

The use of AI algorithms on a macro scale raises many questions and doubts among both public and private sector representatives. Due to the incompletely understood purpose of the use of AI, the arguments of opponents of algorithms and AI are definitely more noticeable. The prominence of the negative position is also related to concerns about the issue of human replacement by machines. When considering the arguments for and against the use of AI algorithms, it would be appropriate to start by introducing the key concepts. At this point, it should be emphasised that fundamental in the context of algorithms is the question of the logical (or mathematical) way of solving a given problem. Obviously, the process of reasoning, associating facts, processing information is a pattern of behaviour that may or may not lead to the completion of a task. Logic hitherto reserved for humans has become part of the activities of AI. In science, the concept of so-called AI algorithms has been introduced, which consists in "intelligent searching of the space of possible solutions (...) automatic inference (...) machine learning (...) deep learning".[9] Algorithmisation by means of AI systems supports the activities of public entities in particular. AI algorithm models are therefore not only abstract, as due to their specific characteristics they can improve the operation of many entities, including influencing (or shaping) mechanisms of a legal or socio-economic nature. It is not without reason that special attention is paid to features such as transparency, i.e. the transparent way in which AI operates and is used, interpretability, i.e. ensuring accurate interpretation of the data generated by algorithms, and explainability, which consists of understanding why the system has made a decision that it has made.[10] Overall, regardless of views on the use of AI algorithms, it should be recognised that they have revolutionised the classical way of doing things. Mechanisms for automatic interpretation and decision-making can improve the quality and speed of public administration and affect its efficiency. On the other hand, if uncontrolled, they can manipulate the actions of individuals and create a different vision of reality.

Undoubtedly, AI is a contrario an intelligence that is not an attribute of a human being, an individual, one that exists alongside natural intelligence. In other words, it should be acknowledged that, with the help of appropriate software, AI systems "can think and act with a certain level of human intelligence", so it can be said that algorithms enable "the design of artificial solutions in computers that recognise similarities".[11]. Article 3 point 1 of the AI Act indicates that an AI system is a machine system that is designed to operate with varying levels of autonomy once it is deployed and that can show adaptability once it is deployed and that, for explicit or implicit purposes, infers how to generate, based on the input received, outcomes such as predictions, content, recommendations or decisions that can affect the physical or virtual environment. Given the above, it must be acknowledged that AI algorithms can improve the quality of the services provided, at the same time as they contribute to socio-economic development. It all depends, of course, on how AI is managed. As indicated above, the advantages of AI include, above all, the automation of processes (efficiency and speed of decision-making, personalisation of services). AI algorithms can support human activity in a wide variety of areas, such as security (including the fight against cyberthreats), finance, the judiciary, environmental protection or health care. For example, AI is used in defence and military activities and supports logistical and decision-making processes. Jasper Schellekens points to the key geopolitical importance of AI, positing that "it stands to be a pillar of military operations in the near future for the United States and China looking to harness the advantages AI could provide the military".[12] It must also be acknowledged that AI is shaping a new model of augmented, so-called smart medicine. Medical technologies are increasingly based on the actions of AI, and computer-assisted surgical navigation systems have become a reality. Algorithms based on AI have found applications in cardiology, pulmonology, endocrinology and neurology and are able to diagnose cancer[13] and surgical robots assist doctors during operations. The context of the fight against cyberthreats also draws attention, although in this field AI can bring both benefits and risks.

Against the background of the above-mentioned advantages, the arguments of the opponents of algorithmisation should be presented. The literature points to certain risks and negative consequences of using AI. One of the most serious objections is the loss of control over algorithms, which may lead to violations of the right to privacy and personal data protection or excessive surveillance of the public. In view of this, discriminatory and unethical behaviour may result from the automation of actions based on pre-programmed rules. The issue of liability for damages caused by AI is also questionable. A serious, if not the greatest, concern relates to aspects of AI acting in opposition to human work. Indeed, there is a high risk of it becoming a technology displacing the activities of individuals and affecting the labour market, which could lead to increased unemployment or fewer jobs.[14] It should be emphasised that discriminatory behaviour by algorithms is of particular concern and may directly contribute to human rights violations. Indeed, algorithms may "engage in unequal treatment

(…) produce unequal impact (…) take into account some factor that is itself a product of past discrimination (…) produce an imbalance that many people find unacceptable".[15] Traits that are deemed dominant on the basis of the algorithm's actions may create unjustified categorisation and selection and lead to divisions and polarisation of society. At the same time, a certain discrepancy is accentuated as to how the actions taken by the algorithms are implemented on two legal and ethical levels. They are also considered in terms of potential questions about the liability (criminal, civil) of AI, the protection of copyright, personal data and basic human rights. On the other hand, benefits for society, entrepreneurs and the public sector are pointed out, as AI supports competitiveness, reliability of e-service provision, sustainable development or actions taken by public administration.[16] The unreliability of new technologies, however, folds in reflections on caring for human welfare and ensuring cybersecurity. In the latter case, algorithms can be both tools for mitigating cyberthreats and a contrario supporting the activities of cybercriminals. After all, one thing remains constant, cybersecurity policy has an impact on socio-economic development.

3.3.2 *Algorithms and cybersecurity*

Given that cyberspace is now an extremely popular channel of communication, attention should be paid to the role of algorithms in the matter of building a secure and friendly place for e-commerce exchange or carrying out public utility e-tasks. Undeniably, algorithms are crucial in the context of creating so-called cybersecurity policies. However, the scope of their use is a matter of debate. It should be noted that cyber actors can use AI for two, completely contradictory purposes. On the one hand, algorithms can be an effective tool against cyberthreats, e.g. "in the context of malware detection, deep learning algorithms can analyse large amounts of data and identify patterns that are indicative of malware",[17] on the other hand, their use may compromise cybersecurity. Assuming the variant of positive impact of algorithms on cybersecurity, it is worth providing a definition of the concept. Well, the Cybersecurity Act emphasises that cybersecurity means the activities necessary to protect network and information systems, the users of such systems and other persons affected by cyberthreats.[18] In turn, in Article 2 point 4 of the Act on the National Cybersecurity System, the Polish legislator indicates that cybersecurity is the immunity of information systems from actions that violate the confidentiality, integrity, availability and authenticity of the processed data or related services offered by these systems. The definitions presented are linked by the context of protection of cyberspace against cyberthreats,[19] understood through the prism of subjective (users – their data and activities performed online) and object protection (networks, systems, electronic devices). The potential of algorithms is particularly noticeable in the use of AI systems in the sphere of cybersecurity development and building and managing ICT infrastructure (networks and systems). AI, machine learning techniques can be useful in, among other things, the creation (and optimisation) of trust and cybersecurity management systems, cyberthreat analysis, critical infrastructure security, risk assessment and digital investigations.[20] AI technologies are regarded as excellent tools for reducing or preventing the effects of cyberthreats. It is worth pointing out that the Polish Act on the National Cybersecurity System identifies four types of incidents: critical, serious, significant, in a public entity.[21] Skilful application of algorithms can negate their adverse impact on cybersecurity. The role of algorithms in the area of cybersecurity assurance also includes monitoring activities to automatically detect and investigate vulnerabilities, automated vulnerability classification, preventive activities and building risk management strategies.[22] At the same time, cognitive intelligence becomes active intelligence, i.e. included in the fight against cyberthreats. A secure cyberspace is currently a sine qua non for socio-economic development.

Another question also arises, namely, can algorithms contribute to the rise of cyberthreats? This question, unfortunately, must be answered in the affirmative. Algorithms can have a significant impact on the number and effectiveness of cyberattacks, which adversely affects socio-economic development. Cyberattacks can be malicious or cybercriminal in nature. The automation of activities is a definite attribute of AI systems. Algorithm-driven cyberattacks are directed towards mass surveillance, data manipulation, lead to privacy violations and, in extreme cases, pose a threat to democracy.[23] Provoking cyberattacks, incidents and facilitating the execution of criminal activities are not the only arguments of opponents of AI. Related to the above, concerns also relate to the loss of control over the use of algorithms. Perhaps the vision of the future is the self-sufficiency of AI, if so, then not only the issue of employment but also the realisation of the individual's interest will become problematic. Given the above, it is fair to say that "the use of artificial intelligence inevitably affects human rights" and unfortunately in a negative aspect, for "it increasingly leads to violations of the principles of transparency, equality, privacy, rationality of decisions, non-discrimination".[24] The protection of human rights and so-called welfare also manifests itself in terms of respect for human dignity. Thus, the ethical aspects of AI play a huge role. In this matter, numerous questions arise about its morality and conscience, ability to think, possession of legal personality or spirituality.[25] It can be noted that aspects of legal, social and even religious nature remain of interest to scientists conducting research on the impact of AI on socio-economic development. In addition to cyberthreats that falsify the image of cyberspace, limit or prevent access to e-services, or violate basic human rights, a serious danger is actions that destabilise democratic mechanisms. These include, for example, disinformation. Algorithms have become part of political action with remarkable effectiveness, supporting every political option, creating information, supporting propaganda, controlling chat rooms and forums, creating comments. Given the use of algorithms also for political purposes, the reduction of disinformation activities should be inscribed as a key objective of cybersecurity policy.[26] Despite the many negative aspects associated with the use of algorithms, they can successfully impact socio-economic development. Concerns about AI arise in every country, including Poland. The European Union, meeting market, but also social needs, has created the AI Act. It is therefore worth considering its potential impact on the national cybersecurity system and socio-economic development in the Republic of Poland, where the National Cybersecurity System Act has been in force since 2018.

3.3.3 *Impact of the AI Act on the national cybersecurity system – opportunities and challenges for socio-economic development in the Republic of Poland*

The Republic of Poland's policy on the digitalisation of public services and cybersecurity has become increasingly important, especially over the past few years. A watershed moment was the implementation of the National Cybersecurity System Act in 2018. It can be said that cybersecurity has become a priority of the digital transformation, as it has been noted that cyberthreats "can become the greatest drag chain"[27] for social and economic development. The goal of the then government was to comprehensively yet transparently regulate the organisation of the national cybersecurity system (including the tasks and responsibilities of its constituent entities). Undoubtedly, it became crucial to define standards related to incident management, which consisted of handling incidents, finding links between incidents, removing the causes of their occurrence and developing conclusions resulting from their handling.[28] The impact of new technologies on socio-economic development determined the necessity of cybersecurity measures, which is, in fact, emphasised in the Cybersecurity Strategy of the Republic of Poland for 2019–2024. Significantly, already in the introduction of the aforementioned document it was indicated that socio-economic development requires fast and unfettered access to services, the public sector and information. Such access (e-access) is provided by the development of information and communication technologies. At the macro level, information systems, and I quote, "serve the development of the national economy, in particular in the areas of communication, trade, transport or financial services". Cyberthreats therefore affect the security of economic transactions and citizens (society).[29] The next stage of technological progress is algorithmisation, which may revolutionise the e-services market, but also expand the catalogue of tasks of those responsible for the security of economic transactions. Why new technologies and AI are so important for the economy and society. In the case of the Republic of Poland, they support the development of industry, introduce a new innovative standard of services, e.g. robotics, drones or autonomous vehicles, and AI is called an intensifying technology, "having transformative potential and determining the nature of the revolution".[30] Algorithms have been in the spotlight not only for industry players but also for lawyers and officials. The European Union has also taken up the topic of AI. Paradoxically, these systems have become increasingly agile and efficient, taking on activities previously performed by humans, which could result in many of them being taken over by intelligent machines or robots in the future.[31] The AI Act is intended to encourage individual European Union countries to step up their efforts to implement algorithms to increase innovation, competitiveness and security of e-services. A well-conducted economic policy, especially between 2015 and 2022, despite the pandemic and the invasion of Ukraine, placed Poland among the top countries with the highest cumulative Gross Domestic Product (GDP) growth since 2015.[32] Already at that time, the issue of algorithmisation became the focus of government and business. According to Article 1 of the AI Act, the purpose of the regulation is to improve the functioning of the internal market and promote the spread of human-centred and trustworthy AI. At the same time, it points out the need to ensure a high level of protection of health, safety, fundamental rights enshrined in the Charter, including democracy, the rule of law and the protection of the environment, against the harmful effects of AI systems in the Union and to foster innovation.

Given the concept of the work, it is important to consider what potential impact the solutions contained in the AI Act may have on the national cybersecurity system. Moreover, what are the opportunities and challenges for socio-economic development in the Republic of Poland in this connection. It is clear that the impact relates to two fundamental issues, i.e. the secure use of algorithms to enhance competitiveness and quality of services, and the ethical and responsible use of AI systems, including respect for human rights (welfare). Competitiveness, reliability, automation of processes, personalisation of services, speed of operation, optimisation of operations and allocation of resources are undoubtedly attributes of AI. However, it should be borne in mind that technological developments can ensure economic development provided that the appropriate organisational and legal conditions are implemented. The AI Act may influence the content of the new Cybersecurity Strategy of the Republic of Poland, which will be in force from 2025. AI should be one of its pillars. Emphasising the role of algorithms in the area of cybersecurity would arguably contribute to "meeting the challenges of maintaining and improving cybersecurity".[33] At the same time, the optimisation of key cybersecurity standards needs to be addressed. In other words, cybersecurity policies need to be updated. The AI Act clearly indicates that special protection should be given to ICT networks and systems as well as to users of algorithms. In the latter aspect, the context of data protection, privacy rights and human well-being draws attention. The essence of protection against the harmful effects of algorithms, e.g. the use of intentional manipulation techniques of biometric categorisation or social scoring, should be taken into account when developing the new Cybersecurity Strategy of the Republic of Poland. The strategy and cybersecurity policies of the competent entities should be in line with the intent of Article 1(2) of the AI Act, i.e. to include solutions for the security of marketing, commissioning and use of AI systems, elimination of unauthorised AI practices, requirements of high-risk AI systems and obligations on operators of such systems, transparency and monitoring of their performance. Algorithms can assist in the activities of identifying reference objects, assessing and classifying threats and risks, and providing a firewall for network security.[34] Moreover, the algorithmisation used to improve the cybersecurity of e-services should be based on a business-competitive approach. In turn, the value of cybersecurity must be mandatory, treated as a public good, particularly protected.

Poland should extract from the AI act all the necessary components that will provide the greatest possible economic and social benefits. There is much talk about so-called algorithmic transparency, i.e. the introduction of mechanisms to identify harm (e.g. discrimination) or to detect errors in input data.[35] Interestingly, ethical issues and those relating to the anthropocentric treatment of AI may pose the greatest challenge. This does not seem to be possible at this stage, or even if it could be, it would be very irresponsible and risk losing control over AI systems. Poland is facing an extremely difficult task, as the Act on the National Cybersecurity System will soon be amended in connection with the implementation of the NIS2 Directive,[36] the period of validity of the Cybersecurity Strategy of the Republic of Poland is also coming to an end, and AI issues are coming to the fore. Changes to the national cybersecurity system are therefore inevitable. De lege ferenda is postulated for socio-economic development:

1 Introduce concepts such as algorithmisation of services provided by key and important entities, cybersecurity of AI systems, management of AI systems, and a chapter on the activities of algorithms to improve cybersecurity as well as prohibited practices in the field of AI into the amended Act on the National Cybersecurity System;

2 In the new Cybersecurity Strategy of the Republic of Poland, indicate a specific objective on the use of algorithms to improve the competitiveness and quality of services provided (socio-economic development) and on the scope and responsible use of AI systems for the protection of human rights. Obviously, the above changes are to be adequate to the technological possibilities of using AI in Poland, as they represent decisions of a sovereign nation state.

3.4 Conclusions

In summary, AI algorithms have modernised the way services are provided at a distance. Undoubtedly, the strengths of AI, such as process automation, personalisation and speed, have improved the competitiveness and quality of services. Moreover, they have found application in a wide variety of areas, such as cybersecurity. The benefits of using algorithms for social and economic development have been recognised by the European Union, as demonstrated by the implementation of the AI Act. The Republic of Poland, as one of the largest economies in the European Union, also does not shy away from algorithmisation of tasks or public services. Nevertheless, a key aspect of managing AI systems is the issue of cybersecurity. On the one hand, algorithms can improve the cybersecurity of ICT networks and systems, on the other hand, they can be used to intensify cyberthreats.

The Polish legislator, given the current legal, socio-economic and geopolitical situation, should reflect on the positioning of algorithms and AI in existing legal regulations, i.e. the Act on the National Cybersecurity System and the Cybersecurity Strategy of the Republic of Poland. This is not an easy task, due to the goals of algorithmisation, which, in addition to economic and social benefits, include ethical issues and human welfare. In other words, the Republic of Poland should make maximum use of the current knowledge on the application of AI algorithms and introduce good practices for their operation also in the theoretical sense (changes, amendment of the law). The solutions indicated in the Act on AI are a guideline in this case. The Republic of Poland has expressed support for the solutions contained in the Act on AI. Poland's position includes the following wording "every artificial intelligence system in its life cycle should fulfil three conditions altogether – be lawful, include principles and ethics for trustworthy artificial intelligence, and be secure and technically resilient".[37] The focus on the issue of cybersecurity is important insofar as it implies further actions that directly affect socio-economic development. The chapter presents de lege ferenda postulates, key to the use of algorithmisation for cybersecurity and Poland's socio-economic development.

Notes

1 AYOUDA, Asma, HADIDENE Sabrina. E-administration: Concept, Enjeux et Avantages. RevueEtudes Economiques (Journal of Economic Studies), vol. 15, no. 3, 2021, p. 595.
2 SATRY, Fadwa, BELKADI, Ez-Zohra. L'administration électronique: Concept, Défis et perspectives. Revue Internationale des Sciences de Gestion, vol. 2. no. 3, 2019, p. 662.
3 Article 7 of Constitution of the Republic of Poland of April 2, 1997 (Journal of Laws No. 78, item 483, as amended).
4 NIŻNIK-DOBOSZ, Iwona. Prawo administracyjne jako czynnik gwarantujący rozwój cywilizacyjny. In: Fenomen Prawa Administracyjnego. Księga jubileuszowa Profesora Jana Zimmermanna, edited by JAKIMOWICZ, Wojciech, KRAWCZYK, Mariusz, NIŻNIK-DOBOSZ, Iwona, Warsaw, 2019, p. 657.
5 HOFFMAN, István, CSEH, Kristóf B. E-administration, cybersecurity and municipalities – the challenges of cybersecurity issues for the municipalities in Hungary. Cybersecurity and Law, vol. 4, no. 2, 2020, p. 200, https://doi.org/10.35467/cal/133999.
6 Regulation (EU) 2024/1689 of the European Parliament and of the Council of June 13, 2024 laying down harmonised rules on artificial intelligence and amending Regulations (EC) No 300/2008, (EU) No 167/2013, (EU) No 168/2013, (EU) 2018/858, (EU) 2018/1139 and (EU) 2019/2144 and Directives 2014/90/EU, (EU) 2016/797 and (EU) 2020/1828 (AI Act) (Journal of Laws UEL of 2024, item 1689), hereinafter AI Act.
7 Act of July 5, 2018 on the national cybersecurity system (Journal of Laws 2024, item 1077).
8 Regulation (EU) 2019/881 of the European Parliament and of the Council of April 17, 2019 on ENISA (the European Union Agency for Cybersecurity) and on information and communications technology cybersecurity certification and repealing Regulation (EU) No 526/2013 (Cybersecurity Act) (Journal of Laws EU No. 151, item 15).
9 CYTOWSKI, Jerzy, GROCHOWSKI, Lucjan. Algorytm. In: Wielka Encyklopedia Prawa, tom XXII. Prawo informatyczne, edited by SZPOR, Grażyna, GROCHOWSKI, Lucjan, Warsaw, 2021, p. 43.
10 ANGELOV, Plamen P., SOARES, Eduardo A., JIANG, Richard, ARNOLD, Nicholas I., ATKINSON, Peter M. Explainable artificial intelligence: an analytical review. Wiley Interdisciplinary Reviews: Data Mining and Knowledge Discovery, vol. 11, no. 5, 2021, p. 4, https://doi.org/10.1002/widm.1424.
11 VERMA, Mudit. Artificial intelligence and its scope in different areas with special reference to the field of education. International Journal of Advanced Educational Research, vol. 3, no. 1, 2018, p. 6.
12 SCHELLEKENS, Jasper. Release the bots of war: social media and Artificial Intelligence as international cyber-attack. Przegląd Europejski, no. 4, 2021, p. 164, https://doi.org/10.31338/1641-2478pe.4.21.10.
13 BRIGANTI, Giovanni, LE MOINE Olivier. Artificial Intelligence in Medicine: today and tomorrow. Frontiers in Medicine, vol. 7, art. 27, 2020, pp. 1–3, https://doi.org/10.3389/fmed.2020.00027.
14 TAEIHAGH, Araz. Governance of artificial intelligence. Policy and Society, vol. 40, no. 2, 2021, p. 138, https://doi.org/10.1080/14494035.2021.1928377.
15 KLEINBERG, Jon, LUDWIG, Jens, MULLAINATHAN, Sendhil, SUNSTEIN, Cass R. Discrimination in the age of algorithms. Journal of Legal Analysis, vol. 10, 2018, p. 139, https://doi.org/10.1093/jla/laz001.

16 OLEKSIEWICZ, Izabela. Artificial intelligence versus human – a threat or a necessity of evolution? Przegląd Europejski, no. 3, 2022, pp. 64–66, https://doi.org/10.31338/1641-2478pe.3.22.4.
17 ZIMOŃ, Michał, KASPRZYK, Rafał. Yet another research on GANs in cybersecurity. Cybersecurity and Law, vol. 9, no. 1, 2023, p. 62, https://doi.org/10.35467/cal/169299.
18 See art. 2, point 1 Cybersecurity Act.
19 Cyberthreat means any potential circumstance, event or action that could damage, disrupt or otherwise adversely impact network and information systems, the users of such systems and other persons – see art. 2, point 8 Cybersecurity Act.
20 ALOQAILY, Moayad, KANHERE, Salil, BELLAVISTA, Paolo, NOGUEIRA, Michele. Special Issue on Cybersecurity Management in the Era of AI. Journal of Network and Systems Management, vol 30, art. no 39, 2022, p. 2, https://doi.org/10.1007/s10922-022-09659-3.
21 Article 2, points 6–9 of the National Cybersecurity System Act, respectively.
22 KAUR, Ramanpreet, GABRIJELČIČ, Dušan, KLOBUČAR, Tomaž. Artificial intelligence for cybersecurity: literature review and future research directions. Information Fusion, vol. 97, 2023, pp. 8–9, https://doi.org/10.1016/j.inffus.2023.101804.
23 CYTOWSKI, Jerzy. Przestępcze i złośliwe wykorzystywanie sztucznej inteligencji. In: Internet. Hacking, edited by GRYSZCZYŃSKA, Agnieszka, SZPOR, Grażyna, WIEWIÓROWSKI, Wojciech R., Warsaw, 2023, pp. 200–201.
24 MARTSENKO, Natalia. Artificial intelligence and human rights: a scientific review of impacts and interactions. Studia Prawnoustrojowe, no. 58, 2022, p. 321, https://doi.org/10.31648/sp.8245.
25 BIEROŃSKI, Michał. Etyczne i moralne wyzwania związane ze stosowaniem sztucznej inteligencji. Kieleckie Studia Teologiczne, nr 19, 2020, p. 23.
26 SKOCZYLAS, Dominika, ŚWITAL, Paweł. The Information Sphere in the Age of Cyberthreats. Disinformation and Cybersecurity. Teka Komisji Prawniczej PAN Oddział w Lublinie, vol. XVII, no. 1, 2024, p. 263, https://doi.org/10.32084/tkp.5812.
27 SULICH, Adam, RUTKOWSKA, Małgorzata, KRAWCZYK-JEZIERSKA, Agnieszka, JEZIERSKi, Jarosław, ZEMA, Tomasz. Cybersecurity and sustainable development. Procedia Computer Science, vol. 192, 2021, p. 26, https://doi.org/10.1016/j.procs.2021.08.003.
28 See Article 2, point18 of the National Cybersecurity System Act.
29 Resolution No. 125 of the Council of Ministers of October 22, 2019 on the Cybersecurity Strategy of the Republic of Poland for 2019–2024 (M.P. 2019 item 1037).
30 ILCIÓW, Adam. Nowoczesne technologie w rozwoju miasta. Strategie – realizacje – oczekiwania. Środkowoeuropejskie Studia Polityczne, no. 2, 2023, p. 29, https://doi.org/10.14746/ssp.2023.2.2.
31 SUSSKIND, Richard. Sądy internetowe i przyszłość wymiaru sprawiedliwości, Warszawa, 2021, pp. 204–205.
32 Ministerstwo Aktywów Państwowych, *Wzrost gospodarczy w Polsce od 2015 r. na tle innych państw Unii Europejskiej*, https://www.gov.pl/web/aktywa-panstwowe/wzrost-gospodarczy-w-polsce-od-2015-r-na-tle-innych-panstw-unii-europejskiej (accessed July 31, 2024).
33 GERCKE, Marco. Cybersecurity Strategy: Why it is necessary to move from Cybersecurity philosophies to true Cybersecurity strategies. Computer Law

Review International, vol. 14, no. 5, 2013, p. 136, https://doi.org/10.9785/ovs-cri-2013-136.

34 TUMKEVIČ, Agnija. Cybersecurity in Central Eastern Europe: From identifying risks to countering threats. Baltic Journal of Political Science, no 5, 2016, pp. 85–86, https://doi.org/10.15388/bjps.2016.5.10337.

35 DATTA, Anupam, SEN, Shayak, ZICK, Yair. Algorithmic Transparency via Quantitative Input Influence: Theory and Experiments with Learning Systems. EEE Symposium on Security and Privacy (SP), San Jose, CA, USA, 2016, p. 598, https://doi.org/10.1109/SP.2016.42.

36 Directive (EU) 2022/2555 of the European Parliament and of the Council of December 14, 2022 on measures for a high common level of cybersecurity across the Union, amending Regulation (EU) No 910/2014 and Directive (EU) 2018/1972, and repealing Directive (EU) 2016/1148 (NIS 2 Directive) (Journal of Laws EU No. 333, item 80).

37 Polskie stanowisko w sprawie AI Act, https://www.gov.pl/web/cyfryzacja/przelomowe-przepisy-dotyczace-sztucznej-inteligencji–parlament-europejski-przyjal-rozporzadzenie (accessed July 31, 2024).

Part IV

The Hungarian perspective

Chapter 4

Using algorithms during the imposition of sanctions in Hungary

István Ambrus

4.1 Introduction

Algorithmic risk analysis based on the use of artificial intelligence (AI) is nowadays – mainly in the Anglo-Saxon legal areas – a tool of everyday use in criminal justice.[1] This can be a significant assistance to investigating authorities, especially in crime detection and investigation, either through facial recognition systems to identify potential perpetrators or through so-called Big Data analysis (e.g. to identify transactions suspected of money laundering or terrorist financing).[2] In addition, the use of algorithms is of particular importance in the field of law enforcement, through risk analysis of the criminal history of prisoners and their behaviour in prison, especially in the question of the likelihood of recidivism and the consequent admissibility of parole.[3]

Here it is necessary to refer to the latest instrument of the European Union, which will essentially determine the legislative processes of the European Union in the coming years in relation to AI, and which has already been disseminated in the Hungarian professional discourse with the abbreviation 'AI Act' during the adoption of the legislation,[4] but which could obviously only be analysed in detail in the context of numerous studies or even monographs.[5] Therefore, I will here only highlight the approach of the above-mentioned EU regulation, which is the approach to algorithms that is also in line with the investigation and law enforcement issues, namely risk-based *decision making*.[6]

There is, however, one – in my opinion very significant – aspect of the possible use of algorithms in criminal procedure, in which the way in which the new technology is used has not yet been developed; moreover, the literature has so far been largely inadequate in exploring the relevant theoretical possibilities: the problem of the use of algorithms in the field of *sentencing (imposition of sanctions)*.[7] In this chapter I will discuss some of the theoretical and practical possibilities and risks of this new field of application.

DOI: 10.4324/9781003531500-10

4.2 About sentencing in a nutshell

Sentencing (for the Hungarian domestic legislation, see in particular Chapter IX of Act C of 2012 on the Criminal Code [hereinafter: Criminal Code]) involves the third of the three main tasks of the sentencing judge. The first is the *establishment of the facts*, which, as a task that presupposes proof, is clearly of a procedural nature. This is followed by the matching of the established historical facts with one or more statutory facts, in short, *classification*. Finally, the last and perhaps the most important (main) task of the criminal judge is the *imposition of sentence*. In this context, the court individualises the abstract statutory penalty, taking into account the abstract statutory gender and the range of punishment, i.e. it applies the specific sanction(s) (imposes a penalty and/or measure) in the light of all the circumstances of the case before it. As Ágnes Pápai-Tarr puts it in her recent, excellent monograph on the importance of this issue: '[the] correct imposition of a penalty [...] is a key issue of criminal law – if not the most important one. In terms of its importance, it is at least as important as the correct classification of the offence. It is the imposition of the sentence that gives life to the sanction in addition to the substantive disposition of the law, the imposition of the sentence that culminates the criminal procedure, and the enforcement of the sentence'.[8]

As can be seen, therefore, the imposition of the sentence (or the application of the measure) is a classic task of the criminal judge, in the context of which – at least in the case of relatively definite sanction systems without exceptions – the judge determines the type and level of the specific sanction, within the legal framework laid down by the legislator, in the exercise of his discretion, taking into account *mitigating and aggravating circumstances*. These circumstances are only briefly defined in the Criminal Code. Article 80(1) of the Criminal Code does not exhaustively list these circumstances, but it does authorise the judiciary to give substance to the provision in specific criminal cases. The main guiding instrument for this activity has long been the 56th Penal Board Opinion of the Supreme Court (hereinafter: 56th BKv) on the factors to be assessed in the imposition of sentences.

In the light of the above, it is therefore not disputed how important the judicial assessment is for the actual sanction imposed. If an offence is punishable by a sentence of imprisonment of two to eight years [e.g. robbery, § 365(1) Criminal Code], the court is entitled to impose a sentence of imprisonment of two, four, five, or even seven or eight years [of course, taking into consideration § 80(2) of the Criminal Code as a guiding rule]. In the following, I will examine the question to what extent AI-based algorithmic systems could facilitate the determination of a truly lawful sentence that is also appropriate to the specific circumstances of the case.

4.3 Scope of the data used by the algorithms

It will of course be a preliminary question, which will require further elaboration, to ask what databases and what data, if any, would be used by the courts in the future to draw conclusions in the context of sentencing, and what new technological tools could be used to draw conclusions in a given case. In this work, this could be summarised briefly for the time being by making available to the AI all the criminal data available to the investigating authorities, the prosecution and the court, the public court decisions available in cases that have been finally concluded, and any additional information that may be requested by these law enforcement agencies.[9] An example of this is the request to the Tax and Customs Directorate of the National Tax and Customs Administration, a matter which is undoubtedly relevant from the point of view of sentencing, in order to ascertain the financial situation of the offender. In addition, the algorithm should take into account investigative documents, including suspect and witness statements, expert opinions, etc.

Finally, the question of what the algorithm should do in the era of the so-called '*limited precedent*' *system* will raise a number of problems in this area and merit further reflection. Thus, it is natural that decisions published as Court Decisions need to be channelled to the AI's position. It is not uncommon, however, that some Supreme Court decisions, even a few years apart, reach diametrically opposed conclusions on essentially the same point of law. A far-reaching problem, but one that needs to be examined in any case, is which decision should be taken by the AI.

4.4 Use of algorithms in the light of the 56th BKv

The 56th BKv can first of all be said to be an old instrument – dating back to the socialist era – but its flexibility has meant that it has basically stood the test of time.[10] Even so, however, it is possible to identify some of its findings which may require amendment, supplementation or even reconsideration and, as a result, possibly even abandonment. This is only natural, since changes in society require not only the legislator but also the administration of justice to monitor them constantly and, if necessary, to revise its previous positions in the light of the changing situation. However, this issue would also require a study in its own right, so I will concentrate here only on those circumstances – and not exhaustively – which are currently declared by the 56th BKv, but which could benefit from an algorithmic analysis. The main reason is that it could put the excessive subjectivity of the judiciary, which sometimes arises, on an objective basis, thereby also serving *the need for legal unity* under § 24(1) of Act CLXI of 2011 on the Organisation and Administration of Courts.

One of the outstanding virtues of the 56th BKv – and, it may be risked, a fundamental guarantee of its durability – is the fundamentally consistent enforcement of *the prohibition of double assessment (ne bis in idem)*.[11] As the eighth paragraph of point I puts it: '[t]he prohibition of double assessment also applies to the assessment of the circumstances which affect the penalty. A circumstance which is regulated by the legislature as an element of the offence or which gives rise to a more serious or less serious classification cannot be assessed separately as a mitigating or aggravating circumstance'. However, this consistency is sometimes compromised, for example in the assessment of simple *recidivism* [§ 459(1) point 31 of the Criminal Code]. In this respect, point II/2 of the 56th BKv merely states that 'it is a aggravating circumstance if the offender is a repeat offender'. I agree with this statement that, since single repeat offences do not have the effect of increasing the penalty, as opposed to specific and multiple (or violent multiple) repeat offences, the former should *generally* be treated as aggravating circumstances in the imposition of a sentence. However, it should not be regarded as an exception that cannot be excluded. It is possible that the court would consider a sanction that could be applied to a non-recidivist, but which is excluded by law in the case of a repeat offender, on the basis of the predominant mitigating circumstances in the specific case. In such a case, if the court chooses another sanction which is applicable by law, and disregards that sanction, the legislative consideration of recidivism has in fact already been taken into account. And if this is true, in such a case it would be a double assessment – and one that would be more detrimental to the accused – to treat recidivism as a separate aggravating circumstance. Examples of such a situation could be the use of probation or reparation measures. A person who is a recidivist cannot be placed on probation [§ 65(2)(a) of the Criminal Code], nor can reparation work be imposed on him [§ 67(2)(a) of the Criminal Code]. Thus, if, instead of these sanctions, the court is obliged to impose, for example, community service or a fine solely because of the recidivist nature of the offender, it is no longer justified to invoke recidivism as an aggravating circumstance. This could also be indicated by the AI, given the data available in the criminal databases.

The *substantive gravity of* the offence is not only defined in the 56th BKv but also in the § 80(1) of the Criminal Code itself as a generally applicable sentencing criterion. Obviously serious bodily injury [§ 164(3) of the Criminal Code] is deemed to have been committed if the injury caused to the victim by the offender heals within 10 days, and even if it takes 100 days to heal. But theft of a higher value [§ 370(3)(a) of the Criminal Code] is also established if the value of the stolen goods is HUF 510,000.00, as opposed to HUF 4,900,000.00. However, practical experience has shown that the weighting of this can be rather subjective, and it would therefore be appropriate to set up a yardstick – by including algorithms in the sentencing process – which would bring the issue into an objective context, for example by recommending a more severe penalty in percentage terms if, for example, the medical condition exceeded the lower limit of serious bodily injury by 10–20–50% etc., or a similar percentage of the higher value.

Similarly, the assessment of *age* may raise problems. When the 56th BKv II/1 states that a young adult is a person 'a few years over the age of youth', it does not provide a firm basis for a concrete assessment of this.[12] Similarly, it is problematic to take into account 'age generally above the retirement age' (56th BKv II/4) as a mitigating circumstance in the light of the fact that the retirement age has been changing continuously and by gender in recent times. The algorithm could, however, calculate all this up-to-date, thus helping the court to make the right decision.

In my opinion I would exclude *the victim's culpable involvement* (56th BKv III/4) from the mitigating circumstances altogether, and therefore I will not discuss its algorithmic assessment here; although if case law wishes to maintain this clearly outdated circumstance, the algorithm could also put it on a more objective basis on the basis of the documents.

The AI would also be able to fill certain gaps in the 56th BKv, in particular with regard to *incitement* [§ 14(1) of the Criminal Code] as a partial form,[13] which is not mentioned in the 56th BKv at all, although it is not unimportant that the future perpetrator would not have committed the offence at all in the absence of the instigator's statement; or that he had already previously considered the idea of committing the offence, but the instigation matured his intention into a firm determination of will, and as a result he finally committed the offence.[14] Thus, incitement may, depending on the circumstances of the case, constitute an aggravating circumstance, but it is not inconceivable that it may have no such effect. On the basis of the conclusions drawn from the investigative file, the AI could also provide appropriate guidance in this area.

Finally, I will turn to two circumstances which I consider to be the most neuralgic, and which have become almost 'mantras'. The *increase in the number of offences* (56th BKv III/11) has always been the subject of controversy, since case-law has not generally demanded and does not demand precise criminal statistics, contenting itself with the 'telling' of the facts in the course of a trial. However, as József Földvári noted in the socialist era, '[t]he reference to an increase or decrease is sometimes unfounded: such an assessment may be based on the personal experience of the presiding council, and does not take into account – because it is not familiar with – cases decided by other courts or councils in the same county'.[15] Therefore, if the practice insists on maintaining this circumstance – which I do not support, since the strengthening of criminal liability by means of a criterion independent of the perpetrator's consciousness hardly seems compatible with the principle of legality – it can only be done on the basis of accurate statistical data on crime, broken down by type of offence and location. Thus, if there are about a third as many burglaries in 2023 as there were ten years ago, this can only be taken into account as an aggravating circumstance if the prosecution can show with accurate (at least uniform police and prosecution statistics, usually abbreviated as ENyüBS) data that this type of crime has become more prevalent in the municipality in question in the last year or so.

The other such circumstance is the *passage of time* (56th BKv III/10), which is mentioned in almost all defence pleadings, but in many cases is of little relevance as a mitigating circumstance. The algorithm could, however, perhaps give an idea of what caused the lapse of time: the fact that the crime remained unsolved for a long time, the defendant's misleading behaviour towards the investigating authority,[16] delays on the part of experts or authorities or the delay of any party to the proceedings (whether culpable or not). In addition, as with the material gravity of the offence, it would be useful to draw more objective lines which would quantify, in relation to the occurrence of the limitation period, the weight to be attached to the time which has elapsed since the offence was committed in a particular case.

4.5 Some further substantive and procedural aspects

The question of the application of so-called *alternative penalties*, which is not included in the 56th BKv, but is of cardinal importance in the everyday application of the law, i.e. under § 33(4)–(5) of the Criminal Code, when should the court depart from the custodial sentence otherwise applicable under the Special Part and apply a lighter sanction (e.g. confinement, community service, fine) instead. From an AI point of view, the most important thing is that the algorithm can make its decision based on the right amount and quality of data. Thus, if the financial situation of the perpetrator does not allow it, do not propose to impose a fine, if his physical condition is such that he is unlikely to be able to work, it should not propose community service, etc. Similarly, in the context of the *preliminary court discharge* [§ 102(1) of the Criminal Code], it may be interesting to consider the merits of the case, which should also be supported by objective arguments.

We may also find Hungarian examples that completely remove judicial discretion from sanctioning *(absolutely determinate sanctions)*. As per § 52(3) of the Criminal Code states, 'in connection with any criminal offence against sexual freedom and sexual morality, if at the time when the crime was committed the victim is under the age of 18 years, the perpetrator must be permanently banned from the exercise of any professional or other activity that involves the responsibility of undertaking the education, care, custody or medical treatment of a person under the age of 18 years, or if it involves a position of authority or influence over such person'. This special case of disqualification from a profession differs from the endangerment of a minor offence mentioned in the category of de facto cogent rules in two respects. First, here it is not only obligatory to disqualify the perpetrator, but this must exclusively be done permanently. Second, the rule allowing the court to avoid this penalty in cases of special commendation is absent. Therefore, the court cannot circumvent disqualification, no matter the preponderance of mitigating circumstances. Also a so-called 'three-strikes rule' that tolerates no deliberation applies to multiple violent recidivists. § 90(2) of the Criminal Code states that, in instances of imprisonment, the upper limit of the penalty range for a multiple violent recidivist's primary offence to establish him as such must be doubled. If the thus-inflated sentence exceeds 20 years or may carry a statutory possibility of life imprisonment, the perpetrator shall be sentenced to life imprisonment. It is important to note that the mutual presence of the aforementioned conditions would mean that the mandatory life sentence is without the possibility of conditional release, because § 44(2)(a) of the Criminal Code precludes the possibility of parole if the perpetrator is a multiple violent recidivist. Therefore, if the application of a particular sanction is mandatory, the AI may be able to impose it in the same way as a human judge.

However the possibility of applying AI would essentially require an examination of substantive legal issues, in practice these are of course also closely linked to *procedural* aspects. Thus, it may be a question of cardinal importance whether, if the first instance decision was taken in accordance with the advice of the AI, the court of appeal should also use AI, or perhaps another AI-based software, or whether the decision on appeal should be based solely on human judgement (I personally see the latter as being supportable).

Finally, the importance of the imposition of a penalty from a procedural point of view is also shown by the fact that the classification of a violation of the law under § 649(1)(b) of the Act XC of 2017 on Criminal Procedure as a general rule only justifies a review if it also means the application of a sanction that violates the law, so the possibility of using algorithms to review final decisions also requires reconsideration.

4.6 Conclusion

Almost coeval with the recent emergence of AI is the question of whether the use of algorithms in criminal proceedings – and in particular, as we have seen, in the area of sentencing, which is one of its 'highlights' – can eventually replace the work of the courts, i.e. whether the issue of sentencing can be entrusted to 'robot judges'. In my view, the answer to this question – sharing the view of Krisztina Karsai[17] – is currently no. However, I am not sure, given the fundamental proliferation of AI-based systems, that this will remain the case forever.[18] The discretion in continental legal systems should of course be vested in the judge, as it has been for centuries. However, if we take into account the proliferation of so-called *absolute determinate sanctions*, such as the before-mentioned 'three strikes' rule [§ 90(2) of the Criminal Code], the mandatory disqualification from a profession [§ 52(3) of the Criminal Code], or recently also the increasing number of cases where conditional release is excluded [§ 38(4)(e), (5) of the Criminal Code] – it can be assumed that all this may contribute to the soundness of the AI-based sentencing. Since if there is no possibility for judicial discretion, then if the offence is proven and properly classified, the imposition of sentence loses its function as an independent judicial task and thus may give way to algorithms. It would of course be worth keeping the possibility of all this to a minimum. For my part, however, I do not see it as a devilish idea to rationalise the assessment of mitigating or aggravating circumstances, which may be too subjective and whose relevance may be questionable, by using algorithms, thereby promoting a more objective sentencing process that better serves the need for unity of justice.[19]

Notes

1 See BIDDLE, Justin B. On Predicting Recidivism: Epistemic Risk, Tradeoffs, and Values in Machine Learning. Canadian Journal of Philosophy, vol. 52, 2022, pp. 321–341.
2 FANTOLY, Zsanett, HERKE, Csongor. A mesterséges intelligencia a hatékonyabb büntetőeljárás szolgálatában. Magyar Jog, vol. 70, 2023, p. 223–238.
3 HAMILTON, Melissa. The Biased Algorithm: Evidence of Disparate Impact on Hispanics. Americal Criminal Law Review, vol. 56, 2019, pp. 1533–1577.
4 REGULATION (EU) 2024/1689 OF THE EUROPEAN PARLIAMENT AND OF THE COUNCIL of 13 June 2024 laying down harmonised rules on artificial intelligence and amending Regulations (EC) No 300/2008, (EU) No 167/2013, (EU) No 168/2013, (EU) 2018/858, (EU) 2018/1139 and (EU) 2019/2144 and Directives 2014/90/EU, (EU) 2016/797 and (EU) 2020/1828 (AI Act)
5 MEZEI, Kitti, TRäGER, Anikó. The European Approach to Artificial Intelligence: Ethical and Regulatory Implications. Acta Universitatis Sapientiae Legal Studies, vol. 11, 2022, pp. 19–34.
6 AI Act Preamble (26)–(27).
7 BRENNAN-MARQUEZ, Kiel, CHIAO, Vincent. Algorithmic Decision-Making When Human Disagree on Ends. New Criminal Law Review, vol. 24, 2021, pp. 275–300.
8 PÁPAI-TARR, Ágnes. A büntetéskiszabás aktuális kérdései. Novissima, Budapest, 2024, p. 5.
9 By analogy, this solution would not contradict paragraph 19 of EU Regulation 2016/69 of 27 April 2016 on the protection of natural persons with regard to

the processing of personal data and on the free movement of such data, and repealing Directive 95/46/EC (General Data Protection Regulation), which states that 'the processing of personal data by competent authorities for the purpose of the prevention, investigation, detection, prosecution or execution of criminal penalties shall not be subject to [this Regulation]'.

10 AMBRUS, István, UJVÁRI, Ákos. Adalékok a büntetéskiszabás elvi és gyakorlati kérdéseihez. Magyar Jog, vol. 67, 2020, pp. 585–591.

11 AMBRUS, István. A ne bis in idem elve a legújabb európai joggyakorlatban, kitekintéssel a princípium érvényesülésére különböző jogterületek találkozása esetében. Európai Tükör, vol. 22, 2019, pp. 122–135.

12 VASKUTI, András. Az életkor és a fiatalkorúak vonatkozó rendelkezések az új Btk.-ban. Jogtudományi Közlöny, vol. 70, 2015, pp. 173–182.

13 For an overview on parties of criminal offences, see MÉSZÁROS, Ádám. A bűncselekmény elkövetői – elméleti és gyakorlati alapkérdések. Ad Librum, Budapest, 2008.

14 NAGY, Ferenc. A magyar büntetőjog általános része. HVG-ORAC, Budapest, 2008, p. 219.

15 FÖLDVÁRI, József. A büntetés tana. KJK, Budapest, 1970, p. 216.

16 Let there be no misunderstanding: the accused has the right to present different 'versions' of the offence under § 185 of the Criminal Code, but if at the end of the criminal proceedings criminal responsibility is established, there is no '*fair trail*' (the Convention for the Protection of Human Rights and Fundamental Freedoms, Rome, 1950). It does not appear to be contrary to the principle of 'human rights and fundamental freedoms' (Article 6 of Chapter I of Act XXXI of 1993 on the prolongation of proceedings).

17 KARSAI, Krisztina. Inkriminált algoritmusok a büntető igazságszolgáltatásban. In: MADAI, Sándor, PALLAGI, Anikó, POLT, Péter (eds.), Sic itur ad astra. Ünnepi kötet a 70 éves Blaskó Béla tiszteletére. Ludovika, Budapest, 2020, p. 259.

18 GLESS, Sabine, SILVERMAN, Emily, WEIGEND, Thomas. If Robots Cause Harm, Who Is to Blame? Self-Driving Cars and Criminal Liability. New Criminal Law Review, vol. 19, 2016, pp. 412–436.

19 See Article 25(3) of the Fundamental Law of Hungary.

Chapter 5

Artificial intelligence and contemporary questions from the aspect of Hungarian criminal law

Máté Hodula

5.1 What do we mean by AI?

In order to examine the responsibility of algorithms in detail, we also need to look in detail at the central area of their use, artificial intelligence (AI). István Ambrus, in his paper on AI, points out *that* 'first of all, the distinction between categories of strong and weak AI, and among the essential characteristics, the ability to learn by machine, and consequently the distinction between simply automatic and truly autonomous action, is considered to be the most significant'.[1]

The latest recent achievement in the codification of AI is the 'AI Act', a piece of legislation adopted by the European Parliament.[2] A detailed description of the AI Act is beyond the scope of this chapter, but many of its provisions are of particular importance to the criminal lawyer with an interest in AI. The AI Act contains a number of administrative provisions (e.g. marketing standards, data protection, etc.), but its definitions are already significant – Article 3 (1) defines AI system as 'a machine-based system designed to operate with varying levels of autonomy, that may exhibit adaptiveness after deployment and that, for explicit or implicit objectives, infers, from the input it receives, how to generate outputs such as predictions, content, recommendations, or decisions that can influence physical or virtual environments'. Paragraph (12) of the preamble highlights the connection between algorithms and AI by stating that 'a key characteristic of AI systems is their capability to infer. This capability to infer refers to the process of obtaining the outputs, such as predictions, content, recommendations, or decisions, which can influence physical and virtual environments, and to a capability of AI systems to derive models or algorithms from inputs or data'.

In relation to the scope of the AI Act, it should be emphasised that it covers not only distributors of AI systems but also users [Article 2(1), and user is defined user as 'a natural or legal person, public authority, agency or other body who uses an AI system under its control, unless the AI system is used in the course of a personal, non-professional activity'].[3] Also, the AI

DOI: 10.4324/9781003531500-11

Act, given that it would apply to all AI, sets out general standards of conduct and could not be a norm-setting rule for a framework disposition fact.

The jurisprudential works also typically include a specific job definition or criteria for AI. Eszteri cites Stuart Russel and Peter Norvig's division between systems that think and act humanly and systems that think and act rationally, where rational thought and action are in some sense more perfect than human thought and action.[4] Eszteri points out that a further distinction can be made between weak and strong AI – the former has no mind, while the latter refers to systems that are truly self-aware.[5]

5.2 Algorithms and the elements of an offence

Although the main focus of this chapter of my research is on AI and the specific issues of liability, I consider it essential to discuss some issues related to the concept of criminal offence along its other parts, specifically the mens rea element.[6]

Analysing the concept of the act within the Hungarian legal system, based on the reduced concept of the action, the actions of robots are not considered to be part of the relevant criminal act, thus, due to the lack of a conceptual element, no crime is committed, given that the basic starting point of the theory of acts is that the act is human behaviour.[7] Shortly – and somewhat cynically – it can be said that the liability of AI cannot be established, as will be seen below, direct liability is merely one theory, so that the liability of natural persons for the acts of AI can also exist.

In their research, Weigend et al. split the question into two sub-questions: can a robot be blamed, and if so, are punishment goals meaningful? The latter question is easier to answer. Generalised prevention does not apply because some 'moral choices' are made on the basis of programming (e.g. self-driving cars should not hit anyone in the process of achieving a goal) rather than as a result of the socialisation process, so deterrence or reintegration, among others, cannot apply.

Prevention also cannot be understood in the sense that an algorithm would not be able to grasp punishments, i.e. they do not have property (at least they cannot perceive property), so a fine would not be imposed, or they do not know the concept of freedom, so a punishment of imprisonment would not achieve its purpose. Complete disconnection might be considered, but since they are not programmed with 'wanting to live' as a goal, this would not deter them either.[8] Should they be provided with such a goal by the designer, it also raises ethical issues to endow an unconscious thing with a will to live for the purpose of arbitrarily taking it (or threatening to do so).

The conclusion of Weigend et al. that the action must arise from self-determination is worth considering, but they do not exclude the possibility that it may fit into a broader notion of action. However, punishability is still absent, since its intrinsic criterion is the recognition of a choice between moral right and wrong (see the case of childhood or pathological mental state).[9]

Regarding the mens rea element behind actions governed by algorithms, Ambrus states that it can be divided into direct liability, covert liability (where the covert offender is a person who instigates the commission of an intentional offense by using a person who cannot be prosecuted for reason of minority or insanity, of for reason of acting under undue influence by coercion or duress, or under misconception), criminal liability similar in case of superior officers and public executives, and liability for breach of duty of care.[10] The autonomy of the algorithm and the complexity of the issue are directly proportional – the more a natural person influences its operation, the easier it is to determine responsibility for its actions.[11]

As regards the acts of algorithms, I agree with the proposal of Ambrus to base liability on the acito libera in causa, on the basis of the human operator's presumed prior conduct, under which intentional or negligent acts could be punished. In this context, Ambrus points out that, although actio libera in causa, i.e. 'the subsequent imputation of guilt as a legal institution', has long been known in domestic dogmatics.[12] In domestic legal literature and practice, this is most often used in determining liability for crimes committed while drunk or intoxicated through one's own fault. However, Ambrus argues that actio libera in causa can be helpful in resolving cases where the culpability (intentionality or recklessness) of the human operator is in question, given the unpredictable decisions of AI.[13]

The above – and the problem of self-driving cars, already referred to above and explained in detail below – can be illustrated by the above-mentioned point IIIa of Appendix 1 of Joint Decree 1/1975(II.5.) of the CPM-MM on the rules of road traffic (hereinafter: KRESZ), according to which the instructor is considered the driver during the driving instruction and the subsequent practical test. Accordingly, the instructor may be held liable for accidents caused during driving instruction and the driving test, even though the vehicle was normally understood to have been driven by the learner/examiner, for causing a road accident under Section 235. In this case, in my view, the instructor can be construed as a quasi-indirect tortfeasor and the learner/examiner is akin to an unpredictable AI situation. And the instructor's responsibility lies in his culpable misconduct in allowing an incompetent learner to drive on the road.[14]

In the context of self-driving vehicles, Ambrus raises the idea of the objectification of liability,[15] 'in the event of which the guilt (intentional or negligent) of a specific person would not even have to be proven in criminal proceedings, only the operator/owner of the vehicle that caused the accident'.[16] In this context, I consider it important to point out that, although objective – private law – liability is an existing formula in common law and French law,[17] it is typically considered feasible only in the context of trivial offences – for example, according to Article 2.05 of the Model Penal Code of the United States, these offences do not fall under the definition of 'crime' and therefore cannot result in a custodial penalty. In view of the above, I am of the opinion that objective liability can be considered as a possible solution in the domestic legal system for offences – not punishable by imprisonment – but not for criminal offences due to the abstract elements of the concept of criminal law.[18]

5.3 Algorithms in certain offences

István Ambrus has also analysed the liability of AI in several articles and in his comprehensive monograph 'Digitalisation and Criminal Law', which has already been referred to, in relation to certain specific elements of the offence, including the liability arising from accidents caused by self-driving cars, autocomplete algorithms (as well as chatbots) and new types of sexual offences.

Ambrus argues that a new definition of sexual offences is also necessary in view of technological developments, arguing that the current Hungarian Criminal Code (HCC) would have difficulties in interpreting the so-called deepfake pornographic videos,[19] or he also includes a number of other algorithm-independent offences, such as upskirting, cyberflashing or revenge porn.[20] The term deepfake is colloquially used to describe the manipulation of images or video footage using AI-based technology with deep learning capabilities, which can be used to lifelike edit anyone's face into a – typically pornographic — footage that does not actually feature them.[21] The AI act defines a deepfake as an 'AI-generated or manipulated image, audio or video content that resembles existing persons, objects, places or other entities or events and would falsely appear to a person to be authentic or truthful'.[22]

In this context, AI can be seen more clearly as a tool than as an agent in its own right, so in my view there is less difficulty in criminalizing this new type of conduct.[23] In the context of deepfake, we refer to the duty to inform under section 50 of the AI Act – subsection (4) specifically requires deepfake users to warn of the artificially created or manipulated nature of the content. It is essential to note that the obligation does not apply where the use is authorized by law for the purpose of detection, prevention, investigation or prosecution of criminal offences. On this basis, for example, the use of an 'agent provocateur' acting in the context of the prosecution of child pornography offenders would also be consistent with the AI act when using a deepfake child pornography recording as 'bait'.[24]

In addition to the above, some so-called 'smart contracts' or the use of bots in trading may also constitute offences related to contract law, for example, embezzlement under Section 372, fraud under Section 373 or even misappropriation of funds under Section 376, while financial transactions with bots may constitute elements of money laundering. However, in the context of fraud, it is important to emphasise that the offence requires the passive subject to be misled or misled, so – if the contract is also 'accepted' by an AI – we may encounter difficulties in establishing certain facts. Therefore I consider that fraud committed by using an information system within the meaning of Section 375(1) can be established – the latter's separation from other offences may also raise a number of additional questions, which can be answered by examining the specific algorithm for concluding the contract and by carefully analysing the authorisations granted for its use and other rules governing the operation of the algorithm. There may also be the question of the use of forged private documents under Section 345, which is also frequently raised in the context of 'classic' contracts, and the so-called intellectual forgery of public documents under Section 342(1)(c), which may be relevant if, for example, the notary's office also uses AI to incorporate certain documents into public documents.[25] Hatfield[26] examines the liability of AI in the context of taxation, but given that the application of AI in domestic taxation is still in its infancy, it is difficult to outline practical problems in relation to any conduct of fiscal fraud under Section 396. It is important to note, however, that based on the Government Decision 1080/2022(23.II) on the Artificial Intelligence Working Group of the National Tax and Customs Administration, a separate working group has been investigating the applicability of AI in the context of domestic taxation since 2022.

A more prominent example would be the behaviour of AI in relation to defamation. A striking example is the problem of crimes 'committed' by artificial search engine algorithms. As Péter Sziládi puts it, 'Google predicts or suggests our search results, which may lead us to results that are related to our interests'.[27] The core of how the algorithm works is that the search engine weights the expected search according to three categories: 'customisation', 'search volume' and 'virality and trending topics'.[28] As the question under examination is also approached in the domestic legal literature from a private law point of view, the research is also oriented towards this point of view, but the facts presented show that the question can easily have a criminal law relevance. For example, in the case of R.S. v. Google, the German Federal Supreme Court displayed the words 'scientology' and 'fraud' (Betrug) after the plaintiff (R.S.) had typed in his full name.[29] In domestic criminal law, the use of fraudulent and similar terms alone may constitute defamation (with particular reference to similar terms used in the case of public figures), it is easy to see how similar automatic additions could easily lead to defamatory or slanderous statements of fact. For example typing the name of an – unnamed – public figure into Google, most of the automatic additions related to his work, the algorithm offered up writings about the public figure's corruption and (unsubstantiated) writings about his extramarital affair, the latter raising the possibility of defamation or slander.[30] In my view, if it is easy to identify the natural person behind the algorithm (e.g. an article written by a journalist falsely accusing the victim of committing a crime, which is then picked up by other newspapers, thus generating interest), an aggravated case of defamation under Section 226(2)(b) in the public domain will be established, alongside a qualified case of substantial damage to interests under (c). However, this would pose further practical difficulties, as one of the principles of autocompletion is personalization, so it would be difficult to determine, even in order of magnitude, how many people Google would similarly supplement the name of the victim. An even greater challenge would be to prove that the defamatory statement originated from a particular person, and even if successful, the additional difficulty would be to establish whether the operation of an algorithm unknown to the lay person is part of the causal chain (even if strict theories of causation are applied). In addition to the above, it is significant that Google's search engine already offers a 'possible way to report inappropriate predictions'; on the basis of the Hungarian practice – using the liability for comments as an analogy – this, in my opinion, fulfils the related expected conduct, as indicated by the Pécs Court of Appeal examined the ECtHR standards in its decision no. Pf. 20.032/2018/5 (also published under BDT2018. 3918.): '[t]he European Court of Human Rights has also emphasized that the operation of the so-called notice-and-take-down system must strike an appropriate balance between the rights and interests of the data subjects'.[31]

A related issue is the area of automatic text recognition software, including ChatGPT and other similar chatbots which topic has dominated all related topics in the last two years. However, in the case of ChatGPT (and bots using similar algorithms), the prior issue of all artificial text generation is amplified. First, I refer back to the duty of disclosure under Section 50 of the AI Act, so that natural persons must be able to detect that they are interacting with an AI (a condition that ChatGPT currently meets). This does not, however, deter users from asking ChatGPT (and other similar chatbots) a number of questions whose 'thought arcs' of answers (particularly because of the black box effect) are not even clearly traceable.[32]

5.4 Algorithms in autonomous vehicles and the criminal law

According to László Viski's (1974) monograph '[assuming] both the full exploitation of the technical possibilities realistically conceivable today and the flawless work of the authorities, it is beyond doubt that the personal performance of the driver will remain the basis of accident-free and orderly, disciplined transport for generations to come'.[33] As today's technological innovations show, for the coming generations, the (primary) basis for accident-free driving will no longer be the personal performance of the driver. As regards to criminal liability for accidents caused by self-driving vehicles, Ambrus stresses that the most appropriate approach would be to create a sui generis offence[34]; he also points out that, given the ultima ratio nature of criminal law, decriminalization could also be a possible solution.[35] In the context of decriminalization, his proposition resonates with Thomas Weigend et al.,[36] which, in my view, is not yet applicable in the near future.

In my previous papers[37] I have dealt in detail with the criminal liability of self-driving vehicles, and while I consider István Ambrus' proposal for a sui generis definition of the facts to be fully logical and well supported, I believe that with the appropriate amendment of the rules on the framework displacement of traffic offences, we can also achieve the appropriate sanctioning of accidents caused by self-driving vehicles.[38] It is important to note that certain concepts and rules on self-driving vehicles have already appeared in Hungarian legislation: Annex 18 to Decree 6/1990(IV. 12.) of the Ministry of Transport, Building and Urban Affairs contains the often cited 5+1 division for the definition of technology.[39] Furthermore, Section 2(4)(k) of Decree No 5/1990(23.Iv.) of the Ministry of Transport and Communications defined the term test driver as 'a driver who supervises the testing of an autonomous vehicle for development purposes while being present in the autonomous vehicle under test and who is capable of taking control of the autonomous vehicle for development purposes at any time without delay'. In addition to the above, Annex 13 of the Regulation provided that 'the test driver, whether the vehicle is in manual or automatic mode, is responsible for the safe operation of the vehicle'. The AI Act self-driving technology per se is not named in the AI Act, but can be categorised as such based on Section 6(1)(a) and Annex I, point 18. On this basis, I believe that the use of self-driving cars without a natural person without a 'remote monitoring' system is, in my view, not compatible with the AI Act.

In view of the above, I am of the opinion that the traffic offences of the current Criminal Code, in particular the offences of dangerous driving under Section 234(1) and road accident under § 235, are a sufficient basis for determining liability, and it may be necessary that at most Section 240(2), which defines the persons who may be offenders of traffic offences.[40] For example, the essence of SAE 3 is that the driver should take control only on command, so it is not inconceivable that in the absence of such a command he could engage in a completely different activity, which would make it inherently more difficult for him to monitor the road. Since the technology itself controls the traffic, I consider it unnecessary (or even counterproductive) to impose an additional strict control task on the driver.

Furthermore, I would consider it unnecessarily complicated to define detailed control obligations (e.g. the driver is obliged to check the correct choice of speed, following distance, etc. even in the absence of a warning), and instead I strongly suggest a more general formulation to be more appropriate (e.g. the driver is obliged to ensure safe participation in traffic even in the absence of a warning); however, in this case the driver is not the only one who is checking, and is essentially expected to detect obvious errors by relying on the machine, so I would suggest that it will be up to the practice to tighten the control obligation more lightly. To give you a concrete example: there is a speed limit of 60 km/h before a slight bend in a main road. If a driver crosses it at 70 km/h and then causes an accident, he will be held liable for the breach of the standard, causality and the relevance of the two. In contrast, a different result can be reached if we take into account the confidence in the correct speed choice of the self-driving technology. There is no significant difference between a speed of 60 and 70 km/h 'by feel' (based on the lateral acceleration forces acting on the human body), so that the liability of a driver who has a reasonable confidence in the correct speed choice of the vehicle will not be established in the absence of illegality.[41] Conversely, if the driver senses an incorrect choice of speed on the bend, a duty to intervene arises.[42]

The 'behavior' of AI typically also raises the responsibility of software designers as well as manufacturers; the rules are expressed through standards designed to protect the interests of consumers as a legal subject. If the manufacturer or distributor is aware that his product is capable of causing the danger (e.g. does not meet the future EU safety or quality requirements), the Hungarian legal system is based on the article 415(1) of the HCC which states that 'any person who places on the market substandard products as if they were good quality is guilty of a felony punishable by imprisonment not exceeding three years'.

In the absence of related EU rules, Act LXXXVIII of 2012 on the Market Surveillance of Products is the framework legislation, which states in Article 3 (2)–(3) that the manufacturer is obliged to ensure the safety of the product and imposes a similar obligation on the importer. Section 2(1) of the same Act defines the concept of a safe product as 'any product which, under normal or reasonably foreseeable conditions of use, does not present a risk or which is compatible with the use of the product, is considered acceptable and presents the least risk compatible with a high level of protection of the safety and health of persons', which is the basis for the prohibition of risk enhancement in the present legislation. The concept of substandard quality product' is already defined in the HCC, Article 415(6), which provides that 'the product does not meet the safety or quality requirements laid down by law or by a directly applicable legal act of the European Union, or, in the absence of such a requirement, if the product cannot be used as intended or if its usability is significantly reduced'. The concept of substandard quality product' is already defined in the HCC; according to Section 415(6) a product is substandard if it is not in conformity with the safety and quality requirements specified by the relevant legislation or by any directly applicable legislation of the European Union, or in the absence of such requirements, if the product cannot be used for its designated purpose, or its use has been diminished considerably. In the case of a car that is not capable of self-driving, this means, e.g. the proper functioning of the braking system, which in the case of self-driving is supplemented by the proper functioning of the software and hardware of the information system. To summarise the above, it can be determined that the manufacturer, as well as the distributor, must comply with certain safety requirements; if he fails to do so intentionally or negligently, as set out in paragraph 4 of the facts, to ensure that the product is safe, he commits an offence.[43]

5.5 Conclusion

Liability for the 'actions' of AI will become an increasingly pressing issue in the near future. While I consider a certain degree of fragmentation of judgments in the forthcoming criminal proceedings to be a realistic and unavoidable possibility, it is of the utmost importance to summarize the basic doctrinal principles so that we manage to avoid, in the words of Thomas Weigend, a liability vacuum.[44] Two journalists expressed the same in a layman's but extremely illustrative way in their podcast on 444.hu: 'We are at the point [...] with self-driving cars that either they can solve all existing trolley problems perfectly, or they should not be allowed on the roads, but the fact is that there is no such thing, there will always be a mistake.[...] What is the problem with self-driving cars? The fact is that they cause far fewer accidents than human drivers in any situation, the only problem is that there is no one to hold responsible. So we are at the moral problem that it is more important to address the liability as an inner emotional need than human lives. So that's where we're at the fundamental problem, isn't it? The reason why they don't allow self-driving cars is because there has to be someone responsible, someone who, if the vehicle hits someone, we put in jail'.[45] Here I suggest visiting the most widely used test, the so-called 'moral machine' website, created with the support of the Max Plank Society, the Massachusetts Institute of Technology and other renowned institutions, which, if completed, can be part of a sample of tens of millions of people: https://www.moralmachine.net.

To address the question of the national legislation, a proper definition of AI is needed, but presumably international law (including Community legislation) will soon provide a normative, clear definition, so that the liability regime of the norms filling the criminal law framework positions will also become clearer. This, however, requires a detailed knowledge and examination of the existing doctrine; in my view, the current liability formulations and facts can provide a largely adequate basis.

Notes

1 AMBRUS (2021, p. 166).
2 European Parliament legislative resolution of 13 March 2024 on the proposal for a regulation of the European Parliament and of the Council on laying down harmonized rules on Artificial Intelligence (Artificial Intelligence Act) and amending certain Union Legislative Acts (COM(2021) 0206 – C9-0146/2021 – 2021/0106(COD)), available at https://www.europarl.europa.eu/RegistreWeb/search/simpleSearchHome.htm?references=P9_TA(2024)0138&sortAndOrder=DATE_DOCU_DESC.
3 Article 3(1)4.
4 ESZTERI (2015, pp. 1–2).
5 ESZTERI (2015, p. 2).
6 see Sections 7 and 8 of the HCC: a criminal offense is committed with intent if the person conceives a plan to achieve a certain result, or acquiesces to the consequences of his conduct. 'Negligence' means when a criminal offense is committed where the perpetrator is able to anticipate the possible consequences of his conduct, but carelessly relies on their non-occurrence or fails to foresee such possible consequences through conduct characterized by carelessness and neglectfulness.
7 VISKI, László: Közlekedési Büntetőjog, Közgazdasági és Jogi KÖnyvkiadó, Budapest, 1974. p. 309.
8 WEIGEND, Thomas – Gless, Sabine – Silverman, Emily: If Robots Cause Harm, Who Is to Blame? Self-Driving Cars and Criminal Liability. New Criminal Law Review, 2016/3. pp. 423–425.
9 WEIGEND, Thomas – Gless, Sabine – Silverman, Emily: If Robots Cause Harm, Who Is to Blame? p. 422. See also HODULA, Máté: Az önvezető járművek és a büntetőjogi felelősség. Jogelméleti Szemle, 2018/3.
10 AMBRUS (2021, p. 172).
11 KLEIN, Tamás: Homonculum regulare necesse est – Adalékok egy jövendő robotjog elé, különös tekintettel a jogalanyiság és a felelősség kérdésére. Jogtudományi Közlöny, 2018/9. p. 388.
12 AMBRUS (2021, p. 44).
13 AMBRUS (2021, p. 174).
14 See also Hodula (2018).
15 Objective criminal liability should not be confused with objective criminal liability; to distinguish between the two see. MÉSZÁROS, Ádám: A bűncselekmény fogalmának alapkérdései, OKRI, Budapest, 2020, p. 72.
16 AMBRUS (2021, p. 196).
17 Strict liability offenses ill. contraventions purement matriels – WEIGEND (2014, p. 491).
18 See also HODULA, Máté: Adalékok a büntetőjog és a digitalizáció kapcsolatához, Magyar Jog, 2022, 6, pp. 351–359.
19 AMBRUS (2021, p. 221).
20 AMBRUS (2021, pp. 221–233).

21 DELFINO, Rebecca A., Pornographic Deepfakes: The Case for Federal Criminalization of Revenge Porn's Next Tragic Act, 88 Fordham L. Rev. 887 (2019).
22 AI Act, Article 3(1)(60).
23 I note that, in my view, instead of Ambrus's codification proposal – which bears Anglo-Saxon traits – containing a wide range of offences, it would be closer to domestic dogmatics to create a more comprehensive set of facts (e.g. abuse of pornographic footage) (HODULA, 2022, p. 357).
24 Provided it does not fall within the scope of prohibited AI practices or other legal prohibitions.
25 See also HODULA (2022).
26 HATFIELD, Michael: Professionally Responsible Artificial Intelligence. Arizona State Law Journal, 2019/3.
27 SZILÁDI, Péter: Személyiségsértés algoritmussal? – avagy a Google automatikus kiegészítő funkciója, Bibó Jog és Politikai Szemle, 2020/1, 95–114, p. 97.
28 SZILÁDI, Péter: Személyiségsértés algoritmussal? p. 99.
29 SZILÁDI, Péter: Személyiségsértés algoritmussal? pp. 102–105; in this particular case, the German court ruled that Google's liability is limited, i.e. the company is obliged to remove the infringing search behavior of which it becomes aware
30 While I could provide an anonymous screenshot during the conference, by the time I have finished this paper, the certain auto-complete suggestion cannot be reproduced – an educated guess would be that the affected person filed a request outlined below.
31 See also HODULA (2022).
32 A memorable case is the New York Times article in which the journalist was persuaded by a Microsoft chatbot that he didn't love his wife and should leave her – the newspaper published the entire conversation. The reasons behind the AI's thinking could not be explained by Kevin Scott, a senior Microsoft executive. ROOSE, Kevin: A Conversation with Bing's Chatbot Left Me Deeply Unsettled, NY Times, 2023.
33 VISKI (1974 p. 69).
34 AMBRUS (2021, p. 196).
35 AMBRUS (2021, p. 197).
36 Relying on these theories, it might be argued that robots are part of the 'normal' risks of life, comparable to lightning or falling trees; Wegiendet al.: If Robots Cause Harm, Who Is to Blame? Self-Driving Cars and Criminal Liability. New Criminal Law Review, 2016/3 p. 433.
37 see Hodula, Máté: Az autonóm járművek hatása a közlekedési büntetőjog fejlődésére, 2021, MTA Law Working Papers 2021/7.
38 Hodula, Máté: Az autonóm járművek hatása a közlekedési büntetőjog fejlődésére, 25.
39 SAE International (2016). US Department of Transportation's New Policy on Automated Vehicles Adopts SAE International's Levels of Automation for Defining Driving Automation in On-Road Motor Vehicles, https://www.sae.org/news/3544/.
40 The cited offences can only be committed by the driver; if a pedestrian is liable for a traffic accident, they may be according to the general offences of crimes against life, limb or health.
41 For the possibility of amendments (i.e. if they are needed), see HODULA (2018, 2021). Also, I have to highlight that I have a different opinion than AMBRUS (2021) – for the comparison, see HODULA (2022).

42 1.5–1.8 m/s^2 lateral acceleration is already noticeable but not/always unpleasant, while more significant (2.5–5 m/s^2) is already impactful. Fülöp – Major, 2 FÜLÖP, ÁGNES – MAJOR, Róbert: A KRESZ értelmezése a joggyakorlatban, HVG-Orac, 005, 63.
43 For a detailed comparison, see HODULA (2018).
44 WEIGEND et al. (2016, p. 432) – István Ambrus mistakenly attributes the term to me in footnote 28 of 'Digitisation and Criminal Law', but in my 2018 paper I also cited Professor Weigend and his co-authors (footnoted as appropriate) – ld. Ambrus (2021, p. 171. 27. footnote). See also HODULA (2018, p. 68. 3. footnote).
45 UJ, Péter, BEDE, Márton, WINKLER, Róbert: Borízű Hang #112.: Az automatizált Boris Johnson és az internetes nimbyzmus (2023) 21:28 [...] 22:08.

References

AMBRUS, István: Digitalizáció és büntetőjog, Wolters Kluwer, Budapest, 2021.

AMBRUS, István: Az autonóm járművek és a büntetőjogi felelősségre vonás akadályai. In: Mezei, Kitti (szerk.): A bűnügyi tudományok és az informatika. PTE ÁJK–MTA TK, Budapest–Pécs, 2019, 9–26.

DELFINO, Rebecca A.: Pornographic Deepfakes: The Case for Federal Criminalization of Revenge Porn's Next Tragic Act, 88 Fordham L. Rev. 887, 2019.

ESZTERI, Dániel: A mesterséges intelligencia fejlesztésének és üzemeltetésének egyes felelősségi kérdései. Infokommunikáció és Jog, 2015/2–3.

FÜLÖP, ÁGNES – MAJOR, Róbert: A KRESZ értelmezése a joggyakorlatban, HVG-Orac, 2005.

HATFIELD, Michael: Professionally Responsible Artificial Intelligence. Arizona State Law Journal, 2019.

HODULA, Máté: *Az önvezető járművek és a büntetőjogi felelősség*. Jogelméleti Szemle, 2018/3.

HODULA, Máté: Az autonóm járművek hatása a közlekedési büntetőjog fejlődésére, 2021, MTA Law Working Papers 2021/7.

HODULA, Máté: Adalékok a büntetőjog és a digitalizáció kapcsolatához, Magyar Jog, 2022/6, 351–359.

KLEIN, Tamás: Homonculum regulare necesse est – Adalékok egy jövendő robotjog elé, különös tekintettel a jogalanyiság és a felelősség kérdésére. Jogtudományi Közlöny, 2018/9.

KŐHIDI, Ákos – Somkutas Péter: Az önvezető autó szoftvere magas szintű szellemi alkotás vagy kifinomult károkozó? In Medias Res, 2017/2. sz., 232–269.

LŐRINCZ György: A mesterséges intelligencia alkalmazásával hozott döntés jogi megítélésének egyes kérdései. Gazdaság és Jog, 2019/3.

MÉSZÁROS, Ádám: A bűncselekmény fogalmának alapkérdései, OKRI, Budapest, 2020.

MEZEI, Kitti: A kiberbűnözés egyes büntetőjogi szabályozási kérdései, PhD értekezés, Pécsi Tudományegyetem Állam- és Jogtudományi Kar Doktori Iskola, 2019.

MISKOLCI, László: A bűnösség alapkategóriái az angol büntetőjogban, Magyar Jog, 2002/2, 100–117.

ROOSE, Kevin: A Conversation with Bing's Chatbot Left Me Deeply Unsettled, NY Times, 2023. [online] accessed: 21 July 2024.

SZATHMÁRY, Zoltán: A mesterséges intelligencia hatása a büntetőjogi felelősségre, Ügyészek Lapja, 2019/3.

SZILÁDI, Péter: Személyiségsértés algoritmussal? – avagy a Google automatikus kiegészítő funkciója, Bibó Jog és Politikai Szemle, 2020/1, 95–114, 97.

UJ, Péter, BEDE, Márton, WINKLER, Róbert: Borízű Hang #112.: Az automatizált Boris Johnson és az internetes nimbyzmus (2023) https://444.hu/2023/03/05/borizu-hang-112-az-automatizalt-boris-johnson-es-az-internetes-nimbyzmus [online] accessed: 21 July 2024.

VISKI, László: Közlekedési Büntetőjog, Közgazdasági és Jogi KÖnyvkiadó, Budapest, 1974.

WALTERS, Robert & NOVAK, Marko: Artificial Intelligence and Law, in: Cyber Security, Artificial Intelligence, Data Protection & the Law, Springer, Singapore, 39–69.

WEIGEND, Thomas: Subective Elements of Criminal Liability, in: The Oxford Handbook of Criminal Law (szerk: Dubber, Markus & Hörnle, Tatjana), Oxford University Press, Oxford, 2014, 490–511.

WEIGEND, Thomas - Gless, Sabine – Silverman, Emily: If Robots Cause Harm, Who Is to Blame? Self-Driving Cars and Criminal Liability. New Criminal Law Review, 2016/3.

ZŐDI, Zsolt & TÖRÖK, Bernát: A mesterséges intelligencia szabályozási kihívása, Nemzeti Közszolgálati Egyetem Ludovika Egyetemi Kiadó Iroda, Budapest, 2021.

Chapter 6

Automated judicial decisions

Is it possible?

Noémi Komporday-Orosz

6.1 Introduction

In our increasingly artificial intelligence (AI)-driven world, many sectors are seeking ways to leverage technology to simplify tasks, improve efficiency, and streamline operations. The judicial field, and particularly the criminal justice system, remains a sensitive area of exploration in this regard. The question arises: can we simplify the judicial process through AI? And, if so, should we?[1]

Automated or AI-based judicial decisions have been subjects of research and discussion in recent years. While AI certainly holds potential for improving many aspects of legal work, such as legal research, document analysis, replacing human judges with AI systems for final decision-making is – hopefully – unlikely to become a reality in the near future. There are significant concerns regarding the capacity of AI to adequately interpret the complexities of law, provide moral judgment, and exercise discretion in ways that align with human ethical standards.[2]

At its core, AI functions as an advanced database, capable of processing major amounts of information and identifying patterns within that data. However, AI systems, despite their computational power, cannot fully interpret legal complexities that human judges are trained to understand.

Legal reasoning involves more than just interpreting laws and regulations; it requires applying legal principles, often with a level of discretion that accounts for the details of human experience, social values, and ethical considerations. These elements of judicial decision-making rely on a nuanced understanding of human behavior, emotions, and the cultural and social context: elements that AI, at present, are not able to comprehend.

Also we have to highlight: legal systems involve complex and unique interpretations of laws, principles, and judicial practice (precedents). AI systems are lacking human-level understanding, contextual reasoning, hence the struggle to navigate complex legal issues properly.[3]

DOI: 10.4324/9781003531500-12

One of the key challenges in decision-making itself is *discretion*. Discretion in legal decision-making is not merely a technical application of rules but is inherently connected to ethics, morality, and human values. Judicial decisions frequently involve balancing competing interests, considering the nuances of individual cases, and making determinations that have profound social and ethical implications. This type of moral reasoning – whether an action is just or fair – requires human judgment. Human judges apply their professional expertise and empathy, something that AI, despite its impressive capabilities, cannot replicate.

The need for human discretion in legal decision-making is further underscored by the ethical implications of AI decisions. AI systems are trained on historical data, which may reflect existing societal biases or inequities. If these biases are not adequately addressed, AI-based systems could perpetuate or even amplify discriminatory outcomes. For example, AI may deliver biased verdicts based on flawed data, which could disproportionately affect certain groups. The ethical considerations in this context are clear: a lack of empathy, the inability to apply moral judgment, and potential for bias present serious concerns for AI's role in judicial decision-making.

Transparency and accountability[4] are other critical issues. AI decision-making systems, especially those based on complex algorithms where the reasoning behind a decision is not always clear. This lack of explainability could undermine public trust in the judicial system and make it difficult to challenge or appeal AI-generated decisions, so it is safe to say that without transparency, the public may lose confidence in the fairness and accountability of the legal (judicial or justice) system, which is built on principles of openness and accountability.

Basically, while some kind of developed AI systems may assist judges or other legal professionals during the process, the final decision-making is highly likely to remain in the hands (and responsibility) of human judges for the foreseeable future.

The proportional and ethical goal might be – in the near future – to enhance the skills and aptitudes of judges with AI tools rather than replace them entirely. In my opinion, AI technology can be helpful in the judicial field, used wisely; we can optimize the processes, by using AI for providing and filtering relevant information, identifying patterns, helping with legal research or other time-consuming, but also simple, monotonous tasks.

6.2 Advantages and disadvantages of artificial intelligence in the judicial decision-making processes

The use of AI in the judicial system has both advantages and drawbacks that need to be carefully considered. This question should be examined from various perspectives.[5]

First and strongest pro is *efficiency*. AI can process huge volumes of legal data quickly and effectively, which can streamline tasks such as legal research and document analysis. This efficiency could potentially reduce the time and resources required to make legal decisions, helping to alleviate case backlogs and reduce delays in the legal process.

In connection with efficiency, we shall mention *consistency*. AI systems can deliver consistent decisions by applying the same legal principles and case law (precedents if you like) uniformly. By analyzing past cases and identifying patterns in legal data, AI is able to uncover insights that human judges might overlook. This could, in theory, reduce disparities stemming from human bias or inconsistencies in interpretation.

While, on the one hand, this could help decrease disparities originating from human biases or variations in interpretation, on the other hand, however the decisions would be consistent and uniform, we would lose the individualized judicial decisions, because we should not forget: there is always a difference between cases, whether it is based on the same criminal offence or legal dispute.

In a judicial system based on the rule of law, access to justice is really important and essential. Unfortunately, there are some regions around the world with limited legal resources or expertise, AI could help enhance *access to justice*. AI-based or AI-driven tools could assist individuals who may not have access to legal counsel, providing them with guidance on legal questions or helping them navigate the judicial process more effectively. Additionally, AI can increase access to justice in regions with limited legal (judicial) resources or expertise.

Other argument advocating for automated decisions – related to easy accessibility – is *promptness* and because undeniably AI is able to process cases faster than human judges, potentially reducing delays. This promptness could help make the judicial process more efficient, particularly in jurisdictions with heavy caseloads.

Some of the cons of automated decisions were mentioned in the introduction but shall be detailed further. First and foremost, the biggest and most relevant argument against AI-based decisions is the *lack of empathy and subjective judgment*. It is safe to declare that AI systems lack the ability to understand and apply human emotions, empathy, and subjective considerations, which are almost always crucial in judicial decisions. These are moral or ethical aspects that an algorithm may struggle to comprehend, while human judges can easily consider and weigh these factors. In conclusion, AI systems, no matter how advanced, lack the ability to understand human emotions or apply empathy in decision-making, emotional and moral considerations are often the core of certain legal decisions, particularly in criminal cases where the personal circumstances of the defendant and the victim, also the circumstances of the act itself must be weighed carefully. As I see, AI cannot replicate and neither will replace in the future the nuanced judgment that professional judges bring to these situations.

The next argument is strongly linked to the previous. *Bias and discrimination*[6] are huge concern, AI systems are trained on and learn from existing (historical) data, which will inevitably contain biases or reflect societal disparities. If these biases are not identified and addressed, AI could perpetuate or even amplified in automated decision-making, potentially creating discriminatory practices, also leading to unfair outcomes.[7]

Transparency and accountability were also mentioned before, so without repeating the abovementioned, it should be stated that it can be difficult to understand and challenge (appeal to) the reasoning behind AI-based judgments and decisions. AI decision-making processes can be opaque, making it difficult for affected individuals to understand how a decision was reached, which fact could potentially undermine the public trust in the judicial system. This also raises concerns about accountability, particularly in a legal system that relies on transparency and the ability to challenge decisions.[8]

Until now, the technology was considered only as an advantage, however in some cases we might face sorts of technological limitations or errors. AI systems, while powerful, are not infallible. They can make errors, particularly when dealing with unknown or unusually complex cases. AI systems are dependent on historical data and may struggle with unprecedented legal challenges that fall outside the patterns found in the data they were trained on.

This limitation highlights the need for human oversight to ensure that AI does not make decisions in cases that require a more flexible, adaptable approach. Relying solely on AI (automated) decision-making could limit the flexibility to address new legal challenges and issues.[9]

6.3 Potential areas for AI-integration in the judicial system[10]

We should examine the question, which field of justice or judicial decisions are most likely to be (or may become) automated or AI based in the future?[11]

While the idea of fully automated judicial decisions remains distant and dystopian (?), there are areas within the judicial system where AI could play a more significant role. These areas, while requiring oversight and human judgment, could benefit from AI's capacity to process and analyze large amounts of data quickly.

These certain areas within the judicial field, which are more amenable to automation, also may experience an increased amount of integration of AI systems and technologies.

One of these areas is *legal research and document analysis*, in which AI systems can assist properly and usefully. By analyzing vast amounts of legal texts, acts, regulations, case law etc., AI might help judges, lawyers, and other legal professionals to access relevant information more efficiently. AI can aid in identifying relevant cases, relevant legal principles, and possibly providing recommendations for legal arguments.

Nowadays AI systems are already being used to assist legal professionals with legal research and document analysis, because they can be used to analyze legal documents, contracts, or other written materials to extract and identify key information.

AI can be used in so-called *case prediction*, because AI can analyze past case outcomes and legal data to predict the potential outcomes of future cases. This tool could help legal professionals understand how similar cases have been resolved and form legal strategies based on existing data.

AI could also assist in providing *recommendations for sentencing* (sentencing guidelines) based on factors such as the severity of the crime, the defendant's criminal history, and relevant legal precedents. However, final sentencing decisions should remain in the hands of human judges, who can apply moral judgment and consider the unique circumstances of each case, AI should always be an orienting tool, nothing more.

While in the areas mentioned above, AI systems can be a useful tool, it is quite important to note that even in these areas, human judgment and oversight shall remain crucial. The use of AI technologies should be seen as a tool to improve human decision-making rather than replacing human judges entirely. The ethical, legal, and societal implications of AI-based decision-making always need careful consideration and appropriate safeguards to ensure fairness, transparency, and accountability.[12]

6.4 Conclusion: The future of AI in the justice system and decision-making

The integration of AI into the judicial system is a complex issue that demands careful consideration of its potential benefits and drawbacks.

While AI holds promise for improving efficiency, consistency, and access to legal services, particularly in areas such as legal research, document analysis, etc., it is unlikely (and this is this author's favored outcome) that AI will replace human judges in the foreseeable future.

The future of AI in the judicial field should be approached with caution. While AI has the potential to enhance the efficiency and consistency of legal processes, it cannot replace the need for human judgment, empathy, and discretion. AI can serve as a powerful tool to assist judges and legal professionals, improving tasks such as legal research, document analysis, and case prediction. However, the final decision-making authority should remain firmly in the hands of human judges.

As we move forward, it is essential to strike a balance between optimizing AI technology and preserving the integrity of the judicial system. As this paper outlined, AI systems excel at processing large volumes of data quickly, identifying patterns, and applying uniform principles, which can aid in streamlining certain aspects of the judicial process. However, the role of judges goes far beyond mechanical decision-making. Judicial decisions are deeply influenced by a human understanding of complex social, cultural, and moral factors that AI systems, despite their sophistication, cannot replicate. Legal reasoning often requires empathy, ethical deliberation, and an understanding of context: factors that are integral to ensuring fairness and justice. As such, AI's current inability to incorporate these subjective and emotional elements in its decision-making processes makes it unsuitable for replacing human judgment in matters of legal consequence.[13]

Despite these challenges, AI has the potential to play a valuable role as a support tool for judges and legal professionals, enhancing their ability to handle complex legal issues, so AI should be seen as a tool that complements and enhances human decision-making rather than replacing it entirely. Ethical, legal, and societal implications must be carefully considered, and appropriate safeguards must be put in place to ensure fairness, transparency, and accountability in the use of AI in the judicial process.

In conclusion, the future of AI in the judiciary should not be centered on replacing human judges but on assisting them in making more informed and efficient decisions. The current limitations of AI, especially its inability to fully comprehend legal nuances, exercise discretion, and make ethically sound judgments, underscore the critical importance of retaining human oversight in judicial decision-making. As AI technologies continue to evolve, their role in the judicial system must be approached with caution, ensuring that the ethical, legal, and social implications are fully addressed.

Human judgment, with its capacity for empathy, ethical reasoning, and understanding of context, remains indispensable in the pursuit of justice. For AI to be effectively integrated into the judicial process, it must be used in a manner that respects the principles of fairness, transparency, and accountability, with robust safeguards in place to mitigate the risks of bias and ensure that justice is truly served.

Notes

1 Same questions arised in: SUSSKIND, R., SUSSKIND, D. The Future of the Professions: How Technology Will Transform the Work of Human Experts. Oxford University Press, Oxford, 2015.

2 See more: LUKÁCS, M. A mesterséges intelligencia etikai kihívásai a jogi döntéshozatalban. Jogi Szemle, vol. 18, 2020, pp. 243–261.
3 See more: AMBRUS, I. Substantive Criminal Law and Artificial Intelligence, in: GRYSZCZYNSKA, A. (ed.) Legal Aspects of Artificial Intelligence. Instytut Wymiaru Sprawiedliwości, Warszawa. 2024.
4 As Cathy O'Neil highlighted in 2016. See O'NEIL, C. Weapons of Math Destruction: How Big Data Increases Inequality and Threatens Democracy. Crown Publishers, New York, 2016. Further details of the topic: Barocas, S., Hardt, M., Narayanan, A. Fairness and Machine Learning: Limitations and Opportunities. The MIT Press, Cambridge, 2023.
5 TÓTH, A. A mesterséges intelligencia hatása a bíráskodásra; A bírói hatalom gyakorlásáról szóló 1869. évi IV. törvénycikk megalkotásának 150. évfordulója: A Kúria ünnepi teljes ülése és tudományos konferenciája, 2021 [https://www.researchgate.net/publication/349252190_A_MESTERSEGES_INTELLIGENCIA_HATASA_A_BIRASKODASRA].
6 See in detail: ANGWIN, J., LARSON, J., MATTU, S., KIRCHNER, L. Machine Bias: There's Software Used across the Country to Predict Future Criminals. And It's Biased against Blacks. ProPublica. 2016 [https://www.propublica.org/article/machine-bias-risk-assessments-in-criminal-sentencing].
7 HARCOURT, B. E. Against Prediction: Profiling, Policing, and Punishing in an Actuarial Age. University of Chicago Press, Chicago, 2015.
8 See more: BINNS, R. On the apparent conflict between fairness and transparency in AI decision-making. Proceedings of the 2018 CHI Conference on Human Factors in Computing Systems. 2018 [https://arxiv.org/pdf/1912.06883].
9 As László Kovács stated in: KOVÁCS, L. Mesterséges intelligencia és jog: Az AI alkalmazása a bírósági rendszerekben. Magyar Jog, vol. 66, pp. 303–318.
10 In Hungarian aspect, see NAGY, A: A mesterséges intelligencia és a digitalizáció jelentősége és lehetséges hasznosítási területei az igazságszolgáltatásban; Infokommunikáció és Jog, 2022 [https://infojog.hu/dr-nagy-adrienn-a-mesterseges-intelligencia-es-a-digitalizacio-jelentosege-es-lehetseges-hasznositasi-teruletei-az-igazsagszolgaltatasban-2020-2-75-e-kulonszam/].
11 For European aspects and concerns, see CEPEJ: European ethical Charter on the use of Artificial Intelligence in judicial systems and their environment [https://rm.coe.int/ethical-charter-en-for-publication-4-december-2018/16808f699c].
12 As mentioned in VARGA, G. (2022). Digitális igazságszolgáltatás: A mesterséges intelligencia szerepe a bíróságokon. Bírósági Szemle, vol. 3, 2022, pp. 50–72.
13 CALO, R. Robotics and the Lessons of Cyberlaw. California Law Review, vol. 103, 2015, pp. 513–563.

Chapter 7

Regulating law enforcement facial recognition and safeguarding against misuse

European Union and Hungarian perspectives

Kitti Mezei

7.1 Introduction: AI-powered surveillance

In this chapter, the aim is to introduce and analyse the legal frameworks surrounding the use of facial recognition technologies, particularly in the context of law enforcement, with a focus on the EU Artificial Intelligence Act (AI Act) and Hungarian regulations. Facial recognition technologies, which are AI-based systems that rely on complex machine learning algorithms to process and identify biometric data, are increasingly employed in various fields, but their use in law enforcement is especially contentious due to the significant privacy concerns and potential for human rights violations. The AI Act, as well as national laws like those in Hungary, have begun to address the challenges associated with these technologies, particularly focusing on high-risk applications such as real-time biometric identification in public spaces, which are seen as high-stakes implementations of AI. I will explore how the AI Act classifies such systems, the compliance obligations it imposes, and the exemptions available for law enforcement under certain conditions. Additionally, I will examine specific cases, such as the legal use of facial recognition technology in Hungary, where national frameworks regulate the collection, storage, and processing of biometric data. Through this examination, I aim to provide a clear understanding of the regulatory landscape, highlighting both the benefits and risks of deploying AI-powered facial recognition technologies in law enforcement, and addressing ongoing debates about their appropriate use and potential abuses.

7.2 Navigating facial recognition in law enforcement under the AI Act

Cases involving law enforcement use have been mainly classified as high-risk AI systems. The AI Act defines law enforcement authority and law enforcement activities.[1] Importantly, the AI Act will exclude AI systems

DOI: 10.4324/9781003531500-13

used for military, defence, or national security purposes from the scope of the AI Act, regardless of whether public or private entities utilise them (Article 2(3)). This exclusion is justified by both international law and the specific competencies governing defence and security within the EU. The exclusion is supported by Article 4(2) of the Treaty on European Union (TEU), which designates defence and national security matters as the sole responsibility of Member States. Additionally, the specificities of the Member States' defence policies, covered by Chapter 2 of Title V of the TEU, are subject to public international law. However, if these systems are also used for non-excluded purposes, such as civilian or law enforcement activities, they must comply with the AI Act. Conversely, AI systems developed for civilian or law enforcement purposes that are subsequently used for military, defence, or national security purposes are not subject to the AI Act. This allows entities engaged in national security, defence, and military activities to use AI systems without being affected by the regulation (Recital 24). Arguably, these rules create a loophole that allows Member States to exempt themselves from the rules for any activity they deem relevant for "national security".[2]

The EU aims to create more stringent restrictions on facial recognition to better protect citizens' rights, especially related to biometric data usage. The use of facial recognition technology affects not only privacy and data protection but also broader fundamental rights, such as human dignity, freedom of movement, and freedom of assembly. This broadens the scope of concerns beyond personal privacy, as these rights are critical for democratic societies. These issues are particularly emphasised in law enforcement and criminal justice, where the balance between security and individual rights is most delicate. Facial recognition's role in policing must therefore align with human rights safeguards.[3]

Facial recognition technology uses algorithms to analyse facial features from images or video to match and verify identities. It is a valuable tool for law enforcement, helping to quickly identify suspects by comparing facial data with criminal databases. It also aids in locating missing persons by matching unidentified individuals with reported cases. Beyond law enforcement, facial recognition enhances security in controlled environments by replacing traditional authentication methods like physical access control. As facial recognition becomes widespread, especially in public spaces, it raises ethical concerns about surveillance and potential misuse. The large databases supporting these systems are also vulnerable to cyberattacks, underscoring the need for strong data protection. Large databases containing facial images are attractive targets for hackers. Data breaches could lead to the theft of sensitive biometric information, which cannot be easily changed like a password.

A key distinction exists between live or real-time facial recognition, which analyses faces in real time against a watchlist, and retrospective facial recognition, used post-event to compare images with lawfully stored databases like criminal records. A remote biometric identification system in the AI Act refers to AI systems that identify individuals at a distance without their active participation, by comparing their biometric data with information in a reference database. These systems can identify multiple people or track their behaviour simultaneously. The regulation excludes biometric verification systems used solely for authentication purposes, such as unlocking devices or gaining access to services, as these have a lesser impact on fundamental rights. Real-time systems capture, compare, and identify biometric data instantly, while post systems perform identification after a delay, using previously captured data like CCTV footage. While live facial recognition can raise data privacy concerns and face technical challenges, such as biases or system overload, retrospective recognition is more controlled. The widespread deployment of facial recognition in public spaces raises significant privacy concerns.[4] The technology can enable mass surveillance, like in China,[5] leading to the continuous tracking of individuals without their consent.

In the Glukhin v. Russia (2023) case, the European Court of Human Rights (ECHR) expanded the interpretation of privacy under Article 8 of the European Convention on Human Rights, which guarantees the right to respect for private and family life. The court acknowledged that even in public spaces, individuals may have a reasonable expectation of privacy in certain interactions, recognising a "zone of interaction" with others that can still fall within the scope of private life. This idea contrasts with the traditional view that privacy is mostly applicable to private settings (such as homes or personal communications), but the court's decision reflects the evolving nature of privacy in modern society, especially in the face of new surveillance technologies like facial recognition and CCTV. The zone of interaction refers to those situations where individuals interact in public but still maintain an expectation of privacy concerning their actions, movements, or communications. For instance, even though someone is in a public space, the use of invasive digital technologies to continuously monitor, identify, and track them could violate their privacy rights. The Glukhin case is important because it demonstrates the court's acknowledgment of the broader implications of surveillance technologies, particularly in maintaining a balance between public safety and personal privacy. The decision underscores the need for proportionality and legality when employing surveillance technologies in public, ensuring that they do not disproportionately infringe on individuals' private lives. The ruling also sets a precedent that encourages further development of legal frameworks to protect privacy in the face of advancing technology.[6]

7.2.1 *Off-limits AI – Prohibited law enforcement applications under the AI Act*

Following its risk-based approach, the AI Act proposes a category of prohibited AI systems. This entails a completely prohibited category (Title II), which includes the prohibition of real-time remote biometric identification for law enforcement purposes in publicly accessible spaces[7] with narrow exceptions where the use is strictly necessary to achieve the public interest, which outweighs associated risks. These situations include searching for victims of crime, addressing threats to life or physical safety, and locating or identifying perpetrators or suspects of serious criminal offences (such as human trafficking or sexual exploitation or for the prevention of terrorist attacks) punishable by a custodial sentence or detention order of at least four years. Thus, the prohibition does not apply where these systems are used for any of the listed specific purposes because the severity threshold for such offences ensures that real-time biometric identification systems are proportionate and justified. In principle, relying on such an exception will require thorough assessments, technical and organisational measures, notifications, and a warrant.[8] However, the AI Act allows the use of real-time and post-event biometric identification for law enforcement and private purposes under certain conditions in general, so there is no ban in these cases.[9]

Since 2015, the French National Police has reportedly used Briefcam's video analytics software, including facial recognition, without public disclosure or legal authorisation. French law only permits facial recognition in limited cases, such as during judicial or administrative investigations related to public order, property, or state authority, as noted in an April 2023 parliamentary report. Investigators can use the judicial antecedent database, containing about eight million facial records as of 2018, or in specific cases like the Parafe system at external borders, which compares travellers' faces to their biometric passports. Briefcam's software, Video Synopsis, offers features like tracking individuals by clothing colour or vehicles by license plates, raising concerns about illegal use of its facial recognition capabilities. Despite being primarily used for post-event analysis, the lack of transparency regarding its facial recognition usage has sparked civil liberties concerns.[10]

Germany conducted trials at Berlin's Südkreuz train station to identify potential criminals and terrorists. The system compares live video feeds with databases of suspects.[11] The Metropolitan Police in London and the South Wales Police have used real-time facial recognition during public events and in crowded spaces to spot individuals on watchlists.[12] Italy's SARI (Sistema Automatico di Riconoscimento Immagini) system uses facial recognition for identifying individuals, particularly migrants. Concerns have arisen over potential bias, as a significant portion of the database reportedly contains images of foreigners.[13]

Moreover, some argue that holding law enforcement to a higher standard than other public or private actors when using real-time biometric identification systems is unjustifiable. Public-private partnerships are common in the development of AI systems. This blurs the lines between their roles and domains, making it challenging to determine when public involvement starts or ends, and where private entities intervene.[14] Similarly, assessing similar risks differently for fundamental rights and values in deploying such systems is unreasonable.[15] Regulatory decisions often prioritise the immediacy of identification, but the focus should be on the use and its implications rather than solely on the timeline. Issues such as scope, consent, and technical architecture are similar in both public and private use of real-time systems, affecting individuals with no reason to be monitored. However, the crucial distinction lies in the fact that private parties are not bound by considerations of the common good, public values, or the checks and balances present in democratic societies.[16] For example, there is a moratorium in force in Italy, until 31 December 2025, on the introduction of video surveillance systems based on facial recognition using biometric data, in public places or places open to the public, by private individuals and public bodies. The use of such systems is currently only allowed to judicial authorities in the exercise of their functions.

The AI Act provides that a judicial body or an independent administrative authority must explicitly authorise AI systems in each Member State for these purposes. Authorisation should typically precede the use of the system, except in urgent situations where obtaining prior authorisation is objectively impossible. In emergencies, system use should be minimal and subject to strict safeguards specified in national law. In such cases, law enforcement must promptly request authorisation, providing reasons for the delay, within 24 hours. If authorisation is denied, system usage must cease immediately, and all related data, except data acquired legally, must be discarded. Additionally, decisions with legal consequences cannot solely rely on system outputs (Recital 35). Arguably, allowing an independent administrative authority, rather than a judicial authority, to authorise the use of real-time remote biometric identification is a controversial choice. While these administrative bodies may be formally independent, they could still be vulnerable to government influence. Without judicial involvement, relying solely on administrative oversight may be inadequate from a checks and balances perspective. The decentralisation of the authorisation framework at the level of the Member States raises concerns, and particularly outlined in the AI Act are situations in which authority is devolved to agencies within Member States, grounded in the legal frameworks of those respective states. This approach raises concerns, particularly in Member

States with questionable adherence to the rule of law. The issue is compounded when pre-authorisation for real-time biometric identification use can be omitted, allowing retrospective authorisation within 24 hours in urgent situations. Such flexibility may increase the risk of misuse, particularly in countries where democratic institutions are weak, the author refers to two countries, Hungary and Poland.[17] The power that facial recognition technology gives to law enforcement can lead to overreach and abuse, especially in countries with weak checks and balances.

One of the major concerns with facial recognition technology is the lack of consent in collecting and storing individuals' biometric data. Another banned use case is databases based on bulk scraping of facial images,[18] since there are cases in which specific harms stem from the online deployment of AI biometric systems.[19] Bulk scraping of facial images can be defined as the automated collection of large volumes of facial images and associated metadata from publicly accessible web sources, using algorithms or bots, typically to build or enhance facial recognition datasets, often without explicit user consent. These images are then used to train facial recognition systems or create massive facial image databases.[20] An issue of considerable controversy revolves around the involvement of private companies in implementing these technologies. For example, in February 2020, media outlets revealed leaked documents indicating that Clearview AI had secured contracts with over 600 law enforcement agencies globally, including in Europe.[21] This technology equips users with the capability to potentially identify every individual they encounter in real time, significantly enhancing law enforcement's ability to swiftly and accurately match faces against extensive databases. The system enables an investigating officer, for example, to submit an image of a person of interest for analysis and conduct a search within a database compiled by Clearview AI. This database purportedly contains publicly accessible images sourced from online postings, which may not necessarily pertain to the individual under investigation, raising concerns about privacy and the ethical implications of such technology.[22]

For example, concerns were raised about racial bias in Clearview's algorithm, as studies have shown that facial recognition systems often struggle to accurately identify people of colour, raising the risk of false positives in law enforcement use. Clearview AI's operations lacked transparency, particularly about who had access to its technology. Clearview AI's method of scraping images without permission sparked significant concern over privacy rights. Many social media platforms, including Facebook, Twitter, and LinkedIn, sent cease-and-desist letters to Clearview AI, arguing that their actions violated terms of service.[23]

Dutch Data Protection Authority imposed a fine of 30.5 million euro and orders subject to a penalty for non-compliance up to more than 5 million euro on Clearview AI. The Dutch authority warns that using the services of Clearview is also prohibited.[24]

7.2.2 *High-risk facial recognition and its legal implications in AI Act*

Annex III categorises post-biometric identification and emotional inference for law enforcement purposes as high-risk applications. As a result, law enforcement agencies must comply with stricter requirements if they plan to utilise these tools. Biometrics, as permitted by relevant EU or national law, encompasses remote biometric identification systems, excluding AI systems used solely for identity verification. It also includes AI systems for biometric categorisation based on sensitive attributes and those used for emotion recognition.

Facial recognition technologies are categorised as high-risk AI systems under the AI Act when used in contexts like law enforcement, border control, and public spaces. This classification imposes strict compliance obligations, such as operators must conduct thorough risk assessments to identify and mitigate risks related to privacy, bias, and potential misuse of biometric data. The use of high-quality, representative datasets is mandated to avoid biased outcomes. The data must be appropriate for the specific use case and must comply with the principles of data minimisation and accuracy (AI Act, Article 10). Users and affected individuals must be informed when facial recognition technologies are in use, particularly in public spaces. Real-time biometric identification systems, like facial recognition in public spaces, are usually banned, but exceptions are allowed for law enforcement. The transparency obligations in Article 50 will not be applicable to the use of AI systems for law enforcement purposes, as it would undermine the interests of crime detection, prevention, and investigation. These exceptions apply when the technology is used for national security, public safety, or to prevent serious crimes (AI Act, Article 5). In these situations, authorities do not have to inform individuals about the use of these technologies if doing so would interfere with the operation or investigation. For national security, authorities can keep the use of AI systems confidential if revealing it would disrupt intelligence work or investigations. Developers and deployers must maintain detailed documentation of the system's design, data sources, testing methods, and compliance measures (AI Act, Article 12). This documentation must be available for review by market surveillance authorities. The AI Act introduces a pre-marketing conformity assessment for high-risk AI systems, subject to an emergency exception that allows "law enforcement agencies to deploy a high-risk AI tool that has not passed the conformity assessment procedure in case of urgency". There will be a post-marketing periodic auditing for

AI systems used in law enforcement and by the judiciary. Post-marketing monitoring required for providers of high-risk AI systems will follow the same methodological approach as continuous auditing.

For high-risk AI systems, such as those in Annex III (point 1a), any action or decision based on the system's identification must be independently verified and confirmed by two qualified human experts before proceeding. This ensures proper human oversight, meaning humans remain responsible for critical decisions, ensuring the system's output is both accurate and appropriate. However, this requirement can be waived for AI systems used in law enforcement, migration, border control, or asylum when EU or national laws deem it disproportionate, especially in situations requiring fast decisions where such oversight could slow down critical operations.

The AI Act will impose an obligation for users of high-risk AI systems to carry out a fundamental rights impact assessment before using such systems. The impact assessment exercise must consider the specific context of the use of the AI system, and it includes the duty to consult the national supervisory authority and relevant stakeholders. Still uncertain is whether deployers will correctly select the relevant fundamental rights. At EU level, a multi-stakeholder project ALIGNER, has published a customised fundamental rights impact assessment template for deploying AI systems for law enforcement purposes.[25]

7.3 Regulating law enforcement's use of facial recognition in Hungary

In Hungary, the Law Enforcement Directive (LED) – Directive (EU) 2016/680 has been implemented as part of the national legal framework governing the use of personal data, including biometric data, by law enforcement authorities. A facial image is defined as personal data under the Hungarian Act CXII of 2011 on the Right to Informational Self-Determination and Freedom of Information, which has been stated by the Hungarian Constitutional Court in several decisions, including Decision 36/2005 (X. 5.), which states that a recording obtained from image surveillance and recorded on some medium is personal data. Since the facial image does not lose this quality even after the transformation, the profile of the facial image from the facial image is also personal data.

The Act CLXXXVIII of 2015 on the Facial Image Analysis Database and the Facial Image Analysis System specifically regulates the creation and use of a national facial recognition system for law enforcement purposes in Hungary. The Hungarian data protection authority had commented on the law before its adoption and stated in its position that it would be constitutionally unacceptable for a state body to secretly monitor citizens on a mass scale using biometric data management, and they propose to amend the rules on secret information gathering by law enforcement agencies and national security services to prevent this. It should be guaranteed that secret information gathering in the public domain based on biometric identification or other compulsory surveillance should not be carried out on a massive scale, should not be stockpiling even in a pseudonymous form, should be strictly limited to a legitimate purpose defined by law, and should be restricted in terms of personnel, space, and time to the extent that a nationwide technical surveillance infrastructure is established, by compulsory external authorisation or otherwise, within the limits set by law.

This law establishes a legal framework for creating a database that stores facial images, particularly for use in criminal investigations. The database is primarily used to help law enforcement agencies identify suspects, locate missing persons, and assist in other law enforcement activities. The law outlines the development and operational use of a facial image analysis system. This system utilises biometric technologies, including facial recognition, to analyse and compare images from the database against new images (such as CCTV footage or photos captured during investigations) to assist law enforcement in identifying individuals. The act ensures that the use of facial recognition technology must adhere to strict data protection regulations, particularly those related to the collection, storage, and processing of biometric data.

The law specifies in a taxatised manner the bodies for which the use of facial image analysis is authorised. Searches of stored facial image profiles may in any case be case-specific. There are two types of facial image analysis activity: one for the identification of an unknown person and one for the verification of identity.

In the case of unknown person identification, the facial image profiles generated from the facial image samples received from the data requesting bodies (e.g., investigative authorities) are compared with all the facial image profiles managed in the facial image profile register. In the case of identity verification, however, the facial image profile generated from the facial image sample of the person will be compared with the facial image profile of the person in the facial image profile register. If a facial image profile cannot technically be generated, the body entitled to receive it will be notified immediately.

In the first phase, the facial image profiles are compared by the IT system, resulting in a second phase, the so-called evaluation activity. If the evaluation is successful, the Central Unit shall transmit to the entitled body, within eight working days of receipt of the request, the technical contact number of the facial image profile obtained as a result of the evaluation and managed in the register.

The evaluation shall be deemed to be successful if the analyst is able to match the input image with one or more elements of the candidate list during the analyst's examination of the candidate list and the input image resulting from the software comparison. The technical contact number associated with these images is then passed to the data requester. If the analyst match fails because the analyst's examination does not suggest a match, the evaluation may be declared ineffective and the data requester will not be provided with a technical contact number or informed of the ineffectiveness. The evaluation activity is not considered to be a matter requiring specific expertise and therefore should not be considered as an expert activity. The analysts employed will also have a high level of anthropological knowledge to support the identification process.

The Decree of the Ministry of Interior 78/2015 (December 23) on the Detailed Rules for the Operation of the Facial Image Analysis System regulates the detailed procedures and operational guidelines for the use of a facial recognition system in Hungary. It sets the technical and legal framework for how facial images are collected, processed, analysed, and stored by law enforcement authorities. Specifying which law enforcement bodies are authorised to use facial recognition and under what circumstances, such as for identifying suspects or verifying identities during investigations. The regulation ensures that such practices comply with data protection laws, including the handling of sensitive biometric data, and outlines the responsibilities of the authorities operating the system.

The implementation of facial recognition is made difficult by the fact that the images sent by requesting bodies of the person to be identified, often from cameras in public places, buildings or inside buildings, are often blurred, at most allowing the recognition of very basic personality traits, such as height, perhaps hair color, facial hair, type of clothing. In many cases this is also the case with footage taken by public surveillance, transport companies, and sometimes the police. Facial recognition algorithms provide probabilities, not definitive identifications, leaving the final decision to users. Rushed decisions without sufficient evidence can lead to errors and legal liabilities. For example, in 2021, a Detroit man sued the police after being wrongly arrested due to a faulty algorithmic match between surveillance footage and his driver's license photo, later proven incorrect.[26] One significant case from the United Kingdom that highlights the dangers of misidentification by facial recognition systems is that the biometric security company Facewatch is being sued after its system wrongly identified a young girl as a shoplifter. Similarly, a community worker was misidentified by the British police and was nearly arrested. These cases show that facial recognition systems carry serious risks of discrimination, especially when used by law enforcement agencies and private companies without proper safeguards.[27] This highlights the potential for misidentification and wrongful actions when relying on facial recognition technology without careful human oversight.[28]

7.4 Criminal law protection against personal data misuse in Hungary

Unauthorised collection and use of facial images, especially for profit or surveillance, violate individuals' privacy rights and can lead to heavy fines and legal consequences under regulations like General Data Protection Regulation (GDPR) or in more severe cases it may result in a criminal law sanction.

In many legal frameworks, including the EU's GDPR, a facial image is explicitly defined as personal data and more specifically biometric data if it is used for identification or verification purposes. GDPR imposes strict rules on how biometric data, including facial images, can be collected, stored, and used, requiring consent from individuals and providing them with rights over how their biometric data is handled. Thus, while a plain facial image may not inherently be biometric data, once it is used in conjunction with facial recognition technology to identify or verify a person, it becomes biometric data. For the processing of personal data for law enforcement, national security, and defence purposes, the Hungarian Act CXII of 2011 must be applied, meaning that in such cases, the data controller is required to act in accordance with Hungarian legal regulations (which largely align with the provisions of the GDPR). In all other cases, where the data processing serves purposes different from the above, the GDPR provisions are applicable.

Misuse of personal data in Section 219 of the Hungarian Criminal Code states that any person who, in violation of the statutory provisions related to the protection and processing of personal data or the binding legislation of the European Union, either (a) engages in unauthorised or improper processing of personal data, or (b) fails to implement necessary security measures to protect data, and does so with the intent of personal gain or causing significant harm, is guilty of a misdemeanor punishable by imprisonment of up to one year.

The criminal law targets only serious violations, meaning that under Section 219(1)(a) of the Hungarian Criminal Code, unauthorised or unlawful data processing constitutes a criminal offence only if it aims to cause substantial harm or seek financial gain. The background legislation for criminal law is the GDPR and the Hungarian Act CXII of 2011. The legal basis for data processing is primarily governed by Article 6(1) of the GDPR and Article 6(1) of the Hungarian Act CXII of 2011. Any processing without these legal grounds is unlawful, making it a matter of legal fact. The purpose limitation principle is a fundamental principle of European data protection law. Data processing must adhere to the principle of purpose limitation (as outlined in Article 6 of the GDPR and Article 4 of the Hungarian Act CXII of 2011), meaning that even lawful data processing becomes illegal if it is misused for purposes other than the original intent.

In cases of personal harm, the damage is objectively determined and there must be a clear link between the action and the result. The term "significant harm" is not precisely defined in the Criminal Code or other legislation, so law enforcement must assess its seriousness based on the specifics of each case. This harm can be both moral (e.g., damage to reputation or personal life) or material (e.g., financial gain from data misuse).

In Decision No 1/2012 BJE, the Curia (Supreme Court of Hungary) clarified that the perpetrator of misuse of personal data, involving the unauthorised and inappropriate processing of such data, is not limited to just a data controller as defined by data protection law but can be any individual responsible for the misuse.

One exception to the scope of the GDPR is household data processing, the Article 2(2)(c) of the GDPR states that the regulation does not apply to the processing of personal data where it is carried out by natural persons solely in the course of their personal or domestic activities.

The Court of Justice of the European Union (CJEU) has ruled that personal data processing is not considered private if it extends into the public domain or is made accessible to an indefinite number of people. This includes activities such as online publication of personal data or video surveillance systems covering public areas. Such processing goes beyond purely private or domestic activities, which are protected under privacy laws, as seen in cases like Lindqvist, Satakunnan, and Ryneš. Therefore, public exposure invalidates the personal or household activity exemption.

Additionally, Section 219(1)(b) of the Criminal Code addresses the failure to implement adequate data security measures. This offense, which includes negligence in implementing technical safeguards like encryption (per Article 32 of the GDPR and Section 25/I of the Hungarian Act CXII of 2011), must be committed intentionally to be punishable.

Under Section 219, the penalties outlined in Subsection (1) are also applicable to individuals who fail to notify data subjects as required by law, thus hindering their rights of access to personal data, and causing significant harm to another's interests. Additionally, misuse of personal data, especially involving sensitive data or criminal records, is punishable by imprisonment of up to two years. If the misuse is carried out by a public official or occurs in the course of public duties, the offense is elevated to a felony, with a maximum imprisonment of three years.

In the case law, the issue of the distinction between misuse of personal data and abuse of authority is most often manifested in the unauthorised provision of data from databases accessible by public officials to third parties. Law enforcement officers have access to sensitive data, including facial recognition databases. If an officer accesses this data for personal reasons (such as for a friend or to track someone outside the scope of official duties), they would be violating the principle of purpose limitation.

The Curia stated that a tax inspector that access to an information system by an official beyond the scope of his or her entitlement on the grounds of a personal favour – and the acquisition of data in this way – constitutes an abuse of authority if the purpose of such access without official cause is to obtain an unlawful advantage or disadvantage. Any public official who, with the intent of securing unlawful gain or causing unlawful harm, either breaches their duties, exceeds their authority, or otherwise abuses their position, is guilty of a felony punishable by up to three years imprisonment (Section 305 of Criminal Code).

If the official's conduct of misuse of personal data for unlawful advantage or disadvantage is also aimed at obtaining profit – based on the principle of speciality – then he or she is committing the crime of misuse of personal data, and a qualified case of misuse of personal data as regulated by Section 219(4) of the Criminal Code. Overall, it can be established in principle that the offence of misuse of personal data can be established in the case of obtaining a benefit or substantial damage to interest, while the offence of misuse of office can be established in the case of unlawful advantage or unlawful damage caused by an official through unlawful data processing. The transmission to another party of data unlawfully retrieved from the police information system without the purpose of gaining benefit does not constitute an offence of abuse of authority, but a misdemeanour of breach of information system.

The distinction between the offence of illicit access to data (personal data) [Section 422(1)(b)–(e), (2)(b) of the Criminal Code] and the offence of misuse of personal data is based on the fact that in the case of illicit access, the conduct is committed by secretly observing or recording the personal data with the use of a technical device or by secretly intercepting the data and recording what is observed with a technical device. Article 422(3) of the Criminal Code, a person who transmits or uses personal data obtained in this way, shall be punishable.

Deepfakes, which involve the use of AI to superimpose or digitally manipulate facial images to create realistic but falsified videos, can lead to various forms of data abuse. Deepfake technology allows for the creation of highly realistic pornographic content by superimposing someone's face onto explicit videos without their consent. For example, a woman's social media photos could be used to create a deepfake video, making it appear as though she is involved in pornographic activities. Revenge porn refers to the non-consensual distribution of intimate images or videos, often as a form of retaliation or coercion. In the context of deepfake technology, revenge porn has evolved to include deepfake revenge porn, where AI-generated synthetic media manipulates facial images (often sourced from social media) onto explicit bodies to create fake pornographic content. This malicious use of facial recognition data exacerbates the emotional and psychological harm caused to victims, even when they never participated in such activities.[29] Deepfake technology can be used to digitally manipulate images or videos, potentially creating child sexual abuse material by placing a child's face on explicit content. This is treated as criminal conduct in many jurisdictions, as it involves the creation and distribution of non-consensual, fabricated material that exploits minors. Under Hungarian criminal law, the creation, distribution, or possession of child pornography, including fabricated material such as deepfakes, is strictly prohibited. According to Section 204 of the Hungarian Criminal Code, any visual representation depicting a minor in a sexual context, whether real or fabricated, is considered child pornography. This applies even if the material is digitally manipulated, as it still represents an exploitative and harmful portrayal of children.[30]

Deepfakes could be used to damage the reputations of individuals by falsely depicting them in embarrassing or illegal situations. The misuse of deepfake technology could lead to impersonate individuals in financial fraud or social engineering attacks. For instance, deepfake video conferencing scams have emerged, where criminals create fake video calls mimicking high-ranking executives to authorise fraudulent transfers. Criminals can use deepfake technology to bypass biometric security systems. For example, by creating a deepfake of a person's face or voice, criminals can deceive facial or voice recognition systems used to access sensitive information or secure facilities.

It is also worth mentioning here that the content used to create the deepfake video of the person to be impersonated, such as images, videos, sounds, will also be considered personal data under the relevant concepts of the GDPR, since – as explained in the previous point – the image of a person is personal data and any operation performed on them constitutes processing. Therefore, when creating a deepfake video, the processing of data of the real person to be impersonated must also comply with the GDPR as a general rule. The use of personal data for such purposes must therefore in principle have a legitimate purpose and an adequate legal basis for the content creator producing it.[31]

In the European Commission's initial proposal of the AI Act, deep fake detection systems were categorised as high-risk, while legitimate use of deep fakes themselves were considered low- to minimal-risk, with transparency requirements. This classification assumed that deep fakes would primarily be handled by the public sector, safeguarding individuals from state surveillance. However, the European Parliament (EP) rejected this, arguing that high-risk technologies should be classified based on potential harm. Experts contend that detection systems should remain high-risk to counteract growing crimes involving deep fakes, such as extortion, impersonation, and fraud.[32] Although, deepfake detection systems would likely fall under high-risk category when used in criminal investigations to verify the authenticity of digital evidence (AI Act, Annex III), helping prevent the manipulation of evidence that could undermine justice or contribute to wrongful accusations. This is crucial in protecting judicial processes, as courts increasingly rely on digital evidence.

7.5 Summary: Balancing security and privacy

Regulating facial recognition technology in law enforcement and safeguarding against the misuse of personal data should emphasise the delicate balance between enhancing public safety and preserving individual privacy. While facial recognition offers promising benefits in improving law enforcement efficiency – such as identifying suspects and locating missing persons – it also poses significant risks if left unchecked. The improper use of facial recognition can lead to invasion of privacy, misidentification, and discrimination, particularly toward vulnerable or marginalised groups.

To address these challenges, robust legal frameworks are essential. Regulatory measures like the EU AI Act and national laws provide a foundation for ensuring that facial recognition system is deployed responsibly and ethically. These laws must clearly define the permissible use, particularly in sensitive areas like law enforcement, where the balance between public security and fundamental human rights is most critical.

Moreover, transparency and oversight are crucial. Facial recognition must be subject to strict, independent review to prevent misuse or overreach. Law enforcement agencies and private entities using this technology must be required to justify its use, and individuals should be informed whenever their biometric data is collected or processed. This transparency builds public trust and ensures that personal data is handled in accordance with legal and ethical standards. Additionally, addressing discrimination and misidentification risks is paramount. Biometric algorithms must be trained on diverse datasets to avoid biases that disproportionately affect people of colour or other marginalised groups. Regular audits and updates to these systems will help minimise false positives and prevent wrongful actions based on erroneous data matches.

Protecting personal data must remain a top priority, with strong regulatory frameworks in place to prevent its misuse. Biometric data, being particularly sensitive, is vulnerable to significant risks such as identity theft or reputational harm in the event of a breach. Legal frameworks like the GDPR and Hungary's Act CXII of 2011 offer robust protections for personal and biometric data. However, in more severe cases, criminal law plays a crucial role in enforcing compliance, ensuring that data misuse is met with strict penalties. This combination of regulatory and criminal measures is essential for effective enforcement and deterring violations, safeguarding individuals' rights and security.

Notes

1 Law enforcement authority "means any public authority competent for the prevention, investigation, detection or prosecution of criminal offences or the execution of criminal penalties, including the safeguarding against and the prevention of threats to public security; or any other body or entity entrusted by Member State law to exercise public authority and public powers for the purposes of the prevention, investigation, detection or prosecution of criminal offences or the execution of criminal penalties, including the safeguarding against and the prevention of threats to public security"; law enforcement "means activities carried out by law enforcement authorities or on their behalf for the prevention, investigation, detection or prosecution of criminal offences or the execution of criminal penalties, including safeguarding against and preventing threats to public security".

2 LEUFER, Daniel, RODELLI, Caterina, and HÍDVÉGI, Fanny. Human Rights Protection ... With Exceptions: What's (Not) in the EU's AI Act Deal, 2023. Available at: https://www.accessnow.org/whats-not-in-the-eu-ai-act-deal/.

3 See more about this: FRA. Facial Recognition Technology: Fundamental Rights Considerations in the Context of Law Enforcement, 2019.

4 FONTES, Catarina, and PERRONE, Christian. Ethics of Surveillance: Harnessing the Use of Live Facial Recognition Technologies in Public Spaces for Law Enforcement. Technical University of Munich Research Brief, 2021.

5 LIU, Tingting, YANG, Bing, GENG, Yan, and DU, Shan. Research on Face Recognition and Privacy in China: Based on Social Cognition and Cultural Psychology. Frontiers in Psychology, 2021.

6 GLUKHIN v. Russia. European Court of Human Rights (Application no. 11519/20), 2023. See LYNCH, N. Facial Recognition Technology in Policing and Security—Case Studies in Regulation. Laws, vol. 13, 2024, p. 35.

7 Publicly accessible space "means any publicly or privately owned physical place accessible to an undetermined number of natural persons, regardless of whether certain conditions for access may apply, and regardless of the potential capacity restrictions". In the context of the AI Act, a publicly accessible space refers to any physical area open to an indeterminate number of people, whether publicly or privately owned, and regardless of its use, such as commercial, service, transport, or entertainment spaces (e.g., shops, banks, gyms, airports). Spaces remain publicly accessible if access requires fulfilling certain conditions (e.g., buying a ticket or prior registration). However, areas restricted to specific individuals by law or authority (e.g., workplaces, company premises, prisons) are not considered publicly accessible. Online spaces are excluded, as they are not physical.

8 Real-time biometric identification is held permissible for law enforcement if the following prerequisites apply: (a) ex-ante permission by a judicial authority; (b) targeted search; and (c) link with the investigation of committed serious crimes listed in Article 83(1) Treaty on the Functioning of European Union (terrorism, trafficking in human beings and sexual exploitation of women and children, illicit drug trafficking, illicit arms trafficking, money laundering, corruption, counterfeiting of means of payment, computer crime, and organised crime).

9 RAPOSO, Vera Lúcia. The Use of Facial Recognition Technology by Law Enforcement in Europe: A Non-Orwellian Draft Proposal. European Journal on Criminal Policy, vol. 29, 2022, pp. 515–533.

10 https://disclose.ngo/en/article/the-french-national-police-is-unlawfully-using-an-israeli-facial-recognition-software.

11 https://www.politico.eu/article/berlin-big-brother-state-surveillance-facial-recognition-technology/.
12 https://homeofficemedia.blog.gov.uk/2023/10/29/police-use-of-facial-recognition-factsheet/.
13 https://www.aiaaic.org/aiaaic-repository/ai-algorithmic-and-automation-incidents/sari-facial-recognition-system.
14 GEORGIEVA, Ilina, TIMAN, Tjerk, and HOEKSTRA, Marissa. Regulatory Divergences in the Draft AI Act – Differences in Public and Private Sector Obligations, 2022. Available at: https://www.europarl.europa.eu/RegData/etudes/STUD/2022/729507/EPRS_STU(2022)729507_EN.pdf.
15 As reported by the Dutch Data Protection Authority (DPA), it issued a formal warning to a supermarket for using facial recognition technology, which the supermarket claimed was for protecting customers, staff, and preventing shoplifting. This technology, connected to entrance cameras, uses biometric data to identify individuals. Such use is prohibited unless explicit consent is given or it is necessary for substantial public interest in security. The supermarket did not obtain explicit consent, as merely informing customers does not suffice, and the DPA did not accept the supermarket's claim that its use met the substantial public interest criterion.
16 VEALE, Michael, and BORGENIUS, Frederik Zuiderveen. Demystifying the Draft EU Artificial Intelligence Act: Analysing the Good, the Bad, and the Unclear Elements of the Proposed Approach. Computer Law Review International, vol. 22, 2021, pp. 97–112.
17 HACKER, Philipp. Comments on the Final Trilogue Version of the AI Act. 2024. Available at: http://dx.doi.org/10.2139/ssrn.4757603.
18 See, in this regard, SOBEL, Benjamin L. W. A New Common Law of Web Scraping. Lewis & Clark Law Review, vol. 25, 2021, pp. 147–207.
19 GEORGIEVA, TIMAN, and HOEKSTRA. Regulatory Divergences in the Draft AI Act.
20 See more: SOLOVE, Daniel J., and HARTZOG, Woodrow. The Great Scrape: The Clash between Scraping and Privacy. California Law Review, vol. 113 (forthcoming 2025). Available at: https://ssrn.com/abstract=4884485.
21 SANZ, M. B. L.: About ClearviewAI's mockery of human rights, those fighting it, and the need for EU to intervene. 2022. https://edri.org/our-work/we-need-to-talk-about-clearview-ai/.
22 GONZÁLEZ FUSTER, Gloria. Artificial Intelligence and Law Enforcement, 2020. Available at: https://www.europarl.europa.eu/RegData/etudes/STUD/2020/656295/IPOL_STU(2020)656295_EN.pdf.
23 https://jolt.law.harvard.edu/digest/clearview-ai-responds-to-cease-and-desist-letters-by-claiming-first-amendment-right-to-publicly-available-data.
24 https://www.autoriteitpersoonsgegevens.nl/en/documents/decision-fine-clearview-ai.
25 https://aligner-h2020.eu/.
26 https://www.technologyreview.com/2021/04/14/1022676/robert-williams-facial-recognition-lawsuit-aclu-detroit-police/.
27 Big Brother Watch Team: BBC – Victims of facial recognition misidentification. https://bigbrotherwatch.org.uk/press-coverage/bbc-victims-of-facial-recognition-misidentification/.
28 See more: RAPOSO, Vera Lúcia. When Facial Recognition Does Not 'Recognise': Erroneous Identifications and Resulting Liabilities. AI and Society, 2024.
29 JACOBSEN, Ben Nicholas, and SIMPSON, Jack. The Tensions of Deepfakes. Information, Communication & Society, vol. 27, 2023, pp. 1095–1109.

AMBRUS, István. The New Sexual Offences in the Light of Digitalisation. Studia Iuridica, vol. 93, 2022, pp. 7–19.

30 AMBRUS, István. Digitalizáció és Büntetőjog. Wolters Kluwer, Budapest, 2021.

31 ESZTERI, Dániel. A Deepfake-Technológia Adatvédelmi Értékelése a GDPR Tükrében. In: ACZÉL, Petra, and VESZELSZKI, Ágnes (eds.), Deepfake: A Valótlan Valóság. Gondolat Kiadó, Budapest, 2023.

32 EUROPOL. Facing Reality? Law Enforcement and the Challenge of Deepfakes. Publications Office of the European Union, 2022.

Part V

The Czech perspective

Chapter 8

The use of artificial intelligence by Police and courts with a focus on Czech law[1]

Lukáš Bohuslav

8.1 Introduction

Artificial intelligence (AI) has been influencing people's everyday lives in the last few years, functioning in many professions, not excluding the legal ones. AI has significant potential and implications for many areas of law, including criminal law. Criminal law, designed to punish only the most serious anti-social acts, requires careful consideration of the potential implications for the current functioning of the criminal justice system. AI is capable of advancing the work of both the Police and the courts in specific ways, but it must do so with a view to preserving human rights and freedoms. The challenge lies in making criminal proceedings more efficient, both in the work of the Police in investigating criminal activity and in the work of the courts in making fairer decisions. However, it is equally important to be cautious and aware of the potential misuse of AI systems and their indiscriminate judgement, ensuring that society is protected from such risks.

First, it is helpful to define AI for the purposes of this chapter. AI can take many different forms and definitions. A suitable definition for criminal law is found by the Czech authors Mulák and Provazník,[2] according to whom critical elements of AI are autonomy of the process, 'other entity' – meaning an entity different from an entity for which the process of autonomous problem solution is natural in a biological sense, intelligence – as the ability to solve problems in external environment by interacting with it and finally autonomy and intelligence are what make AI different from robotization or mere automatization of a particular process.

It should be stated at the outset that the Czech Republic suffers from a generally strong deficit in the electronization of justice. If we look at criminal proceedings, no electronic system will enable all subjects or parties to criminal proceedings to work with electronic files. At present, the situation is so dire that parties to criminal proceedings, typically the accused represented by a defence lawyer, must physically go to the workplace of the

DOI: 10.4324/9781003531500-15

law enforcement agency and photograph the file page by page on a mobile phone, portable scanner or digital camera when they need to consult the file. This is a fundamentally unprofessional activity, where a criminal defence attorney wastes his or her time when he or she could perform much more sophisticated work than slavishly securing information in a criminal file. However, this activity must also be paid for by the defence counsel and is thus a very financially demanding activity for which the accused must reimburse his defence counsel. Suppose the accused is acquitted or the criminal prosecution against him is discontinued. In that case, the financial compensation for this activity is borne by the State, which is obliged to reimburse the accused for the costs incurred for effective defence, pursuant to Act No. 82/1998 Coll., on liability for damage caused in the exercise of public authority by a decision or an incorrect official procedure. Given the relatively bleak economic situation in the Czech justice system, defendants are then awarded by the Ministry of Justice or, subsequently, by the civil courts much lower sums than those spent by the defendant on his defence. In the absolute minimum of cases, the police authority can hand over an existing file to the defence electronically, but only if it scans the entire file itself. This is certainly not an electronization that we should be excited about. From this point on, the use of AI systems in the Czech justice system is very far away.

Now, it is necessary to highlight the key areas of AI and their manifestations in criminal law. For the purposes of my post, I have divided them into two categories:

a Use of AI by criminal Police
b Use of AI in justice

8.2 Use of artificial intelligence by criminal Police

AI can assist Police in recognizing people and objects, establishing models of existing relationships between information (so-called relational links), detecting inconsistencies, for example, between testimonies using semantic tools or AI, and automation also helps through automated complaint tools (for example, with cybercrimes).[3] Whether two facial images depict the same person is important regarding facial recognition. AI does this by extracting biometric data from a digital image and then comparing that data against biometric data from images in a database, such as a watch list. If enough biometric data appears similar, a 'match' is declared between the face on the footage and the face on the watch list. A 'similarity score' is generated, with a higher number indicating a greater likelihood of a positive match. A human decision is required regarding where to fix the software's threshold to indicate a match-fixing this threshold too high or too low risks high false positive or false negative rates, respectively.[4]

These mechanisms are also used in crime mapping. It is based on all the data, the tool which determines precisely where and when these offences could be committed, and to reproduce this information on a geographical map in the form of hot spots monitored in real time by police patrols. This procedure's important elements include the Aho Corasick pattern (a method of using AI to identify suspects). In this algorithm, one must first use a midpoint circle algorithm to set the boundary area for the crime analysis.[5] AI is also used in crime hotspot detection to help identify where crime is most concentrated. In this context, it is very important and appropriate to address the basic legal framework that allows the Czech Police to use AI.

European Parliament resolution of 6 October 2021 on AI in criminal law and its use by the police and judicial authorities in criminal matters (2020/2016(INI)) deals with police and judicial authorities and the impact of decisions they take for the prevention, investigation, detection or prosecution of criminal offences or the execution of criminal penalties that the use of AI applications has to be categorized as high risk in instances where there is the potential to significantly affect the lives of individuals (bod three preamble). This European Parliament resolution states that it is dangerous to use AI by law enforcement authorities to make behavioural predictions on individuals or groups based on historical data and past behaviour, group membership, location, or any other such characteristics, thereby attempting to identify people likely to commit a crime (bod 24 preamble).

Next, Regulation (EU) 2024/1689 of the European Parliament and of the Council of 13 June 2024, laying down harmonized rules on AI (further in this chapter), provides that the use of 'real-time' remote biometric identification systems in publicly accessible spaces for law enforcement, unless and in so far as such use is strictly necessary for one of the following objectives:

- i the targeted search for specific victims of abduction, trafficking in human beings or sexual exploitation of human beings, as well as the search for missing persons;
- ii the prevention of a specific, substantial, and imminent threat to the life or physical safety of natural persons or a genuine and present or foreseeable threat of a terrorist attack;
- iii the localization or identification of a person suspected of having committed a criminal offence for the purpose of conducting a criminal investigation or prosecution or executing a criminal penalty for offences referred to in Annex II (of the resolution) and punishable in the Member State concerned by a custodial sentence or a detention order for a maximum period of at least four years.[6]

The key regulation for the work of the Police regarding the possible use of AI systems is currently in Czech law, Act No. 110/2019 Coll, on the processing of personal data.[7] The key part of the Act on the processing of personal data is Title III of this legislation, entitled 'Protection of personal data when processing them for the purpose of preventing, searching for or detecting crime, prosecuting criminal offences, executing penalties and protective measures, ensuring the security of the Czech Republic or ensuring public order and internal security' (Sections 24–42 of the Act). These norms mainly regulate the principles of personal data processing, the essence of which is the fact that when processing personal data, the administering authority, in our particular case, the police authority (a), determines the specific purpose of processing personal data in connection with the performance of a task for the purpose of preventing, searching for or detecting crime, prosecuting criminal offences, executing penalties and protective measures, ensuring the security of the Czech Republic or ensuring public order and internal security, including the search for persons and things, (b) take measures to ensure that personal data are accurate in relation to the nature and purpose of the processing, and (c) retain personal data in a form that permits identification of the data subject only for the time necessary to achieve the purpose of the processing (Section 25 of the Act). The regulation also provides in its Section 26 that, where possible, the managing authority shall (a) attach to the personal data processed information on the status of the data subject in criminal proceedings or, where appropriate, information on final decisions of law enforcement authorities concerning such data, if justified by the purpose of processing, and (b) identify inaccurate personal data or personal data based on personal assessments. From the point of view of the specific subjects who are the subject of the processing of personal data, the focus should then be on the right of access to personal data of these subjects, which is, however, limited if it could jeopardize (a) the performance of the task of preventing, preventing and detecting crime, prosecuting crime, the execution of penalties and protective measures, ensuring the security of the Czech Republic or ensuring public order and internal security, including the search for persons and things, (b) the conduct of proceedings concerning an offence, disciplinary offence or conduct which has the characteristics of an offence, (c) the protection of classified information, or (d) the legitimate interests of a third party (Section 28 of the Act). This regulation also regulates, for example, the right to rectification, restriction of processing or erasure of personal data (Section 29 of the Act). The administering authority, in our case, the Police of the Czech Republic, taking into account the nature, scope, circumstances, purposes and risks of processing personal data, the development of technology and costs, shall adopt technical and organizational measures in order to (a) protect personal data as effectively as possible, (b) restrict unreasonable processing of personal data, (c) restrict processing of personal data which is not necessary due to its scope, the amount of data, the duration of its storage or its availability, (d) provide the necessary safeguards for the rights of the data subject, and (e) prevent the automatic disclosure of personal data (Section 32 of the Act). The law also addresses automated record-keeping, which directly impacts the use of AI in criminal law. If automated processing of personal data is carried out, in our case, the Police of the Czech Republic make records of at least the operations of collection, insertion, alteration, combination, consultation, transmission, disclosure, and deletion of personal data. The records of the operations of collection, insertion, consultation, or communication referred to in paragraph 1 shall make it possible to identify and verify the reason and time of these operations, the identity of the person carrying out the operation and the identity of the recipient unless the identification of these persons is not possible for technical reasons (Section 36 of the Act).

A specific regulation which is related to the Act on the processing of personal data is Act No 273/2008 Coll., on the Police of the Czech Republic, which provides that the Police may process personal data if it is necessary for the purpose of preventing, searching for and detecting crime, prosecuting crime, ensuring the security of the Czech Republic, or ensuring public order and internal security, including the search for persons and things. A significant limitation, however, is that data on racial or ethnic origin, religious, philosophical or political beliefs, trade union membership, health, sexual behaviour or sexual orientation may only be collected if it is necessary for the purposes of investigating a specific crime or offence or in providing protection of persons (section 79). It follows that the Police may, if necessary for the performance of their tasks, make audio, visual, or other recordings of persons and things in places open to the public and audio, visual, or other recordings of the course of action. Where permanent automated technical systems are set up to make recordings pursuant to Section 62, the Police shall publish information on the setting up of such systems in an appropriate manner. Regarding the use of AI systems, the above provision is the legal basis for surveilling persons using CCTV systems. Based on this provision, it is possible to obtain information on a blanket basis, so it will most often be used to obtain information on general crime, where a particular place open to the public is 'monitored' to detect the possible commission of crime.[8]

It should be added that currently, according to publicly available information, there is only one object in the Czech Republic that the Police of the Czech Republic constantly monitor. This is the Václav Havel Airport. Currently, an amendment to the Police Act of the Czech Republic is in the legislative process, which would be in the framework of exchanging information in police cooperation within the European Union.

Within the above context, the request under Act No. 106/1999 Coll. for free access to information is exciting. The applicant has requested the following information: is AI currently used by the Police of the Czech Republic, and in what processes or areas? The Police replied to the applicant and published its answer in June 2024, stating that the Police of the Czech Republic are currently using AI in two areas: to ensure the safety of citizens, for example, at the airport (for authentication), and in support activities (speech to text systems, software for sorting so-called big data, automatic reading of traffic signs, etc.). In its reply, the Police stated that all systems are used according to standard ethical principles now common within the European Union. AI at the Police of the Czech Republic is extremely robust, explainable, and responsible, and it respects the principle of the necessity of handling personal data to the maximum extent possible, thus placing an extraordinary emphasis on the privacy of every citizen.[9]

If we summarize the above information into a partial conclusion, the Police have powerful tools for using AI in a general legal environment. It is challenging for the public, not only the public but also the professional public, to know now whether the Police of the Czech Republic are following the legal framework. An amendment to the Police Act of the Czech Republic is now in the legislative process, which, based on Regulation (EU) 2024/1689 of the European Parliament and of the Council of 13 June 2024 laying down harmonized rules on AI, should refine and probably also tighten the conditions for the use of AI, particularly in relation to biometric recognition of persons. The draft law refers to creating a reference database of persons, with the explanatory memorandum stating that 'The importance of the reference database lies in the fact that persons who are not included in it cannot, by nature, be identified by the system. It is not technically possible. The impact on unlisted persons' human rights and freedoms is not zero but comparable to that of CCTV systems not using biometric identification. This means that a facial image is captured and processed, and the processed image is compared with a reference database, but no identification of the person or specific alert on the unidentified person is made due to the failure to find a reference facial image. However, no decision with adverse consequences for a particular person should be made solely based on the output of biometric identification, i.e. the use of an AI system'.

8.3 Use of artificial intelligence in justice

When discussing how AI can help courts and judicial decision-making, the term predictive justice is worth mentioning. The definition of predictive justice is according to the European Ethical Charter on the use of AI in judicial systems and their environment – Adopted at the 31st plenary meeting of the European Commission for the Efficiency of Justice (Strasbourg,

3–4 December 2018) – *the analysis of large amounts of judicial decisions by artificial intelligence technologies in order to make predictions for the outcome of certain types of specialized disputes (for example, redundancy payments or alimentary pensions).*[10] Generally, predictive justice concerns the process before the judicial process or before the court.

Regarding judicial decision-making, it is advisable to focus on the legislative background in the Czech Republic and the European Union. First, it is worth mentioning the European Parliament resolution of 6 October 2021 on AI in criminal law and its use by the police and judicial authorities in criminal matters (2020/2016(INI)), which states in its preamble that, among other promises:

- increasing use of AI in the criminal law field is based in particular on the promises that it would reduce certain types of crime and lead to more objective decisions, whereas these promises, however, do not always hold;
- AI has the potential to be a permanent part of our criminal justice ecosystem, providing investigative analysis and assistance;
- AI technology in law enforcement can have vastly varying degrees of reliability and accuracy and impact on the protection of fundamental rights and the dynamics of criminal justice systems;
- AI tools and applications are also used by the judiciary in several countries worldwide, including supporting decisions on pre-trial detention, sentencing, calculating probabilities for reoffending, and probation.

Further, Regulation (EU) 2024/1689 of the European Parliament and of the Council of 13 June 2024 laying down harmonized rules on AI and amending Regulations (EC) No 300/2008, (EU) No 167/2013, (EU) No 168/2013, (EU) 2018/858, (EU) 2018/1139 and (EU) 2019/2144 and Directives 2014/90/EU, (EU) 2016/797, and (EU) 2020/1828 (Artificial Intelligence Act). This regulation, which generally shall apply from 2 August 2026, lays down some basic rules for the use of AI also in criminal justice.

The regulation sets out in its preamble the general principles that:

- The use of those systems for the purpose of law enforcement should, therefore, be prohibited, except in exhaustively listed and narrowly defined situations where the use is strictly necessary to achieve a substantial public interest, the importance of which outweighs the risks. Those situations involve the search for certain victims of crime, including missing persons; specific threats to the life or the physical safety of natural persons or a terrorist attack; and the localization or identification of perpetrators or suspects of the criminal offences listed in an annex to this regulation, where those criminal offences are punishable in the

Member State concerned by a custodial sentence or a detention order for a maximum period of at least four years and as they are defined in the law of that Member State. Such a threshold for the custodial sentence or detention order in accordance with national law contributes to ensuring that the offence should be severe enough to potentially justify the use of 'real-time' remote biometric identification systems. Moreover, the list of criminal offences provided in an annex to this regulation is based on the 32 criminal offences listed in the Council Framework Decision 2002/584/JHA (article 33 of the preamble).

- In line with the presumption of innocence, natural persons in the Union should always be judged on their actual behaviour. Natural persons should never be judged on AI-predicted behaviour based solely on their profiling, personality traits or characteristics, such as nationality, place of birth, place of residence, number of children, level of debt or type of car, without reasonable suspicion of that person being involved in criminal activity based on objectively verifiable facts and without human assessment thereof. Therefore, risk assessments carried out regarding natural persons to assess the likelihood of their offending or to predict the occurrence of an actual or potential criminal offence based solely on profiling them or assessing their personality traits and characteristics should be prohibited (article 42 of the preamble).

The regulation then goes further in its standards by prohibiting, inter alia, the following practices:

- the placing on the market, the putting into service for this specific purpose, or the use of an AI system for making risk assessments of natural persons in order to assess or predict the risk of a natural person committing a criminal offence based solely on the profiling of a natural person or on assessing their personality traits and characteristics; this prohibition shall not apply to AI systems used to support the human assessment of the involvement of a person in a criminal activity, which is already based on objective and verifiable facts directly linked to a criminal activity [(article 5(1)(d)].

Regarding the risks of using AI in judicial decision-making in criminal justice, some authors call the help of AI in the process '*speedy justice*'. That means that failure to engage with the suspect as an agent and the risk of persons being treated as guilty based on inaccurate and unchallenged evidence[11] because algorithms are partially based on statistics – the criminal proceedings may be more prone to coming back to deterministic doctrines instead of supporting the principle of the individualization of sanction. This drift is endangering the privacy and freedom of all citizens and, most perniciously, that of the '*usual suspects*'. Reliance on databases 'that locate, identify, register, record, classify and validate or generate grounds for suspicion' results in a broadening from the traditional targeting of a specific suspect to '*categorical suspicion*'.[12] Both issues are naturally related to the issue of discrimination.

AI is summed up in the fact that criminal history, work, family and other backgrounds may determine or decide the fate of an individual, who is, of course, a unique human being with a specific social background, education, skills, degree of guilt and distinctive motivations for committing a crime.[13] However, what is still most important is that AI lacks societal skills. For example, a judge could decide to order the bail of a female offender who has a risk of recidivism based on a hierarchy of values, for example, by setting greater store by her role as a mother and protector of her children. In contrast, the algorithm would be able to determine the risk of reoffending more accurately but not operate such a hierarchy of priorities – which is essential to fully guarantee respect for the principle of equality of arms and presumption of innocence.[14]

Research done by Fair Trials found fundamental flaws in AI in criminal justice. Predictive and risk modelling systems – these systems operate in a grey area, using data to draw correlations between certain factors and 'guilt', data which is often directly or indirectly used as a proxy for other specific factors, such as *race or socioeconomic class, labelling people as criminals or making de facto findings of guilt as a result.*[15] It undermines the presumption of innocence.

We cannot allow police officers, the judge or the jury to be reduced to the long arm of the algorithm. The former has the decision-making prerogative whilst making judgements under uncertainty.[16]

The use of AI tools could also lead to a negative effect. Judges may become reluctant to decide against the algorithm (so when the algorithm says the sentence should be from five to seven years, the judge might not want to say four years) – as it would bear greater responsibility – especially in systems where judges' terms of office are not permanent but subject to popular vote, or in which their liability (disciplinary, civil or even criminal) is likely to be incurred, especially if their statutory guarantees in disciplinary matters are insufficient.[17]

Before enacting something like that into criminal proceedings, we need a clear ethical framework, in-depth public debate, and clear mechanisms to prevent bias and discrimination in its design processes (as private companies create the algorithms). The choice of the learning technique used, the ethics of design, the absence of bias, and the absolute necessity of being able to explain the arguments that allowed the tool to make a particular decision are all prohibitive elements in the initial construction of these support tools.[18]

The case State of Wisconsin v. Loomis[19] says that algorithmic assessment in sentencing did not violate the defendant's right to a fair trial, even though the methodology used to produce the assessment was disclosed neither to the court nor to the defendant – as it is an ineffective means of altering judge's evaluations.[20] Scholars warn that the assessments are often biased – discrimination based on demographics and socioeconomic status (people of colour are more likely to get a longer sentence).[21] There is, thus, potentially a pronouncement of the sanction 'in abstentia' based on exogenous mechanical elements without the litigant having any means of ex-ante contradiction.[22] It could happen that a judge would admit the (so-called) mitigating circumstance and probably limit the impact of a conviction to the pedagogical understanding that not respecting road safety constitutes a danger. The machine will automatically condemn and make the person pay a fine before allowing a possibly contradictory procedure to be launched.[23]

In the context of possible decision-making by AI in criminal justice, the most serious anticipated effect of the whole decision-making process appears to be the lack of human factors. AI will probably not be able to make sufficiently precise decisions regarding the individualization of sentencing conditions. This is one of the basic elements of decision-making on punishment, as it can be found in the provisions of Section 39(1) of the Czech Criminal Code.[24] However, from the point of view of the Czech situation, this is merely a theoretical, or perhaps better said, academic question. As it has already been mentioned in the introduction of this chapter, the Czech legal environment and the Czech justice system is in a situation where the basic computerization of the justice system has not been carried out, where it is not possible to consider the deployment of AI systems that could independently make decisions or at least assist in decision-making.

In this respect, we cannot overlook the relative rigidity of the Czech judiciary, which often reluctantly accepts trends that emerge in criminal law. Here we can mention the criminal liability of legal persons (2012) or the adoption of the institute of plea bargaining (also 2012). Some representatives of the judiciary have tried to ignore these trends until today. Can one imagine how they would accept decision-making through AI?

An equally important issue that would need to be resolved for the future is the consistency of the fundamental principles of criminal procedure, which would necessarily be affected by the AI decision-making process. These include, for example, the principle of the free evaluation of evidence, particularly the principle of the presumption of innocence. The concern that the AI's decision may not be sufficiently reviewable is entirely valid. Legislation at the European Union level dealing with AI is a step in a good direction, as it highlights precisely the possible conflict with the principle of the presumption of innocence and emphasizes the prevention of possible discrimination in the broadest sense.

8.4 Conclusion

Criminal law must still be exposed to its proven principles, but it must adopt some additional ones, such as the increased expression of the principle of non-discrimination, the principle of transparency, or the principle of human control of AI. As with all progress, it must be the case that progress in AI must be within reasonable limits that will benefit not only the criminal law but, more importantly, the running of society. This must be reflected in a balance between fairness in criminal proceedings and decision-making, efficiency, and savings in staff capacity and financial resources. Finally, in the regards of application of AI, there must be especially focused on the presumption of innocence. We also cannot ignore the prevention of discrimination based on the use of AI systems. Finally, the threat of AI predictively assessing a person as susceptible to committing a crime must be eliminated. These are all challenges that need to be dealt with effectively.

Notes

1 This chapter was prepared within the framework of the Cooperatio Law at the Faculty of Law of Charles University.
2 MULÁK, Jiří, PROVAZNÍK, Jan. Roboti za mřížemi – je české trestní právo připraveno na rozvoj umělé inteligence? In: GŘIVNA, Tomáš, RICHTER, Martin, ŠIMÁNOVÁ, Hana (eds.), Vliv nových technologií na trestní právo, 2022, pp. 257–258.
3 GANS-COMBE, Caroline. Automated Justice: Issues, Benefits and Risks in the Use of Artificial Intelligence and Its Algorithms in Access to Justice and Law Enforcement. In: O'MATHÚNA, Donál, IPHOFEN, Ron (eds.), Integrity and Policymaking. The Value of the Case Study, 2022, p. 185.
4 KOTSOGLOU N., Kyriakos, OSWALD, Marion. The long arm of the algorithm? Automated Facial Recognition as evidence and trigger for police intervention. Forensic Science International: Synergy, vol. 2, 2020, p. 87.
5 ENIGO, Felix V.S. An Automated System for Crime Investigation Using Conventional and Machine Learning Approach. In: RAJ, S. Jennifer, KAMEL, Khaled, LAFATA, Pavel. Innovative Data Communication Technologies and Application, 2022, p. 112.
6 These include also terrorism, trafficking in human beings, sexual exploitation and child pornography, trafficking in drugs, weapons, ammunition and explosives, nuclear material, murder and grievous bodily harm, trafficking in organs and tissues, kidnapping.
7 It incorporates which incorporates Directive (EU) 2016/680 of the European Parliament and of the Council of 27 April 2016 on the protection of natural persons with regard to the processing of personal data by competent authorities for the purposes of prevention, investigation, detection, or prosecution of criminal offences or the execution of criminal penalties, on the free movement of such data and repealing Council Framework Decision 2008/977/JHA, and which builds on Regulation (EU) 2016/679 of the European Parliament and of the Council of 27 April 2016 on the protection of natural persons with regard to the processing of personal data by competent authorities for the purposes

of prevention, investigation, detection, or prosecution of criminal offences or the execution of criminal penalties, and repealing Council Framework Decision 2008/977/JHA. April 2016 on the protection of natural persons with regard to the processing of personal data and on the free movement of such data, and repealing Directive 95/46/EC (General Data Protection Regulation) and to fulfil everyone's right to privacy, regulates the rights and obligations when processing personal data.

8 BÍLEK, Milan, HLAVÁČOVÁ, Kateřina, ŠLESINGER, René, ŠTEINBACH, Miroslav, ZIMMERMANN, Miroslav. Zákon o Policii České republiky. Komentář, Section 62, 2024.

9 Police response to a request for information under Act No. 106/1999 Coll., on free access to information. https://www.policie.cz/article/published-informations-2024-artifialinteligence.aspx.

10 EUROPEAN COMMISSION FOR THE EFFICIENCY OF JUSTICE. European ethical Charter on the use of Artificial Intelligence in judicial systems and their environment, p. 74.

11 AMBER, Marks, BOWLING, Ben, KEENAN Colman. Automatic Justice? Technology, Crime, and Social Control. The Oxford Handbook of the Law and Regulation of Technology, OUP, Forthcoming, Queen Mary School of Law Legal Studies Research Paper, vol. 211, 2015, p. 11.

12 AMBER, Marks, BOWLING, Ben, KEENAN Colman. Automatic Justice? Technology, Crime, and Social Control, p. 8.

13 EUROPEAN COMMISSION FOR THE EFFICIENCY OF JUSTICE. European ethical Charter on the use of Artificial Intelligence in judicial systems and their environment, p. 55.

14 EUROPEAN COMMISSION FOR THE EFFICIENCY OF JUSTICE. European ethical Charter on the use of Artificial Intelligence in judicial systems and their environment, p. 55.

15 FAIR TRIALS. Automating Injustice: the use of artificial intelligence & automated decision-making systems in criminal justice in Europe, 2021, p. 30.

16 KOTSOGLOU N., Kyriakos, OSWALD, Marion. The long arm of the algorithm? p. 89.

17 EUROPEAN COMMISSION FOR THE EFFICIENCY OF JUSTICE. European ethical Charter on the use of Artificial Intelligence in judicial systems and their environment, p. 56.

18 GANS-COMBE, Caroline. Automated Justice, p. 185.

19 Loomis v. Wisconsin, 881 N.W.2d 749 (Wis. 2016), cert. denied, 137 S. Ct. 2290 (2017).

20 Criminal Law – Sentencing Guidelines – Wisconsin Supreme Court Requires Warning before Use of Algorithmic Risk Assessments in Sentencing. – "State v. Loomis", 881 N.W.2d 749 (Wis. 2016). Harward Law Review, vol. 130, 2017, pp. 1530–1531.

21 Criminal Law – Sentencing Guidelines – Wisconsin Supreme Court Requires Warning before Use of Algorithmic Risk Assessments in Sentencing. — 'State v. Loomis', 881 N.W.2d 749 (Wis. 2016). Harward Law Review, vol. 130, 2017, p. 1534.

22 GANS-COMBE, Caroline. Automated Justice, p. 182.

23 GANS-COMBE, Caroline. Automated Justice, p. 182.

24 The wording of this provision: In determining the type of punishment and its amount, the court shall take into account the nature and gravity of the offence committed, the personal, family, property, and other circumstances of

the offender and his/her previous way of life and the possibility of his/her rehabilitation; it shall also take into account the offender's behaviour after the offence, in particular his/her efforts to make good the damage or to eliminate other harmful consequences of the offence; it shall also take into account his or her attitude towards the offence in the criminal proceedings, whether he or she has negotiated a plea bargain, pleaded guilty or identified the relevant facts as undisputed, and, if he or she has been designated as a cooperating defendant, also the significant contribution he or she has made to the clarification of the crime committed by members of an organized group, in association with an organized group or for the benefit of an organized criminal group. It shall also take into account the effects and consequences which may be expected from the sentence for the future life of the offender.

Chapter 9

Use of algorithms in securing electronic evidence in the Czech Republic

Radka Čihulková[1]

9.1 Introduction

As diverse as the crimes committed through the information technology are, the evidence used to uncover these crimes and convict perpetrators is also extremely variable. Not only this diversity but also their nature of being intangible, volatile, complex, hard to access and easy to alter or manipulate present investigators with a huge challenge in not only securing them, as it requires specialized technical knowledge and skills, but also in proving their authenticity. What is more, legal systems in most cases lag behind, and for the purposes of securing electronic evidence law enforcement authorities must use not very convenient institutes created originally for the purposes of securing physical evidence. A further complication in solving this type of crime and securing electronic evidence is the very frequent cross-border nature of cybercrime, while the very instruments of international cooperation, their rigidity, and lengthiness very often cause cybercrimes to go unpunished. All these aspects contribute to the length of the criminal proceedings and may ultimately result in the loss of electronic evidence.

For the above reasons, it would be most highly appropriate to establish in the legal regulations institutes directly intended for securing electronic evidence and to create a procedure for law enforcement authorities to ensure the authenticity and integrity of the secured data, which can subsequently be proven in court proceedings. Experts also stress the need to negotiate international agreements on cooperation in the development and exchange of computer and information technology aimed at preserving electronic evidence from destruction and to commit countries to implementing and complying with these agreements because in many cases effective international cooperation is a key aspect for the successful detection and punishment of perpetrators.[2]

9.2 Evidence, electronic evidence, and data

Evidence can take different forms and its legal definition is very broad. In the Czech legal system, evidence is defined in Section 89(2) of the Criminal

DOI: 10.4324/9781003531500-16

Procedure Code ("CPC"), which merely provides that anything that may contribute to the clarification of the case may serve as evidence. Any further definition is then left to doctrine. The only limit set out in Section 89(3) CPC is that the evidence must not be obtained by unlawful compulsion or a threat of such compulsion. Although doctrine and case law have come up with guidelines for determining whether evidence is admissible in criminal proceedings, the final assessment of the evidence, its weight, and particularly its credibility still rests with the discretion of the judge in accordance with the principle of the free evaluation of evidence. Thus, although the evidence was obtained in a lawful manner, from a source of evidence which is provided for, or at least permitted by the law, by an authorized procedural body, at the relevant procedural stage of the criminal proceedings, and the evidence relates to the subject matter of the evidence in the criminal proceedings in question,[3] the judge may nevertheless assess that the evidence is not credible and give it no or very little weight. One of the aspects which will determine, among other things, the weight to be given to a particular piece of evidence is clearly its authenticity, i.e. the extent to which the evidence in question is immutable and truthfully testifies to the subject matter of the criminal proceedings, without being capable of being altered or falsified in any way.

Electronic evidence does not have one generally accepted definition and the numerous definitions vary to a lesser or greater extent; however, on the substance of the definition, most of them agree. In the Czech Republic, the CPC does not define electronic evidence or means of evidence nor does it contain any specific procedures or institutes that would be aimed at the specifics of obtaining electronic evidence.[4] The Council of Europe defines electronic evidence as "*evidence obtained from data contained in or created by any device, the operation of which depends on software or data stored or transmitted through a computer system or network*".[5] Experts provide a very similar definition stating that electronic evidence is any evidential information stored electronically on any type of electronic device that can be used as evidence in a lawsuit.[6,7] A generally relatively accepted definition of the term is offered by the EU Evidence Project,[8] which defines electronic evidence as "*[...] any data that is the output of an analogue or digital device of potential evidential value that is generated, processed, stored or transmitted by any electronic device. Digital evidence is that electronic evidence that is generated or converted to a numerical format*".[9] This definition is broader and includes both digitally born evidence and that which during its life is transformed and then stored or exchanged in electronic form.[10] Finally, probably the most famous definition is "*all digital data through which the crime can be proven, or the relationship between the crime and its perpetrator and the victim is proven. Numeric data is a set of numbers from various texts that include writing as well as graphics, maps, audio, and drawing*".[11]

In this context, it is also necessary to distinguish between the concept of electronic evidence and the concept of data. Data can be understood as raw facts and figures without added interpretation or analysis. Evidence itself, i.e., information, is data that has been interpreted in such a way as to be meaningful to the processor, or in this case to the evidence in criminal proceedings.[12]

9.3 International and European legal regulation

There is no complex legal framework for electronic evidence at the international or European level. The collection, preservation, use, and transmission of evidence are thus carried out in accordance with national criminal legislation, which were often written many years ago, before the internet, let alone electronic evidence, even existed.

However, national legal systems and their approach to the securing of electronic evidence vary significantly, which causes, among other things, considerable complications in terms of international judicial cooperation and cross-border handling of electronic evidence. Significant differences were also found in the UN study on cybercrime between countries with otherwise similar legislation.[13] Thus, the challenge for international organizations in recent years has been to harmonize, at least in part, procedures relating to electronic evidence.

The most important international document is undoubtedly the Cybercrime Convention concluded in the framework of the Council of Europe ("Convention"). The Convention is currently the only international treaty that defines the specific acts that signatory states must consider as (cyber) crimes and provides a framework for procedural regulation of these crimes, while also addressing electronic evidence. The Convention contained very general and vague requirements concerning electronic evidence, most of which were already met by the signatory States at the time of their accession to the Convention.

Additional Protocols have therefore been prepared and the ratification process for the Second Additional Protocol to the Convention on Cybercrime on enhanced co-operation and disclosure of electronic evidence is currently pending ("Second Additional Protocol").[14] The Second Additional Protocol was adopted by the Council of Europe and opened for signature on 12 May 2022. Regarding the current status, 44 states (including the Czech Republic) have signed, and two states have ratified the Protocol, with five ratifications required for its entry into force. The official reason for the adoption of the Second Additional Protocol is the ever-increasing proliferation of cybercrime and the increasing complexity of obtaining electronic evidence that may be stored in foreign, multiple, changing, or unknown jurisdictions. At the same time, the powers of law enforcement authorities are limited by territorial boundaries and, as a result, only a very small proportion of cybercrime that is reported to law enforcement authorities leads to judicial decisions.[15]

The main areas covered by the Second Additional Protocol that should contribute to greater success in detecting and punishing cybercrime and more effective international cooperation are as follows. The first and probably the most crucial area is strengthening of the international cooperation in criminal proceedings. The Second Additional Protocol introduces new tools and mechanisms to improve and accelerate international cooperation between states in cybercrime investigations and the seizure of electronic evidence. The second main area is enabling direct access to data as the Second Additional Protocol allows direct access to certain data, such as account information and operational data, without the need for traditional legal aid tools. The last major area mentioned (although the protocol also deals with others) is the protection of personal data and fundamental rights since it introduces measures to protect personal data and ensure respect for fundamental rights in line with international standards.

At the time of the drafting of the Second Additional Protocol, mutual assistance requests were the primary method to obtain electronic evidence of a criminal offence from other States, including the mutual assistance tools of the Convention. However, mutual assistance is not always an efficient way to process an increasing number of requests for volatile electronic evidence. Therefore, it was considered necessary to develop a more streamlined mechanism for issuing orders or requests to service providers in other Parties to produce subscriber information and traffic data.[16] The Czech Republic signed the Second Additional Protocol on 20 June 2024; however, it has not ratified it yet. Based on the ratification of the Second Additional Protocol, more extensive amendments to the CPC and the International Judicial Cooperation Act would have to be adopted and these changes are undoubtedly desirable.

9.4 Securing electronic evidence

Electronic evidence processing refers to the collection, preservation, use, and transfer of evidence in criminal proceedings. Evidence collection refers to the collection of relevant devices, repositories, and data that contain electronic evidence.

Under the Czech legal system, the evidence collection can be done through several procedural tools, including seizure and searches, in the context of searches, in the context of surveillance of persons and things, but it can also involve obtaining such evidence, for example, from internet service providers, through various mechanisms of cooperation with the private and public sectors.

The Czech legal regulation does not contain an explicit regulation of electronic evidence, except for two sections (Section 7b regulating so-called data freezing and Section 88a regulating the order to seize evidence of telecommunications traffic), and therefore it is necessary to use traditional procedural tools to secure electronic evidence. Computer data can be accessed in essentially three basic ways: either by securing the devices or data carriers on which the computer data is stored, gaining direct access to computer data stored on computer systems, or obtaining computer data from service providers.

The procedural tools used to secure electronic evidence are then applied based on the following aspects. The first deciding factor is the nature of the electronic evidence to be obtained, for example, whether it is a message in transit, message already delivered, or data stored on a fixed medium etc. The second crucial factor is the way the electronic evidence is obtained, for example, whether the data is extracted directly from an electronic device or whether it is obtained from an electronic communication service provider, etc. Lastly, the point in time at which the seizure takes place, for example, whether the messages were delivered before or after the moment of the seizure, also represents a decisive factor.

For evidence to be admissible in criminal proceedings, it must first be secured and preserved in a form that ensures that it can be subsequently taken. At this stage, it is essential to approach electronic evidence precisely regarding its nature, i.e. its volatility, changeability, and ease of alteration. Based on Article 16 of the Convention, Section 7b of the CPC was adopted, which regulates the order to preserve or make data unavailable, i.e. data freezing. In practice, this provision replaced the previously used institution of Section 8(1) of the CPC, under which electronic evidence was seized by means of a simple request for information.[17]

The first way in which electronic evidence can be secured is by seizing the item on which it is located, typically an information carrier or computer system – mobile phone, computer, flash drive, etc. This method of seizure is implemented through Section 78 of the CPC governing the obligation to produce or surrender the item (or Section 79 of the CPC governing the confiscation of the item).

The second way is to secure electronic evidence through data from remote storage. In this respect, it is necessary to distinguish whether the data is network-accessible or secured – typically with a login and password. Freely accessible data can be secured without further ado. Secure data can be seized on the basis of Section 158d(3) of the CPC, i.e. by an operational means of surveillance of persons and things, i.e. on the basis of prior authorization by a judge. This is because secure data are regarded as documents and records kept in private and therefore enjoy a higher level of protection.

The last way of securing data is through information service providers. In this respect, the nature of the data to be secured and the level of data protection should always be reflected. Ordinary data not covered by the obligation of confidentiality or not secured may be obtained based on a routine request pursuant to Article 8(1) of the CPC. However, if the data is subject to a certain security mechanism, it is again necessary to use Section 158d(3) of the CPC on surveillance of persons and things. Traffic and location data within the meaning of Sections 90 and 91 of the Electronic Communications Act can only be obtained and secured under the procedure under Section 88a of the CPC, i.e. after a judge has ordered their release at the request of the public prosecutor, and only for enumerated offences. A similar regime applies to data that is the content of telecommunications traffic (which is subject to telecommunications secrecy and can be seized through Section 88 of the CPC).[18]

9.5 Approach to electronic evidence in the Czech Republic

The basic procedures or institutes currently used for the seizure of electronic evidence in the Czech Republic are the seizure institutes – extradition and confiscation of property pursuant to Sections 78 and 79 of the CPC, searches, searches of non-residential premises and land, and personal searches pursuant to Sections 82 to 85b of the CPC. Furthermore, the institutes of interception and recording of telecommunication traffic pursuant to Section 88 of the CPC, requesting data on telecommunication traffic pursuant to Section 88a of the CPC, as well as cross-border interception (Section 64 of the Act on International Judicial Cooperation), or inspection (Section 113 of the CPC), use of expert opinion or expert statement pursuant to Sections 105 to 111 of the CPC.[19] The foregoing shows that almost none of these institutes was created specifically for the purpose of electronic evidence, and thus their use is more or less ad hoc and in some cases very impractical and burdensome.

The seizure of electronic evidence can be problematic because in some cases it is directly linked to the seizure of the physical medium, and in other cases it is data that is discoverable and seizable even without access to the physical medium (typically stored on clouds), both of which are subject to a different legal regime and require a different approach. At the same time, it is also challenging to legally handle a situation where some evidence arises before the moment of the seizure of the tangible medium and some evidence arises after the seizure, typically when a person receives a text message on a phone without the sender's knowledge that the phone has been seized by law enforcement authorities.

This question was addressed in the case law and its solution was reflected in a resolution of the Supreme Court of the Czech Republic. It follows from the court practice on this issue that electronic evidence in the form of a communication that "has already arrived" on its tangible medium before the seizure of that tangible evidence can be seized without further delay, whereas electronic evidence that was recorded on the tangible medium after its seizure is subject to the special regime of Sections 86 to 88 of the CPC regulating interception and recording of telecommunication traffic. If the data is not in the nature of a communication and is present on the tangible medium before its seizure, then no special regime for its seizure is required, regardless of the degree of its privacy; however, if the data existed independently of its tangible medium and was, for example, in an application that required a password to enter, the law enforcement authorities would be required to proceed in accordance with Section 158d(3) of the CPC regulating the surveillance of persons and things. On the other hand, for data in the nature of a communication, which is not on a tangible medium (e.g. e-mails), the regime of Section 158d(3) of the CPC applies when they are seized before the seizure of electronic evidence, whereas Section 88 of the Criminal Procedure Code applies when they are seized after the seizure of electronic evidence; the regime of Section 88a of the Criminal Procedure Code applies to the metadata relating to this electronic communication.[20]

It follows from the foregoing that in practice, two institutes of criminal procedural law are most frequently used in the Czech Republic, namely Section 88 CPC on interception and recording of telecommunication traffic and Section 158d CPC on surveillance of persons and things. For content and metadata related to electronic communications, the institute stated in Section 88 CPC on interception and recording of telecommunications traffic is used as well as Section 88a CPC the procedures for obtaining traffic and location data on telecommunications traffic. Whereas the past content of electronic communication (emails, messages via social networks, email box) is secured either through the institute of surveillance of persons and things stated in Section 158d(3) CPC, to which is used if the addressee has already had access to the content or communication. If the addressee has not yet had access, then an interception and recording of telecommunication traffic in the Section 88 CPC is used.

This distinction raises several controversies, one of which is the inability of the user to influence in some cases whether data is stored in the device's memory or not. This issue is essential to assessing which evidence preservation regime applies to a given piece of electronic evidence. At the same time, the different modes of seizure differ in the degree of "seriousness" with which the fundamental rights and freedoms of users, in particular the right to privacy and confidentiality of letters, are interfered with, while the modes also differ in terms of procedure and, for example, the need for prior approval by a judge, and thus the procedural protection of fundamental rights.

9.6 Risks and pitfalls of current practice

Since data as such is intangible, to secure and execute it, it must be materialized, i.e. secured on a tangible medium. Electronic traces are different in nature from other criminal traces, as they exhibit characteristics such as latency, temporal determinacy, short-term durability, large data volume, extreme dynamics of their environment, and, finally, heterogeneity and complexity of their environment.[21] For the purposes of securing electronic evidence, so-called forensic digital analysis (FDA) is used, which deals with both the digital record of information on recording media and the technical parameters of these media.[22]

There are several risks involved in securing electronic evidence that need to be reflected and ideally should be avoided by setting up the proper processes. These risks arise due to the different nature of electronic evidence and its characteristics. The main risks include:

- Altering or damaging evidence as it is possible to intentionally or unintentionally alter or damage electronic evidence when handling it.
- Unauthorized access: electronic evidence can be compromised by unauthorized access to electronic systems or accounts where evidence is stored.
- Technical complexity of electronic evidence since electronic evidence can be technically complex, especially when it comes to extracting data from different electronic devices.
- Authenticity and integrity as electronic evidence must be authentic to be admissible in legal proceedings. This means that it is important to verify that the evidence has not been tampered with and to ensure that it has not been damaged or altered during the process of securing and preserving it.

When securing and evaluating electronic evidence, several interpretation and application issues may arise, particularly concerning the originality and integrity of the data. The question of the originality of the data is related to the fact that it is the copy of the data that gave rise to the electronic evidence that is examined in court, not the original evidence itself, since it is always necessary to record it on a tangible medium and only then to examine it. Since the evidence may be damaged in the process of securing or executing it, it is never the original data that is dealt with, but copies of it. However, it is absolutely crucial to ensure that the original data and the copy presented to the court are exactly the same and that no changes have been made in the course of making the copy. The content of the data must always remain identical – the machine-readable code that makes up the data remains the same even when the data is transferred to a recording medium, so the only thing that effectively changes is the location of the data. Data consistency, the guarantee of the integrity of electronic evidence, is a requirement for preserving the evidence in its original form. It is, therefore, necessary to handle the data in such a way that consistency and integrity can be demonstrated; otherwise, the evidence would be inadmissible in court. It is these aspects that are the most common reasons for doubting the credibility of electronic evidence and, therefore, for judges being less likely to take it into account and to base decisions on it.

To assess the originality and credibility of evidence, it is always necessary to first examine the background from which the evidence was obtained and, at the same time, whether the evidence may have been altered or tampered with during the trial. That is, for example, whether any external interference or influence may have occurred after the data was secured, typically by editing, correcting or deleting a message in various chat applications, screenshots of which are very common evidence in criminal proceedings. For a screenshot to be admissible as evidence in criminal proceedings, at least the date of its creation is required.[23] However, as it can be seen from the above, the date alone does not ensure the originality of the content in question. Therefore, to determine whether the evidence has been tampered with, certain steps must be taken to verify its authenticity.

9.7 Use of algorithms in securing electronic evidence

One way to verify the originality of the data is to use algorithms during the process of securing it, namely hashing functions. The purpose of the hash functions is primarily to ensure data integrity, security, and efficient data retrieval. A hash function is a mathematical algorithm that takes an input and produces a fixed-size string of characters, which is typically a sequence of numbers and letters. It means that each unique input produces a unique hash value, and, at the same time, the hash function is deterministic, meaning that for a given input, it will always produce the same hash value. This feature ensures consistency and reliability in generating hashes. Based on these functionalities, hashing is very convenient to verify data integrity by the process of comparing the hash of the original data with the computed hash of the received or stored data, since it is possible to determine if any changes or corruptions have occurred. Even a slight alteration in the input data will produce a completely different hash value.

Specifically, the procedure would be as follows: law enforcement authorities would have hash values of the original files created for each file when securing the data. Subsequently, during the criminal proceedings, when the data would be presented to the court as evidence, the hashing function would be performed again and if the hash value of this evidence matches the hash value created at the beginning, it would be obvious that the data has not been manipulated or tampered with in any way. At the same time, to ensure that it is obvious at what point in time the hash value was created, it would always be advisable to timestamp the hash value to definitively confirm the originality and record the state of the data at a specific point in time.

9.8 Conclusion

The importance, relevance, and prevalence of electronic evidence have been increasing with each passing year. The concerns of law enforcement authorities about the use of electronic evidence are largely justified, particularly in view of the nature of the digital traces seized, their intangible nature, their easy changeability and modifiability, as well as the often-impossible verification of whether they are actually the same data that has been seized. All these aspects, as well as the above-mentioned ones, contribute to the fact that electronic evidence is often overlooked and that law enforcement authorities still try to base their decisions on tangible traces. At the same time, these risks reduce the evidentiary value of electronic evidence or make it easy to challenge it. However, with the increasing number of electronic evidence and cases that are based solely on it, it is crucial that a consistent methodology to secure it is provided to ensure that lawful and procedurally usable evidence is obtained. The different nature of electronic evidence requires a different approach to securing and handling it. Only adopting existing institutions for these purposes is certainly not an appropriate solution. Algorithms, and specifically hashing functions, could be used for the purposes of appropriate and reliable securing of electronic evidence, as they can easily verify the origin and authenticity of electronic evidence.

If a hash value was always created for all the data being secured and timestamped at the same time, and this value matched the original value when it was re-run, it would ensure that the data had not been tampered with and was reliable. Such a finding would clearly contribute to the confidence of judges in this evidence and facilitate their decision-making, the overall transparency of the handling of this evidence, and the justification of judicial decisions.

Notes

1 This chapter was prepared within the framework of the student research project "Criminal Procedure Code de lege lata and de lege ferenda in constitutional law contexts" implemented in 2023 at the Faculty of Law of Charles University, SVV 260 620/2023.

2 Moussa, A. F.: Electronic evidence and its authenticity in forensic evidence. In: *Egypt J Forensic Sci* 11, 20 (2021).

3 Repík, B. Procesní důsledky porušení předpisů o dokazování v trestním řízení. Bulletin advokacie, 1982, červenec-srpen, s. 129.

4 Polčák R., Púry F., Harašta J. et al.: Elektronické důkazy v trestním řízení. 1. vyd. Brno: Masarykova univerzita, Právnická fakulta, 2015. page 253. In: *Spisy Právnické fakulty Masarykovy univerzity, řada teoretická, Edice Scientia č. 542.*
5 Council of Europe. Guidelines of the Committee of Ministers of the Council of Europe on electronic evidence in civil and administrative proceedings. <https://search.coe.int/cm/Pages/result_details.aspx?ObjectId=0900001680902e0c>. Accessed 19 October 2023.
6 Casey E.: *Digital evidence and computer crime: forensic science, computers and the Internet.* Academic Press, Cambridge, USA, 2000.
7 Volonino L.: Electronic evidence and computer forensics. In: *Commun Assoc Inf* Syst 12 (1), 27, 2003. <https://aisel.aisnet.org/cgi/viewcontent.cgi?article=3193&context=cais>.
8 It is an EU-funded research project entitled European Informatics Data Exchange Framework for Court and Evidence, which comprehensively addressed the issue of electronic evidence.
9 Viz EVIDENCE PROJECT CONSORTIUM. EVIDENCE Semantic Structure. 2015, s.7.
10 Biasiotti M. A., Cannataci J. A., Bonnici J. P. M., Turchi F.: Introduction: opportunities and challenges for electronic evidence. In: *Handling and exchanging electronic evidence across Europe.* Springer, Cham, Switzerland, 2018, pages 3–12.
11 Casey E.: repeated citation.
12 Polčák R., Púry F., Harašta J. et al.: repeated citation, page 94.
13 See UNITED NATIONS OFFICE ON DRUGS AND CRIME. Comprehensive Study on Cybercrime (draft) [online]. Vienna: United Nations, 2013, p. 158 [cited 2023-10-20].
14 Data valid as of July 2024.
15 See Council of Europe, Treaty Office. Details of Treaty No.224. Second Additional Protocol to the Convention on Cybercrime on enhanced co-operation and disclosure of electronic evidence [online].
16 See Council of Europe, Treaty Office. Explanatory Report to the Second Additional Protocol to the Convention on Cybercrime on enhanced co-operation and disclosure of electronic evidence [online]. Paragraph 23.
17 Dostál, O.: Zajišťování důkazů u počítačové kriminality – dožádání, vydání věci a prohlídky (1. díl). Trestněprávní revue. 2019, (3), s. 66.
18 POLČÁK, Radim, František PÚRY a Jakub HARAŠTA. Elektronické důkazy v trestním řízení. Brno: Masarykova univerzita, 2015. s. 100–108.
19 Polčák, R., Púry F., Harašta J.: *Elektronické důkazy v trestním řízení.* Brno: Masarykova univerzita, 2015. s. 73–74.
20 Resolution of the Supreme Court of the Czech Republic of 15 December 2000, Case No. 7 Tz 9/2000, and subsequently in the interpretative opinion of the Supreme State Prosecutor's Office No. 4/2005, and the subsequent opinion of the Supreme State Prosecutor's Office No. 1/2015.
21 Rak, R., Porada, V.: Vlastnosti digitálních stop a jejich dopady na forenzní šetření. Soudní inženýrství, č. 4, roč. 16, s. 183–192, 2005.
22 Porada, V., Šedivý, P.: Kriminalistické a forenzní aspekty počítačové (kybernetické) kriminality. Karlovarská právní revue, č. 2, s. 12, 2011.
23 Judgment of the Supreme Administrative Court of the Czech Republic of 12 April 2011, Case No. 1 As 33/2011.

Chapter 10

Algorithmic automation in criminal proceedings

A general discussion and Czech perspective[1]

Daniel Oborák

10.1 Introduction

The utilisation of computer automation in everyday life is on the rise, reflecting the increasing prevalence of algorithmisation and mathematisation in our society. The advent of computer automation has also caused changes in the legal domain, including the introduction of new technologies in criminal procedure. The rationale for the incorporation of contemporary software applications in the context of criminal proceedings is self-evident. The utilisation of algorithms in the context of criminal proceedings is motivated by a number of factors, including fast processing of information, elimination of errors resulting from the imperfections inherent to human analysis of vast quantities of data, exclusion of the possibility of corruption or personal biases and, last but not least, acceleration of the entire process. Conversely, the automation of criminal proceedings, most notably in the context of decision-making, can give rise to a number of practical, legal and ethical questions.

This chapter addresses the subject of computer algorithms in criminal procedure, with particular reference to their application in the decision-making process at various stages of the criminal justice system. The following pages will present the benefits of automated decision-making in criminal procedure, before outlining its limitations. Finally, the possibilities for the use of computer algorithms in the context of Czech criminal procedural law will be evaluated, taking into account the fundamental principles of criminal procedure and the value settings of the European Union as a whole.

10.2 Algorithms in criminal proceedings

It is first necessary to define the terms "artificial intelligence" and "computer algorithm". A computer algorithm is a set of instructions that lead to the solution of a specific problem or task. The term "artificial intelligence",

DOI: 10.4324/9781003531500-17

on the other hand, is far more ambiguous. From a philosophical perspective, we may conceptualise artificial intelligence (AI) systems as technologies that are capable of exhibiting cognitive processes analogous to those inherent to humans.[2] However, our perception of AI is heavily influenced by the sci-fi department, where AI softwares are usually self-aware, sometimes even capable of experiencing emotions similar to those perceived by a person. In today world, we use term AI mostly for software that uses machine learning methods or artificial neuron network model. Technological concepts used in today world are still miles away from the science fiction visions of self-aware machines.

The correct implementation of any computational algorithm must be based on three core requirements. The first requirement is an existing scientific theory that explains why and how a set of facts can occur. Such a theory must meet the minimum requirements of validation as defined by the scientific community. The second core requirement is a translation of this theory into a specific algorithmic language. By algorithm we mean a normative procedure, a mathematical model, that processes data on the input and delivers desired results on the output, while adhering to the scientific theory on which it's based. The third and final core requirement is where modern technologies come in, because the final level of complexity is a complete automation of the algorithm. Only when used with sufficient computing power are algorithms at the peak of their potential, because at this point the software is able to process huge amounts of data needed to produce relevant results.[3]

Several jurisdictions around the world are already using software algorithms at various stages of the criminal justice process. Initially, AI-driven algorithms are used as policing and risk assessment tools that are applied prior to the commission of a crime. Computer automation can also be used to detect, obtain and preserve evidence and to evaluate it in court proceedings. For example, the use of AI-driven technologies for facial recognition, DNA analysis and gunshot detection has been widely documented, particularly in China. Computational algorithms are also an invaluable tool for legal research and summarisation, as they can process huge amounts of data in a matter of seconds. For example, they can be used effectively to analyse and summarise the entire body of case law on a particular issue. Finally, automation can be used in the sentencing process or other forms of decision-making. It has the potential to act as an actual decision-maker, a "computer judge", or as a tool to assist a human judge, who often follows its recommendations in his or her decision-making. For example, risk assessment tools can be used in the decision-making process in criminal proceedings to predict recidivism. This chapter focuses mainly on the final form of implementation of computer algorithms, as an aid to sentencing.

10.3 Computer as a judge

Algorithmisation in criminal proceedings is often used to make an assessment of the offender's risk and likelihood of reoffending, which can be useful at various stages of criminal proceedings, such as when deciding on probation, remand in custody, sentencing or parole. Algorithms help human judges to assess data about the offender, usually in the form of a score, which represents the likelihood that a particular offender will continue his criminal behaviour or reoffend. The algorithm categorises the offender on the basis of a number of determinants and gives the judge a probability score based on statistics about other previous offenders who have been placed in the same categories. This categorisation is based on the real or perceived psychological characteristics of the offenders.[4]

The automatised decision-making can be viewed as peak of implementing AI into criminal proceedings. But, as it is the most critical part of criminal proceedings, which most infringes upon the rights of individuals, the use of AI in this area is hugely controversial. As it was already stated, the undiscutable benefit of computer-ran algorithms is that they can process large amount of data. In decision-making this means that software can make its decision on the basis of hundreds and thousands of previous court decisions and can compare hundreds and thousands of other statistical data relevant for the purpose of decision-making.[5]

A significant issue arises from the very nature of the decision-making itself. From the standpoint of legal theory and philosophy, a significant question arises as to whether sentencing should be based on the outcomes of big data analysis at all. The processes of human decision-making and algorithmic decision-making are based on different patterns of reasoning. The decision-making process of humans is rooted in the recognition of personal experiences, which translates into more individualistic and personalised outcomes. In contrast, automated decision-making is based on a statistical approach, which leads to more generalised outcomes. It could be argued that the human mind, based on human experience, is a key aspect of justice, despite inherent limitations. A lack of human empathy and sentiment could be seen as a limitation of computer algorithms in this regard. While computer algorithms are superior at complex analysis, they are not capable of considering questions of equitable discretion and mercy.[6]

Decisions made by human – judge in this debate – are made upon syllogistic approach to reasoning, on deductive logic. Human being is able to process much smaller amount of data at given time, which can be seen as disadvantage. On the other hand, when using big data, which by its nature can be analysed only in purely statistical way, the small details of every particle of given set of data disappears in the pool of regularities and similar elements.[7] The problem with criminal law is that it lies in that details.

Individual details about given offender make a complete narrative, which is essential for the purpose of making right decision in criminal matter, most notably in the case of sentencing.

Another problem connected with algorithmical decision-making is the opacity of algorithms. The software is usually subject to trade secret of the company that owns particular tool and is not publicly disclosed. What is even more alarming is the fact that the detailed calculations behind the algorithms are not usually known even to court and law enforcement agencies. The main reason that legitimises the outcomes is the pure faith in the algorithm itself and in the science theory that the algorithm lies upon, not the effectiveness and fairness of the outcome in form of given sentence or other decision made in criminal proceedings.

The legitimacy of algorithm-driven decision-making is a topic of considerable academic debate in its own right. The legitimacy of criminal sentencing in the eyes of the public is derived not only from the institutional framework that comprises a court but also from the public's trust in the professional, competent and morally upright conduct of a judge as an individual. In this context, society accepts human judges as authoritative figures and acknowledges their legitimacy.[8] From this perspective, the concept of a "computer judge" is controversial, as the legitimacy of algorithms is based on different philosophical premises than that of human judges. Society may place its trust in the scientific principles that underpin the algorithm. It may also have confidence in the company that developed the software, assuming that it did so with good faith and in accordance with the highest standards of quality. Furthermore, society may accept the trustworthiness of the statistical methodology that forms the basis of the results in a given case. Nevertheless, the legitimacy of judicial decision-making is distinct from the belief in the accuracy and flawlessness of the software.

In criminal sentencing, there is a pronounced moral disapproval of the offender's criminal conduct which, by its nature, cannot be made by machine itself. Software itself has no sense of morality, only an algorithmic approach that analyses the given data, even if the variables are chosen on the basis of morality of the creators of the algorithm. As Simmons stated, criminal law carries with it a moral judgement that the perpetrator has broken the social contract, and it is inappropriate for machines to make that moral judgement.[9]

The concerns described above persist even when considering the main role of the human judge in the decision-making process. Some might argue that judge can choose whether or not to accept the result of the computer analysis in his decision and that he still maintains the judicial power in this regard. Predictive algorithms give factors that algorithm takes into account a "scientific" veneer, so that judges give them too much weight and rely less on individual characteristics that are not taken into consideration by the algorithm.[10] There is a significant concern that human judges may be inclined to defer to the recommendations of predictive algorithms, potentially undermining their own intuitive and insightful decision-making abilities. The algorithm provides a result with a mathematical and scientific foundation that is challenging to dispute, particularly when the methodology is not transparent to the judge, as it is often protected by the trade secrets of the company that developed the software.

10.4 Where does the COMPAS lead us?

One of the most mentioned and also one of the most controversial algorithmical tools used in criminal proceedings is "Correctional Offender Management Profiling for Alternative Sanctions", also known as COMPAS. COMPAS is a risk assessment tool made by company Northpointe used in several jurisdictions in United States, specifically in New York, Wisconsin, Florida and California. It's used as a help for the judge during sentencing and during deciding on probation as a tool for calculating probability of recedivism of defendant.

For a decade, there has been a robust academic debate surrounding the question of whether the utilisation of software tools in sentencing and other forms of decision-making within the criminal justice system is inherently discriminatory, even when there are no criteria based on race, sexual orientation or religion present in the input form of given software. In 2016, journalists from the American journal ProPublica published an article offering an opinion on the inherently discriminatory nature of the COMPAS tool. The journalists' investigation revealed that the algorithm is, in fact, biased against Black individuals, assigning them high-risk scores based on the colour of their skin. The research conducted by the journalists indicates that the algorithm has the propensity to exacerbate pre-existing bias, as it assesses the colour of the skin to be a statistically significant factor in previous decision-making processes.[11]

It is important to note that COMPAS is not openly discriminatory against the Black minority, as it does not include skin colour as a variable. However, some of the variables are indirectly related to the ethnic background of the offender, which gives rise to the issue that Black individuals are assigned higher risk scores in comparison to Caucasian individuals accused of the same crime. In another words, although the data used by COMPAS do not include an individual's race, other aspects of the data may be correlated to race that can lead to racial disparities in the predictions.[12]

But the discriminatory nature debate extends beyond the question of racial discrimination. COMPAS input form is made of 137 questions list which range from obviously important variables, such as whether offenders have any criminal history or if they violated probation or parole, to less predictable ones, such as if the offenders moved in last year or if they have an alias.[13] Some of the variables are not affected by offenders actions in the present or in the past, and are uncontrollable by the offenders, such as criminal history of their family members or dangerousness of the neighbourhood they currently live in.[14] As Harcourt stated, the algorithm works with information on who the defendant is and what he is expected to do in future, rather than just what he committed.[15]

One of the strong factors that come into place when assessing dangerousness of offender is a gender. According to Starr, many of the risk assessment tools are used for sentencing incorporate gender between its attributes.[16] The reasoning behind this is that women have substantially lesser recidivism risk than males. The Supreme Court of the United States has consistently rejected the use of statistical discrimination in its case law, even outside of criminal matters. According to a decision made in case United States v. Virginia (1996),[17] any gender-based government action must demonstrate "exceedingly persuasive justification" and cannot rely on stereotypical assumptions about characteristics of given gender. According to Starr, implementation of risk assessment algorithm that uses gender as one of its attributes on which the score is granted is based on subordination of individual to particular group, which is in opposition to anticlassification and anti-statistical discrimination policies that Supreme Court has been holding.[18]

It can be argued that the issue of discrimination in risk assessment tools is largely dependent upon the selection of attributes, which may, in some cases, be either directly or indirectly discriminatory. It is also possible that the issue does not lie with the attributes themselves, but rather with the dataset comprising previous court rulings and convictions, which could be discriminatory in nature. This could result in the introduction of biases into the results generated by the software tool. However, the discriminatory nature of software risk assessment is not limited to these two factors, although they may be relevant considerations.

As previous authors that dealt with ethical aspect of risk assessment tools stated, ethical questions that rise when dealing with the use of algorithms for risk assessment of given individual in the context of criminal prosecution are not simply one of bias or accuracy, rather it's one of purpose.[19] According to Fialová, the source of discrimination is not only a faulty dataset, but in the basic principle of algorithmic decision-making itself. Fialová discusses that the mathematical models are based on group profiling, which leads to punishing members of particular group more than members of other groups, all that on basis of statistical probability.[20] Individualistic approach, which courts should uphold in their decision-making, is replaced by assessing a combination of various groups that the offender falls into.

It can be argued that even a human judge assesses an individual based on certain attributes, selecting them according to their opinion of their relevance. This process is similar to that of a computer algorithm, but less consistent and with a smaller amount of data. The difference lies in what was already stated before in the third section. A human judge is able to consider a person in their entirety and is equipped with the ability to perceive subtle nuances between different cases that a machine would be unable to take into account. Furthermore, the judge is able to draw upon human characteristics such as emotions, compassion and empathy in a subconscious manner. This can be favourable to defendants as much as it can be unfavourable.[21] These are the variables that cannot be quantified because human experience and emotions are difficult to define using a mere set of data. In other words, the issue lies in the limitations of communication between humans and machines, which must be encoded in machine-readable code.

As it was already stated before, the problem with algorithms such as COMPAS lies also in its proprietary and nontransparent nature. In 2016 in the case of Loomis v. Wisconsin, Supreme court of Wisconsin tackled the question whether the proprietary nature of COMPAS and similar tools violates defendant's constitutional rights to due process. The court ruled that the unpublicity of the algorithm does not violate the right to due process as it is a mere tool used by the court and the court is free to rely on portions of the assessment while rejecting other portions. Supreme court of the United States then denied the writ of certiorari in 2017 so the Supreme court so to speak missed the chance to give opinion about risk assessment tools and about use of algorithms in criminal matters in general.[22] In consecutive cases, namely People v. Johnson (2018) and State v. Hill (2019), courts upholded the findings of Supreme court of Wisconsin.

The academical community has been less lenient towards risk assessment software in regard of its opacity. Much discussed topic is a practical limitation of the right of defence. If the defendants do not exactly know how exactly the processes behind the result in the form of sentence work, they cannot effectively defend against its results, even if there is a judicial reasoning included in the decision.[23] This is caused by a fact that the outcome is not based on thought process of a judge, but is generated by the nontransparent algorithm and then legitimised by ad hoc reasoning of the judge. The defence is unable to exert any meaningful influence over the algorithmic process. Consequently, should the judge choose to adhere unquestioningly to the algorithm's output, any argument advanced by the defendant is essentially meaningless. This argumentation leads to the question of how appellate courts should examine a disputed decision when the part of the decision-making process in question is not included in the judicial reasoning and is covered by the unpublic code of the algorithm.

It can be argued that the utilisation of computer algorithms to assist judges in making decisions regarding criminal cases represents a significant departure from the conventional notions associated with criminal procedure. Moreover, it can be observed that the current institutions of criminal law have not yet fully reflected the profound shift in discourse that this technological advancement has brought about, even in those jurisdictions where the software tools have already been implemented.

The opacity problem rises as a risk assessment algorithms are improving from technological point of view.[24] Machine learning software, AI tools, which are more accurate and effective than programmes that don't use machine learning technology, are less explicable, because the algorithm is autopoietic, as it uses computational power to enhance its capabilities and writes its code by itself. Even the creators of the software do not fully comprehend its processes after the initial launch of the programme, because the machine itself is making those processes more complex during periods of time. The heavy philosophical debate lies in the questions if we should allow application of algorithms which are practically unknown to anyone and constantly change to make decisions in criminal matters. If we are allowing using of algorithms in criminal proceedings in general, shouldn't we use the ones that are objectively best at assessing risks, so we protect the rights of the defendants, who would get worse punishment just because of an inferior risk prediction software, even if the cost of that is practical unreviewability of results that came out of machine learning based software?

10.5 European and Czech perspective on algorithmical decision-making

On 6 October 2021, the European Parliament adopted a resolution addressing the use of AI in criminal law. Resolution acknowledges "extraordinary promises" and also the risks that the implementation of AI brings to the table. European parliament declared that AI systems need to be designed as non-discriminatory, safe and their decisions must be explainable and transparent. It also declared that the AI technology must be worthy of public trust. According to the resolution, European union, as well as its member states, bear responsibility that decisions surrounding in implementation of AI in judiciary and law enforcement sector are made in "transparent manner, fully safeguard fundamental rights, and in particular do not perpetuate discrimination, biases or prejudices where they exist".[25]

European parliament has also taken into account a debate from other jurisdictions concerning bias and discrimination of algorithms, as was the case of aforementioned COMPAS controversy. Resolution states that "biases can be inherent in underlying datasets, especially when historical data is being used, introduced by the developers of the algorithms, or generated when the systems are implemented in real world settings". It also "points out that the results provided by AI applications are necessarily influenced by the quality of the data used, and that such inherent biases are inclined to gradually increase and thereby perpetuate and amplify existing discrimination, in particular for persons belonging to certain ethnic groups or racialised communities".[26]

European parliament calls out for specific, clear and precise legal framework that regulates the use of AI in law enforcement and judiciary field, which would include safeguards in the form of easily available complaint and redress procedures and also stresses the right of parties to have access to data collection process and the assessment itself.

Resolution also stresses that decision with legal effect must be taken by human, who is accountable for his decision-making. In European context, a person has a right not to be subject of a decision, which is based only on automated data processing, nor can be subject of decision-making based on categorisation of personal data, unless there are suitable safeguards of his rights and freedoms and there is a legitimate interest for these measures. European law prohibits profiling that leads to discrimination based on the membership of individual in any special category of personal data.

To some extent, the implementation of algorithmic decision-making has already occurred in several member states of the European Union, including France, Belgium, and the Netherlands. Consequently, the declarative resolution of the European Parliament represents a significant statement that outlines the discourse chosen by the European Union and its members, influencing the present and future direction of member states' policies and their application in this matter.

To date, no form of algorithm-based tool has been employed in the context of criminal sentencing in the Czech Republic. In this regard, it is necessary to examine purely theoretical possibility of utilising methods similar to COMPAS risk assessment tool in Czech criminal proceedings, with reference to the aforementioned discourse set by the European Parliament. In the absence of a legal framework that would specifically regulate the use of algorithms, this section will primarily address the question of compliance of these methods with the basic principles of Czech criminal procedure as well as with the principles of substantial criminal law.

The initial question that must be addressed in order to assess the viability of utilising an algorithmic tool for the purpose of sentencing is whether it would be consistent with the general principles applying to imposition of punishments, as set forth in sections 37, 38 and 39 of the Criminal Code.

According to section 39 paragraph 1, "when determining the type and extent of the punishment, the court shall take into account the nature and seriousness of the criminal offence committed, of the personal, family, property and other relations of the offender and his/her previous way of life and the possibility of his/her personal reform; furthermore, the offender's behaviour after the act shall also be taken into account, in particular their efforts to compensate any damage or mitigate any other detrimental effects of the act, and where the offender has been designated as a co-operating accused".

As a commentary to Criminal Code argues, the type, combination and intensity of penalties must be determined by the court in each individual case in such a way that they correspond to all the specific features of the case.[27] In contrast to the more binding approach to sentencing that is characteristic of United States criminal law,[28] Czech criminal law places a strong emphasis on the individuality of each case and each perpetrator. This is reflected in the legislative framework itself, which provides numerous instruments that guarantee increased judicial discretion in specific modalities of particular cases. Such instruments include the extraordinary mitigation of a sentence and its opposite, the extraordinary increase of a sentence, as provided by sections 58 and 59 of the Criminal Code. These regulations are a direct manifestation of the aforementioned principle of individualisation of penalties.

In light of the Criminal Code's emphasis on an individualistic approach to determining the type and extent of punishment imposed on offenders, it can be concluded that there may be a conflict with the methodologies employed by risk-assessment tools such as COMPAS, whose foundations are rooted in statistical analysis. The hypothetical computer algorithm would have to comply with a more individualistic approach to sentencing present in Czech criminal law, which is in direct contradiction to the current mode of operation of these tools, as was presented in previous subchapters. In theory, risk-assessment tools could be better employed in determining whether probation, parole or other similar legal instrument is an appropriate course of action for a particular offender.

According to Fialová, algorithmic decision-making could be contrary to the principle of free evaluation of evidence, which binds Czech criminal proceedings.[29] According to section 2 paragraph 6 of The Criminal Procedure Code, the authorities involved in criminal proceedings shall evaluate the evidence according to their inner beliefs based on careful consideration of all circumstances of the case individually and also in their summation. As has been previously indicated, there is a possibility that the subjective beliefs of the judge may be overruled by the presumed objectivity of the algorithm as well as inability of a judge to fully comprehend the processes that lead to an outcome of the algorithm and that other evidence pertaining to the perpetrator's personality may be rendered inconsequential.

It can be argued that this point also applies to expert opinions, as experts naturally possess superior knowledge on a given specialised issue compared to the court. This could be considered analogous to the analytical and computational superiority of algorithm-driven tools. The distinction lies in the fact that even in cases of highly complex scientific and technical issues, expert opinions adhere to the principles of reviewability and transparency in the methodology employed in formulating the expert opinion. Moreover, the judge shall interrogate the expert, should the judge identify any unclear elements within the expert opinion or have doubts regarding the methodology employed by the expert to reach their conclusion. Should the judge have reservations regarding the reliability of the expert opinion, he is at discretion to request the assignment of a new expert. This is not the case with regard to risk assessment tools as they are currently understood. In contrast to risk assessment tools, expert opinion may be presented by the defendant, in addition to the prosecution or court. In the event of significant discrepancies between experts regarding matters relevant to criminal proceedings, a revisory expert opinion may be employed to clarify the contradictions between the experts. Furthermore, experts are held strictly liable for their actions, whereas algorithms are not. We note that the use of experts who may have a significant impact on a court's decision-making process due to their professional expertise is subject to rigorous regulation as a counterbalance. Therefore, it is the court itself that ultimately determines guilt and sentence.

The implementation of algorithmic tools in the Czech criminal justice system would require the establishment of rigorous regulatory frameworks governing their utilisation as evidence in criminal sentencing. Such frameworks would need to be as robust as those governing the involvement of experts, or even more stringent, given the heightened risks associated with algorithmic decision-making. Unlike experts, algorithms are not subject to the same degree of accountability, ethical constraints and personal motivations, which could potentially lead to more significant implications.

There is an argument that algorithmical sentencing, based on the settings of the monitored parameters and their influence, does in fact occur during the compilation of the algorithm by engineers, sociologists, IT specialists and other persons involved in the development of the algorithm rather than during court hearing.[30] It can be argued that this setting could be in conflict with the principle of statutory judge, as well as with the principle of an independent and impartial judge. According to article 38 paragraph 1 of the Charter of Fundamental Rights and Freedoms of Czech Republic, "nobody shall be denied his or her statutory judge. The jurisdiction of the court and the competence of the judge are set by law". According to article 40 paragraph 1, "only a court shall decide on guilt and on the penalty for criminal offenses". When other individuals, unknown to the defendant, significantly impact the decision-making process, it is reasonable to conclude that the aforementioned constitutional rights would be violated.

As previously indicated, additional concerns have been raised regarding the compliance of algorithmic decision-making with the rights of defence and fair trial. It has been previously stipulated that the non-transparent nature of the algorithm leads to unreviewability of the decision, as the defending party is unable to comprehend the precise method by which the algorithmic outcome was generated and is therefore unable to challenge the results. This represents a further challenge that would have to be addressed before the potential implementation of automated decision-making in Czech criminal proceedings with the introduction of a robust and complex regulatory framework.

10.6 Conclusion

Computer algorithms, notably machine learning software, are useful tools in many challenges facing modern society. As evidenced by their use in criminal proceedings, notably in the form of automated decision-making, the current form of these algorithms is subject to legitimate controversy. There are questions of fundamental importance concerning inherent discrimination, opacity and legitimacy of such algorithms, as well as the questions that arise from these core problems linked to automated decision-making. Frequently discussed COMPAS tool, which is widely used in the United States, is an illustrative example for many problems a controversies that arose with expansion of automatic decision-making around the globe.

It can be agreed with the Supreme Court of Wisconsin that gave its opinion on the use of COMPAS software that the algorithm is a mere tool and that it is the judge who is responsible for sentencing, and thus must articulate the reasoning behind the sentence. However, as the judge himself is unaware of the specific factors that informed the assignment of a risk score to a particular individual, and as he is basing his reasoning on this score, it is unclear whether the constitutional rights of the defendant have been adequately protected.

Furthermore, there is a significant question of the accountability and legitimacy of decisions made by computer algorithms. In the contemporary era, at least within the context of Western society, the human judge remains the primary decision-maker within the criminal legal system, even when they utilise algorithms as a tool during the sentencing process. However, in the future, new ideas and opinions may emerge that could prompt a re-evaluation of the necessity of human involvement in the judicial process. In such a scenario, who would be the ultimate decision-maker? The algorithm's creator? The software's proprietor? Or the AI itself? These are the questions that will require resolution in the near future.

Notes

1 This chapter was prepared within the framework of the student research project "Criminal Procedure Code de lege lata and de lege ferenda in constitutional law contexts" implemented in 2023 at the Faculty of Law of Charles University, SVV 260 620/2023.
2 RYBERG, Jesper, ROBERTS, Julian V. Sentencing and artificial intelligence. 2022. p. 5.
3 QUATTROCOLO, Serena. Artificial Intelligence, computational modelling and criminal proceedings. 2020. p. 15.
4 FIALOVÁ, Eva. Využití algoritmů při profilování v trestním řízení a důsledky pro lidská práva. Časopis pro právní vědu a praxi, XXVI, vol. 2. 2018. p. 231.
5 LIPERT-RASMUSSEN, Kasper. Algorithm-Based Sentencing and Discrimination. In: RYBERG, Jesper, ROBERTS, Julian V. Sentencing and Artificial Intelligence. 2022. p. 74.
6 SIMMONS, Ric. Big data, machine judges, and the legitimacy of the criminal justice system. UC Davis Law Review, vol. 52. 2018. p. 1095.
7 There is a question if the algorithmical tools are more precise in their risk assessments more than human judges. According to a study made by Dressler and Farid, COMPAS tool is no more accurate or fair than predictions made by people with little or no criminal justice expertise. DRESSLER, Julia, FARID, Hany. The accuracy, fairness, and limits of predicting recidivism. Science Advances, vol. 4. 2018. p. eaao5580.
8 SIMMONS, Ric. Big data, machine judges, and the legitimacy of the criminal justice system, p. 1071.
9 SIMMONS, Ric. Big data, machine judges, and the legitimacy of the criminal justice system, p. 1095.
10 SIMMONS, Ric. Big data, machine judges, and the legitimacy of the criminal justice system, p. 1098.
11 ANGWIN, Julia, LARSON, Jeff, MATTU, Surya, KIRCHNER, Lauren. Machine Bias. ProPublica. 2016. https://www.propublica.org/article/machine-bias-risk-assessments-in-criminal-sentencing.
12 DRESSLER, Julia, FARID, Hany. The accuracy, fairness, and limits of predicting recidivism,p. eaao5580.
13 The form with questions is available on: https://www.documentcloud.org/documents/2702103-Sample-Risk-Assessment-COMPAS-CORE.html.
14 ANGWIN, Julia, LARSON, Jeff, MATTU, Surya, KIRCHNER, Lauren. Machine Bias. ProPublica. 2016. https://www.propublica.org/article/machine-bias-risk-assessments-in-criminal-sentencing.
15 HARCOURT, Bernard E., Against prediction: Profiling, policing, and punishing in an actuarial age. 2007. pp. 31–34, 188–189. Similary to Harcourt, Lippert-Rasmussen stated that offenders are punished not simply on the basis of their crime, but also for who they are, based on statistical properties of the classes to which they were categorised. LIPERT-RASMUSSEN, Kasper. Algorithm-Based Sentencing and Discrimination, p. 74.
16 STARR, Sonja B. Evidence-Based Sentencing and the Scientific Rationalization of Discrimination. Stanford Law Review, vol. 66. 2014. p. 823.
17 United States v. Virginia, 518 U.S. 515, 531, 1996.
18 STARR, Sonja B. Evidence-Based Sentencing and the Scientific Rationalization of Discrimination, p. 827.

19 BARABAS, Chelsea, DINAKAR, Karthik, ITO, Joichi, VIRZA, Madars, ZITTRAIN, Jonathan. Interventions over Predictions: Reframing the Ethical Debate for Actuarial Risk Assessment. Proceedings of Machine Learning Research, vol. 81. 2018. pp. 1–15.
20 FIALOVÁ, Eva. Využití algoritmů při profilování v trestním řízení a důsledky pro lidská práva, p. 240.
21 ZAVRŠNIK, Aleš. Algorithmic justice: Algorithms and big data in criminal justice settings. European Journal of Criminology, vol. 18(5). 2021. p. 634.
22 Loomis v. Wisconsin, 881 N.W.2d 749 (Wis. 2016), cert. denied, 137 S. Ct. 2290, 2017.
23 FIALOVÁ, Eva. Využití algoritmů při profilování v trestním řízení a důsledky pro lidská práva, p. 256.
24 RYBERG, Jesper. Criminal justice and artificial intelligence: How should we asses the performance of sentencing algorithms? 2024. p. 2.
25 European Parliament resolution of 6 October 2021 on artificial intelligence in criminal law and its use by the police and judicial authorities in criminal matters (2020/2016(INI)).
26 European Parliament resolution of 6 October 2021 on artificial intelligence in criminal law and its use by the police and judicial authorities in criminal matters (2020/2016(INI)).
27 ŠÁMAL, Pavel a kol. Trestní zákoník. 3. vydání. Praha: C. H. Beck, 2023. p. 796.
28 In the United States, the sentencing of individuals is guided by the United States Sentencing Commission Guidelines. These regulations restrict the judicial discretion regarding the type and extent of punishment in specific circumstances.
29 FIALOVÁ, Eva. Využití algoritmů při profilování v trestním řízení a důsledky pro lidská práva, p. 244.
30 Fialová refers to this phenomenon as "the faceless judges". FIALOVÁ, Eva. Využití algoritmů při profilování v trestním řízení a důsledky pro lidská práva, p. 255.

Part VI

The Slovak perspective

Chapter 11

Perspectives of use of algorithms in criminal proceedings in Slovakia[1]

Radovan Blažek

11.1 Introduction

The use of algorithms in criminal proceeding has in some countries already long history and artificial intelligence (AI) is used already for decades. These tendencies are primarily coming from the US, where they were firstly used already in 1933 in Chicago.[2] In the US the intelligent technology is rapidly expanding with the use of algorithmic risk assessment tools in criminal proceedings. This might be explained by the more limiting data protection and privacy laws in Western Europe. However, the use of algorithms spread widely in the 20th century also in European countries. "Algorithmic tools is often an expression of a trend generally observable in Western legal orders."[3]

However, we can ask what is the purpose of using algorithms in criminal proceedings, how it could work and how could the human brain be replaced by the computer when deciding about man's destiny in criminal proceedings. Algorithms in criminal proceedings could be defined as "the use of technology in the criminal justice system based on algorithmic decision-making and the collection, analysis, and processing of big data."[4] They are mainly not used for deciding on who is guilty and who not. "Algorithms are gaining importance in criminal justice because they are part of the decision-making processes, even though they mainly serve as support for the humans in charge."[5]

The algorithms are mainly used for collecting data about accused or convicted persons and they help to evaluate them quicker. "The ability of algorithms to process large amounts of data allows them to evaluate more information more quickly than any officer, crime analyst or individual department, and at a time of growing public demands for fairness and responsibility, this becomes a value in itself."[6] "*Algorithms promise to predict delinquent behaviour, identify potentially dangerous persons, and support crime investigation.*"[7] Actually, the computer only does the same work as would the human evaluators do, but the outcome is more precise,

DOI: 10.4324/9781003531500-19

accurate and without mistakes that could do the human brain. "*Algorithms were used to help structure the human assessment process, and especially to ensure that all relevant factors were taken into account.*"[8] "In particular, judges should interpret law in such a way as to maximize certain desirable features of a legal system, including justice, fairness, and due process, as well as the system's 'integrity' (in essence, its moral coherence). Risk assessment algorithms, however, ... provide the same recommendation given the same demographic information, precluding the possibility to reinterpret legal rules. ... Here it is worth considering the prevalence of cognitive biases in human reasoning. ... Efforts to reduce bias and discretion in sentencing are not unique to the current move toward algorithmic decision-making."[9] "*The use of automated systems will minimize such issues as the inconsistency of standards, difficulties in the practice of their application. Also, it will be possible to avoid subjective interpretation of the law.*"[10]

"*Artificial intelligence can be used as a mediator of the judiciary and increase the level of efficiency and fairness of court decisions.*"[11]

The good practice from other state shows, that algorithms are used mainly for following purposes:[12]

a precrime phase[13]

1 spatio-temporal predictive policing (i.e., the identification of possible crime scenes and times);[14]
2 predictive policing regarding individuals (i.e., the identification of potentially dangerous persons and subsequent threat management).

b postcrime phase:

3 advanced technology in police investigations;
4 advanced technology in criminal proceedings;[15]
5 forensic-psychiatric assessment of defendants during criminal proceedings;[16]
6 the assessment of convicts in the penal system.[17]

Comparing these practical using of algorithms the chapter presents, how the "good practice" from other states could be introduced in Slovak criminal proceedings. Obviously, there are also criticisms of the use of algorithms in criminal proceedings.

The aim of this chapter is not to discuss the possible errors that could appear when using the AI and algorithms in criminal proceedings, but to analyse the conditions in Slovak Republic, if the legal order is capable of incorporating such tools into criminal proceedings. There are also evaluated some practical aspects of such legal changes.

11.2 Slovak criminal proceedings in the view of algorithms

To find the possible scope of use of algorithms in criminal proceedings, we need to explain the basic stages and progress of the criminal proceedings in Slovakia. The criminal proceedings is ruled mainly by the Slovak Criminal Procedure Code[18] and is divided into two main parts: pre-trial stage and stage before the court.[19] These parts are distinguished by the subjects that are active during this part and to whom is entrusted the decision-making procedure.

In the pre-trial stage the police officers and prosecutors are playing the main role. They are collecting evidence and decide about the case and mainly they decide, whether the case will be sent into further stage to the court or if the case will be terminated already in this pre-trial stage.[20]

If the case continues before the court, then court itself decides about the guilt and punishment and usually the prosecutor loses his position of "decision-maker" in the case. The main hearing (trial) is followed by the possible remedy stage and afterwards the execution part follows. In the theory the "execution of the sentence" is part of the "court stage;" however it is a specific part of the criminal proceedings, where the decisions and subjects are significantly different to the previous part of the court stage and for the purpose of this chapter, the execution part of the proceedings is analysed separately.

In the next sections, the analysis is focused on those parts of the Slovak criminal proceedings that are suitable for the use of algorithms because there is not enough space in this chapter to present the whole aspects of the Slovak criminal proceedings. When thinking about the possible scopes of the use of algorithms in criminal proceedings, as the most suitable parts for Slovak criminal practice were identified those aspects: predictive policing regarding individuals (i.e., the identification of potentially dangerous persons and subsequent threat management), forensic-psychiatric assessment of defendants during criminal proceedings and the assessment of convicts in the penal system.

11.2.1 Pre-trial proceedings

When we think about the possible applicability of algorithms in Slovakia, we need to concern on the final stage of the pre-trial proceedings, where the documents and materials for the final decision are presented and evaluated. In this stage the prosecutor could decide not to submit the case to the court, but decide about the perpetrator with his own decision. We call it as "alternative dispute resolution" and in Slovakia, there are two main tools that the prosecutor could use:

- § 216 SCPC – conditional termination of the criminal proceedings,
- § 220 SCPC – reconciliation.[21]

They are different in their conditions, which must be accomplished, if these tools should be applied which also limit their usage in the criminal proceedings. The conditional termination of the criminal proceedings and reconciliation are part of the so-called restorative justice, where the aim is focused on the restoration of the damage and the agreement between the accused and the victim. "Restorative justice is a process in which all parties with a material interest in a particular crime come together to collectively agree on how to deal with the consequences of that crime and its consequences for the future."[22] "The term restorative process refers to the process by which the damaged party and the victim and, if necessary, another person or member of society (community) who has been affected by a criminal offense, actively participates in the joint assessment of the causes of the crime and its consequences with a view to find a common solution."[23]

The aim of restorative justice, including procedural alternatives way of dealing with criminal cases, is ultimately an alternative punishment for the offender of criminal offence, in particular non-custodial sentences. The purpose of the alternatives is to help a fair trial but at the same time to resolve criminal cases quickly, which would take into account the interests of all the subjects of the proceedings concerned, achieved by the specific procedural process without holding a formally demanding and complicated main hearing.

The conditional termination of the criminal proceedings is the chance for the criminals, which committed their first crime, which could be deemed as the exemption for otherwise ordinary citizen, to have terminated their proceedings without sanction and only with the probationary period. The primary goal of this procedure is to create the conditions for the offender to live ordinary life without having his life influenced by the negative effects connected with the criminal conviction. The main aim of this form of the decision is to control the behaviour of the offender for the specific time (1–5 years) to create the conditions for him not to re-offend again, at least during this probationary period. This tool should help to the young or occasional offenders to meet the standards of society and live without criminal activities.

According to the § 216 SCPC, the conditions of ADR (Alternative dispute resolution) procedure in the form of conditional termination of the criminal proceedings are as following:[24]

- it could be used only for minor offences with the – highest penalty rate of five years,
- not possible for the criminal offences resulted in the death of a person, corruption cases and criminal prosecution against a public official,
- accused must admit he committed the act,

- the outcome is the possible termination of proceedings without a sanction,
- certain duties and obligations may be imposed on the accused in order to maintain his/her proper life and avoid conducts causing the criminal offence,
- the proceedings are conditionally terminated,
- the probation period from one to five years is ordered for the accused,
- damage party must have the damage restored – e.g. prior to the decision or after the decision about conditional termination, but there must by the obligation to restore the damage during the probation period,
- considering the person of the accused, taking into account his previous life and the circumstances of the case, such a decision can be considered sufficient.

Reconciliation is the tool mainly focused on the restoration of damage. For this tool the priority is the agreement between offender and the victim. This tool is presumed for the cases, where the wrong caused to the public interest is of a little value, however, the private interests of victim could be sufficiently influenced. Thus, the main goal is the absolute and 100% of clearing of the damaged caused to the victim. If the offender is able to satisfy the victim's claim, then the state renounce from the right to punish the perpetrator of the crime and the proceedings should be finally terminated without any probationary period.

According to the § 220 SCPC the conditions for reconciliation are as following:[25]

- it could be used only for minor offences with the highest penalty rate of five years,
- not possible for the criminal offences resulted in the death of a person, corruption cases and criminal prosecution against a public official,
- accused must admit he committed the act,
- the outcome is the final termination of proceedings without sanction,
- payment of a sum of money for the protection of victims of crimes,
- damage party must have the damage restored prior to the decision,
- considering the person of the accused, taking into account his previous life and the circumstances of the case, such a decision can be considered sufficient.

Both of the previous mentioned tools have as their condition that this decision must be sufficient for this person and also for protection of society. The evaluation of the person of the perpetrator could be done prior to the decision. The algorithms could evaluate how probable is that this person will reoffend during the next couple of years and thus, upon this evaluation the prosecutor could decide, if he would apply those tools. There is no legal claim for application of these tools. So, the perpetrator could propose to apply them in his case, but only a prosecutor decides whether he/she will apply them or no. If the outcome of the algorithm would be not favourable for offender, prosecutor could simply decide not to apply these tools even when the other conditions for their application would be fulfilled. There is no sanction for "not-using" these tools, so prosecutor could easily decide without any danger that his decision will be questioned in the next stage of proceedings.

11.2.2 *Trial proceedings*

The main outcome of the trial proceedings should be the decision about the guilt and punishment. In the Slovak Republic the focus was given on the alternative punishments in accordance with restorative justice in the last years. Since the adoption of the new criminal codes in 2005, a new trend has been established within the criminal policy – decriminalization and depenalization, within which one of the goals was the focus on alternative punishments, which should take precedence over the imposition of a prison sentence.[26] "*From the second half of the 20th century in the European area occurs the significant development of restorative justice and also more intensive imposition of alternative punishments, i.e. punishments alternating imprisonment. The mentioned situation is also connected with the crisis of imprisonment in the low preventive and re-socializing effectiveness of imprisonment as of the traditional retributive approach of punishing criminals. The aim is to keep the convict outside of prison and to impose him the kind of punishment which will have a preventive effect against the commission of further criminal activity, protect society and, last but not least, satisfy the interests of the victims of a crime.*"[27]

The decision, if the non-prison sentence should be suitable and accurate for the particular perpetrator, could be also the question of use of algorithms.

According to § 34(1) of Slovak Criminal Code,[28] "***A penalty serves the purpose of protecting the society from the perpetrator of crime by preventing him from continuing to commit crime, and creating conditions for his re-education with a view to making him lead a regular life*** *and, at the same time, discouraging other persons from committing crime; moreover, a penalty expresses moral condemnation of the offender by the society.*"

According to § 34(4) of Slovak Criminal Code, "*A court determines the type and the degree of penalty in particular on the basis of the mode of the commission of crime and its consequence, culpability, motive, aggravating circumstances, mitigating circumstances,* ***the person of the offender, his personal situation and rehabilitation potential.***"

The general provisions ruling the mode, how the punishment should be imposed, explicitly define, that the punishment should be appropriate, on one side, to protect the society against further crimes of this particular perpetrator, and, on the other hand, the court should take into consideration the person of the offender, his personal situation and rehabilitation potential. These prescriptions for imposing a punishment explicitly call for using of some tools, how the court should evaluate, if the sentence is suitable and severe enough for this perpetrator to protect the society against his new crimes after execution of this punishment or even during the term of execution. The court is obliged to have some prior evidence and documentation which will be considered and taken into account when deciding about this issue. The same should be evaluated by the possibilities for rehabilitation of the offender and when assessing his personal situation and family life. These particular elements could be the part of his evaluation incorporated in the algorithms used.

The sentences, which could be considered to use the algorithm before imposing them, should be as following:

- conditional imprisonment,
- house arrest,
- community services,
- financial sentence.

All the above-mentioned sentences should be considered as the replacement for the unconditional prison sentence and should be imposed when the unconditional sentence is not imposed. Other sentences could be imposed also together with unconditional prison sentence (e.g. forfeiture of property, forfeiture of an item, prohibition to undertake certain activities, prohibition of participation in public events, prohibition of residence, loss of honorary titles and distinctions, loss of military and other rank, expulsion), and their character lacks the possibility of use of any algorithms methods, because this second group of sentences is oriented to reach certain purpose (e.g. to disable the perpetrator in performing further criminal activities – forfeiture of an item, prohibition to undertake certain activities, prohibition of participation in public events, prohibition of residence) or are special consequence of a crime, which should be imposed to a perpetrator without consideration of his possibility of future reoffending (forfeiture of property, forfeiture of an item, loss of honorary titles and distinctions, loss of military and other rank). For the second group of sentences, there are directly and explicitly described the conditions, when these sentences are to be imposed and the court has not too much opportunities to take into consideration previous life of an offender or the chance of reoffending or the possible rehabilitation during the execution procedure.

For the first group of sentences, where the applicability of algorithms is viable, the Criminal Code prescribe the condition for their imposition as follows:

According to § 49(1)(a) of Slovak Criminal Code, the conditional prison sentence could be imposed if: "*The court may impose a conditional imprisonment sentence if the imprisonment sentence does not exceed two years* (or 3 years under the § 50 SCC) *and if considering the personal situation of the offender, in particular his previous life and work circumstances and the circumstances of the case, the court reasonably believes that* ***it is possible to protect the society, and guarantee the rehabilitation of the offender even if the sentence is not executed.***"

According to § 53(1)(a) of Slovak Criminal Code, the house arrest could be imposed if: "*The court may impose a house arrest sentence of up to four years on the perpetrator of the crime if considering the nature of the crime referred to in paragraph 2, the person and circumstances of the perpetrator,* ***the imposition of this punishment is sufficient,***"

By the community services sentence, there is no explicit provision that this sentence should be sufficient for not reoffending and for protection of the society. According to § 55(1) of Slovak Criminal Code, there is only a provision how the court could influence the rehabilitation procedure of the offender during the execution of the sentence: "*The court may also impose reasonable restrictions or obligations on the offender for this period as specified in § 51 sec. 3 and 4, aimed at leading an orderly life, usually imposes on him to make up for the damage caused by the crime according to his strength and abilities.*"

According to § 56(1) SCC, the financial penalty as the "independent punishment" could be imposed if: "*Without fulfilling the conditions specified in paragraph 1, the court may impose a financial penalty if it imposes it for a misdemeanour and,* ***considering the nature of the offense committed and the possibility of correction of the offender, does not impose a prison sentence.***"

All above mentioned provisions somehow implicitly incorporate the obligation and necessity of considering the fact, if the sentence is "sufficient" for this particular perpetrator. All these sentences also prescribe the possible change of the sentence for the unconditional prison sentence, if the perpetrator will not live orderly life and won't fulfil the conditions, restrictions and obligations imposed by the court:

According to § 50(4) SCC, the conditional prison sentence could be changed to unconditional prison sentence: "*If the convicted person led a normal life during the probationary period and fulfilled the obligation to compensate for the damage caused by the crime or to pay the debt or arrears of alimony, if they were imposed, the court will pronounce that he has proven himself; otherwise,* ***he will decide, possibly already during the probationary period, that the prison sentence will be carried out.***"

According to § 53(6) SCC, the house arrest could be changed to unconditional prison sentence: "*If* ***the convicted person does not comply with the restrictions or obligations arising from the house arrest sentence or obstructs the execution of the control by technical means, the court will convert the sentence into a non-conditional prison sentence*** *in such a way that the unserved day of the house arrest sentence is equal to one day of the non-conditional prison sentence, and at the same time decides on the method of execution of this sentence.*"

According to § 55(4) SCC, the community service sentence could be changed to unconditional prison sentence: "***If at the time of serving the sentence of community service, the convicted person did not lead a proper life or culpably did not perform work in the specified range, or did not fulfil the imposed restrictions or obligations, the court will convert the sentence of community service or its rest into an unconditional prison sentence*** *by ordering one day for every two hours of work not performed of an unconditional prison sentence and at the same time decides on the method of execution of this sentence.*"

According to § 57(3) SCC, the community service sentence could be changed to unconditional prison sentence: "*If the court imposes a financial penalty,* ***it shall establish an alternative penalty of imprisonment*** *for up to five years in the event that the execution of the financial penalty could be intentionally thwarted.*"

On all above-mentioned provisions could be seen, that those punishments are replacing the unconditional prison sentence, but in case of not-fulfilling the conditions of this punishment, it could be again diverted into unconditional prison sentence. Thus, even when using algorithms and producing the result that will lead to imposition of one of these sentences, if at the end this will turn out as wrong outcome, an "inappropriate" result of algorithm could be always "corrected" with change of the already imposed non-prison punishment into the unconditional prison sentence. Thus, using of algorithms by these sentences could not lead to any danger of misuse or mistake of algorithms, because any wrong outcomes that will in reality turn out to be not correct, will be corrected by the court decision on change of such punishment into prison sentence.

11.2.3 Execution procedure

In the phase of execution procedure is relevant the part of execution of prison sentence. In this case, conditional release from prison is possible.

According to § 66(1) SCC: "The court may release the convicted person conditionally, if the convicted person has shown improvement during the execution of the sentence by fulfilling his duties and his behaviour and can be expected to lead an orderly life in the future."

For this purpose, the use of algorithms is welcomed. The danger of reoffending is one of substantial aspects which should be evaluated during the whole process of execution of prison sentence: "*Committing a criminal offense by a person who has been subject to criminal penalties in the past and intervention aimed at correction, not only threatens the interests protected by criminal law but in particular, it undermines confidence in the ability of existing criminal law to contribute to the protection of society means of resocialization.*"[29]

During the execution of prison sentence, the responsible body for re-education and rehabilitation of offender is the Prison and Judicial Guard. The activities Prison and Judicial Guard are ruled by the particular Act No. 4/2001 Coll. on Prison and Judicial Guard, as amended. Under this law, the Prison and Judicial Guard is an armed security corps that performs tasks during execution of custody and during serving a prison sentence.[30] During these tasks, they, e.g.

- provide penitentiary care for convicts serving a prison sentence, and cooperates in providing post-penitentiary care for convicts with state authorities, local self-government bodies, legal entities, natural persons, citizen interest associations, churches, religious societies, foundations and charitable organizations,
- ensure activities aimed at employing accused and convicted persons.[31]

The activities, under which the influence on offender is performed, are mainly ruled by the Act No. 475/2005 Coll. on Execution of Prison Sentence, as amended. In the execution of the sentence, such attitudes and abilities of the convict are supported that will help him to reintegrate into society and respect the legal order. For each convicted person, a so-called "treatment program" is created that is individual for each convict. It is summary of activities, the purpose of which is to ensure, in a differentiated manner, for each convict:

- respecting his rights and at the same time fulfilling his obligations according to laws,
- to support and develop a sense of responsibility, compliance with laws and social norms,
- to support positive personality features of the convict,
- to strengthen his respect for others, self-esteem and positive relationship with his family.

The members of the Prison and Judicial Guard are subjects of a specific education which could be acquired in a specialized study program at Academy of Police Force in Bratislava. Between educational subjects there are also Execution of detention and criminal sanctions, Penitentiary psychology and pedagogy 1+2, Theory of penitentiary treatment and protection of Prison Guards' objects 1+2 and Theory and practice of detention and punishment.[32] In the scope of Penitentiary psychology and pedagogy the graduates "*gain knowledge in the field of penitentiary pedagogy, they will gain knowledge about the issue of pedagogical diagnostics and the application of pedagogical methods in penitentiary practice, as well as the entire pedagogical activity in the conditions of penitentiary facilities. Furthermore, they will be able to specify the pedagogical methods and forms applied in the process of dealing with convicts. By completing the subject, students will gain knowledge about the importance of effective and systematic pedagogical action on persons who have been sentenced to imprisonment.*"[33] All this knowledge gained they will use during their work with convicts. When working with convicts, care is also taken to limit the negative effects of the prison environment.[34] Furthermore, as part of the treatment program, a plan of activities focused on the development of the convict's personality, his appropriate behaviour and value orientation is drawn up.[35] The treatment program establishes a purposeful, complex and structured action on the convict according to his personal characteristics, professional knowledge and level of education in accordance with the purpose of serving the sentence.

The means of dealing with convicts in prison are the following methods: pedagogical and psychological action, methods of social work, constitutional order, disciplinary authority, placement in work, education, cultural and educational activities.[36]

All above-mentioned processes are intended to change the starting positions and features of offender and are prepared, if successful, to readapt the offender after prison sentence on the life outside the prison without committing of crimes. The process of "re-adaptation" of the offender could be finalized also prior of the end of the sentence. This is the point, where the offender is prepared for conditional release. Obviously, he/she must serve at least prescribed part of the sentence stated in the § 66 sec. 1 of the SCC:

a if it is a person convicted of a misdemeanour after serving half of the imposed non-conditional prison sentence or a reduced non-conditional prison sentence by decision of the President of the Slovak Republic,
b if it is a person convicted of a felony after serving two-thirds of the imposed non-conditional prison sentence or by the agreement of the President of the Slovak Republic to a reduced non-conditional prison sentence,
c if it is a person convicted of a felony who, before committing the crime, was not serving a prison sentence after serving half of the imposed non-conditional prison sentence or a reduced non-conditional prison

sentence by the decision of the President of the Slovak Republic; the court will also order an inspection by technical means.

The decision about the conditional release is performed by the court. According to § 415(1) of the SCPC: "*The court decides on a conditional release from imprisonment on the proposal of the prosecutor, the director of the detention centre or the director of the prison in which the sentence is being served, a non-governmental organisation or on the proposal of the convicted person in a public session.*"

For the purpose of the decision on conditional release, the court needs to have the evaluation report from the prison. According to § 64(1) of Decree No. 368/2008 Coll. on Prison Order, as amended: "*In order to demonstrate the fulfilment of the conditions for the conditional release of a convicted person according to a special regulation, the prison prepares an evaluation report. The assessment requested by the court on the proposal for conditional release of the convicted person contains, in addition to personal data, also the data specified in the court judgment and data showing the status of fulfilment of the conditions for conditional release, in particular*

a *assessment of the behaviour of the convicted person in detention and serving the sentence,*
b *the convict's activity and fulfilment of the treatment program,*
c ***resocialization prognosis according to the assessment of the risk of social failure.***"

"*The evaluation according to paragraph 1 must be objective and specific. At the end of the evaluation, the recommendation of the director of the institution, whether the convicted person is given*

a *demonstrates compliance with conditions for conditional release and whether parole is recommended,*
b *partially demonstrates compliance with conditions for conditional release and whether supervised parole is recommended,*
c *partially demonstrates fulfilment of conditions for conditional release and whether parole is not recommended,*
d *does not demonstrate compliance with conditions for conditional release and whether parole is not recommended.*"[37]

It is clear that the Prison and Judicial Guard should submit to the court the evaluation report, which should incorporate also the data, that could be presented by the algorithms. The Prison and Judicial Guard collects all these information during the whole execution of prison sentence, thus could simply "fill in" the database used by algorithms by the appropriate data about the convicted persons and then the "risk of social failure" could be the outcome of the AI than only by the subjective evaluation by the employee of the Prison and Judicial Guard.

11.3 Problems connected with introduction of algorithms in Slovakia

When we are discussing the possible introduction of using of algorithms into Slovak legal order, we need to think also about the obstacles *de facto* and *de iure* that could appear, when such change should be made. We need to analyse, if there are some legislative obstacles that hinder the possible use of algorithms and if the necessary changes of law must be performed prior to introduction of these algorithms in Slovak criminal proceedings (problem no. 1). Then we need to think also about the practical part of such project, because each project is connected also with material and technical support, it needs its time, finances and other organizational or technical changes prior to introduce such mechanism into practice (problem no. 2). Finally, then there is a question of practical application of the new mechanisms, which is always made by the people – judges, prosecutors, police officers, Prison and Judicial Guard, administrative and technical staff. These people need to be prepared and educated to implement these changes into practical life (problem no. 3).

11.3.1 Legislative problems

In Section 11.2 of this chapter, the possible points and stages of Slovak criminal proceedings were identified where the algorithms could be used. Before implementing such procedure, there must be made an analysis, if there are not current legal provisions that bar these activities and tools in criminal proceedings.

When we are discussing the outcome of the algorithm as the information that should be used in criminal proceedings by any subject and in any stage, it needs to be defined as a particular element, that is falling under specific provision of the Slovak Criminal Procedure Code, because according to Slovak Constitution, "State authorities can act only on the basis of the constitution, within its limits and the scope established by law."[38] So the use of algorithms must fall under specific current provisions of law or the new law should be adopted to introduce such procedure.

Each decision in criminal proceedings must be made upon evidence. The definition of "evidence" is incorporated in § 119(3) of SCPC: "Everything that can contribute to the proper clarification of the subject matter and that was obtained from the means of evidence according to this law or according to a special law can serve as evidence. Means of evidence are, in particular, the questioning of the accused, witnesses, experts, opinions and expert statements, verification of the statement on the spot, reconnaissance, reconstruction, investigative attempt, inspection, things and documents important for criminal proceedings, notification, information obtained by using information and technical means or means operatively - search activity."

As it is clear from the above-mentioned definition, the definition of evidence is quite wide and as evidence could be used anything what was taken from any evidence source. These "sources of evidence" are not explicitly enumerated in Slovak Criminal Procedure Code, but only exemplarily. As the source of evidence could serve also the outcome of AI report. However, the procedure of obtaining AI result must be somewhere defined and ruled by the particular provisions of Slovak Criminal Procedure Code or other specific law, because also second condition must be fulfilled – to be obtained "according to this law or according to a special law." Thus, prior to adopt the algorithms into Slovak criminal proceedings, the most lawful way is to do necessary changes in Slovak Criminal Procedure Code or in other law to implement this new "means of evidence" into the criminal proceedings, otherwise the condition of "lawfulness" of this evidence is doubtful. However, we can discuss, if there is a possibility to define the outcome of algorithms with the current terms of "means of evidence," e.g. *opinions and expert statements*. If there will be special experts empowered to use these algorithms, it could fall within the meaning of "opinion." On the other side, we can also state, that the report from this program is only a "document," which could fall within the meaning of documents, what is quite wide term and any report written on the paper could be labelled as a "document." From this point of view, the wider discussion of experts will be suitable, in which will be resolved, if the outcome of algorithms is a specific new tool of evidence or if it is only a form of "opinion" or "document."

When we are discussing the particular provisions ruling the legal tools described in Section 11.2 of this chapter (e.g. conditional termination of the criminal proceedings, reconciliation), they have no specific level of evidence that must be collected, nor they have any demands on quality of this evidence. It is upon the decisive body (in this case mainly prosecutor), what will he/she take into consideration. Thus, from this point of view, the provisions of § 216 SCPC and § 220 SCPC ruling these tools are not creating any obstacle for using of algorithms.

When we are talking about the imposing of punishment in the trial phase of the proceedings, also the court decides upon the evidence of the case. According to § 168(1) SCPC: "*If the judgment contains a justification, the court will briefly state in it, which facts were taken as proven,* ***the evidence on which the findings of fact are based on, and what considerations were***

used when evaluating the evidence presented, *especially if the proofs contradict each other. From the justification,* ***the relevant evidence must be indicated,*** *why the proposal to take additional evidence is not suitable and what legal opinions were expressed when assessing the evidence according to the provisions of the law in question of guilt and the penalty.*"

From this point of view, it is not a problem to indicate also on the AI report as the "evidence" on which is based the decision on the sentence. The court must only explain and clarify why the court decided in this way and how this decision results from the court's findings.

During the execution procedure, the situation is similar. In this part of proceedings, the court decides also upon the evidence and the decision should according to § 176(2) SCPC incorporate: "*In the justification, if it comes into consideration according to the nature of the matter, must be stated the facts that are considered to be proven, the evidence on which the findings of fact are based, the considerations by which the decision-making authority was guided in evaluating the evidence, as well as legal considerations, on the basis of which, according to the relevant provisions of the law, the decision-making authority assessed the proven facts.*"

The final answer on the question, if there are any "legal" obstacles for the introduction of algorithms in Slovak Criminal proceedings, should be that there are no significant legal obstacles barring the introduction of algorithms into Slovak legal order.

11.3.2 Material and technical problems

When we are thinking about practical introduction of algorithms into criminal proceedings, couple of problematic issues arise.

Firstly, we need to think who should create the applicable software and where the money will come from. There is necessary to mention, that criminal proceedings is the procedure financed by the state budget and that the state processes should be financed by using the public procurement procedure, which is quite complicated and long procedure. This could result to a very long and complicated process where will be hardly possible to find the suitable "supplier" for such a project. We can mention the former process in Slovak Republic connected with the supply of the "electronic monitoring system." In this case to public procurement was announced in the year 2013 and only two suppliers applied for the public procurement, from those only one fulfilled the conditions for the contract.[39] Thus, it could take years to find the suitable supplier for such specific product. And also, we need to have the calculation prior to the public procurement, how much should this "business" cost and what should be actually the attributes of the software, which must be defined in the offer for the public procurement, that the companies actually know what they should provide for the contractor.

After creating the suitable software, the question should be answered who should be responsible for collecting the data, upon which will be performed the assessment of offender. These data could be not collected by the creator of the software, because the data usable in criminal proceedings about the citizens could be collected only by the specific state authorities (e.g. police force, prosecutor, court) and need the appropriate legislative scheme under which they will be collected. "*All research on criminal law and related contents needs a large number of criminal law contents as support. Therefore, the target data to be collected includes various criminal law provisions.*"[40]

When we think about the possible use of algorithms, these could be used before a decision in criminal proceedings is reached. Thus, these data should be collected about the persons and their life outside of the prison prior to committing of the crime (sometimes it could be also after committing of a crime), but the facts should be from the time prior to the prosecutor's or court's decision. The responsibility for such data collecting could be entrusted only to the police, which could make operative activities or surveillance to collect the information about the persons from the "criminal environment" even before they commit the crime. These activities could fall within the "preventive measures" what is one of the priority tasks of the Police force:

> In fulfilling its tasks, the police force cooperates with public authorities, armed forces, armed security forces, armed corps, the Slovak Information Service, legal entities and natural persons; cooperates with local self-government authorities especially in determining the priorities of crime prevention, protection of public order and the focus of the fight against crime.[41]

Other persons responsible to add data into the database could be also probationary and mediation officers of the court. According to § 3(1) of the Act No. 550/2003 Coll. on probationary and mediation, as amended officers: "*The probation and mediation officer helps ensure that, in appropriate cases, the criminal case* ***can be finished in one of the special methods of criminal proceedings or that a non-custodial sentence can be imposed and properly carried out,*** *or that detention can be replaced by another appropriate measure. For this purpose, the probation and mediation officer*

a ***procures documents related to the person of the accused about his family, social and work environment,***
b ***creates the conditions for a decision on the conditional suspension of criminal proceedings or reconciliation,***

c *carries out actions for the purpose of concluding an agreement between the victim and the accused on compensation for damage caused by a criminal offense or for the purpose of removing damage caused by a criminal offense,*
d *supervises the behaviour of the accused during the probationary period and controls the execution of sentences not associated with imprisonment,*
e *performs other actions in criminal proceedings during probation and mediation.*"

Any information collected by the police in the view of the Act No. 171/1993 Coll. on Police Force, as amended or by the probationary and mediation officers under Act No. 550/2003 Coll. on probationary and mediation, as amended could be inserted into the database and with such database would then work prosecutors and judges when reaching the particular decisions described in Sections 11.2.1 and 11.2.2 of this chapter.

However, the situation is different for the decisions about the conditional release from prison sentence (Section 11.2.3), because for this purpose also the information about the life of the convicts in the prison should be taken into consideration. These data could be collected only by the Prison and Judicial Guard. From this point of view, maybe two databases should be created – one for prosecutors and judges in the pre-trial and trial proceedings, where the life outside the prison should be considered and the second database used in the execution procedure, where mainly the life in prison should be evaluated and the reports from the execution of prison should be considered.

From the above-mentioned analysis is clear, that before the real implementation of the algorithms into criminal proceedings, couple of technical and material questions should be resolved and discussed throughout the expert community.

11.3.3 Personal problems

After creation of the software and after filling in the data into database there is the question of real usage of this new tool by the prosecutors and judges.

The current legal order doesn't recognize this special tool as the explicit evidence in criminal proceedings. From this point of view, under current legislative situation, the prosecutors and judges could use the AI and algorithms for their decisions, however they are not obliged to do that. There are not provisions that explicitly enumerate the evidence and documents that the prosecutor or judge should have before reaching the decision. "*The law enforcement authorities and the court evaluate the evidence obtained lawfully according to their internal belief based on a careful consideration of all the circumstances of the case individually and in their connections, regardless of whether it was obtained by the court, the law enforcement authorities or any of the parties."*[42]

There is no obligation that prosecutor should have a particular document or evidence before he/she will decide according to § 216 or § 220 SCPC. There is also no provision, what the judge shall have for disposal prior to impose the "alternative punishment." The only case, when the court is obliged to have certain special documents, is the decision about the "order life" after probation period: "*The court monitors the behaviour of a person sentenced to imprisonment, the execution of which has been conditionally suspended with probation supervision during the probationary period. In particular, it finds out how the convict fulfils the obligations and restrictions resulting from the imposed probation supervision;* ***for this purpose, he mainly makes written requests to the state administration bodies or the municipality and the interest association of citizens in the place of residence of the convicted person and the convicted person's employer. Before issuing a decision, the court always requests a copy of the criminal record of the convicted person and from the Police Department in whose district the convicted person resides, a report on whether criminal prosecution is being conducted against him, and from the authority that hears offenses whether he has been in a probationary period punished for a similar offence."***[43]

Without necessary changes to Slovak Criminal Procedure Code and Slovak Criminal Code, there is only little hope that the prosecutors and judges will use voluntarily new tools, that they are not used to work with until today. The studies and findings from the UK showed, e.g. that police officers have "*sceptical attitude towards predictive technologies and, in a few cases, these officers have expressed a reluctance to use predictive technologies."*[44]

"There are also many inhibitors to adoption, primarily consisting of a general scepticism regarding algorithmic systems and their effectiveness, as well as a rather negative, mistrustful attitude towards the automation of decisions. ... Study confirmed that the complexity of an algorithmic tool can become a problem for users if they are not able to understand the decision process."[45]

The same attitude could be awaited also in other countries, where the algorithms should be implemented. Obligatory educational trainings and other promotion activities need to exist to create the confidence in such tool in persons, that were used for decades to decide only upon the "paper evidence." The same situation occurred with the imposition of "electronic monitoring" in criminal proceedings in Slovak Republic. Even with couple of tools, where these new electronic devices could be used for monitoring of accused and convicted persons, the judges only very rarely used them,[46] because they had no prior experience with it and it was for them "*too complicated and time consuming,*" so they refused to use them.[47]

11.4 Conclusion

The positive impact of algorithms in criminal proceedings could be summarized as following: "*The implementation of algorithmic tools was described as promoting general reflection on processes and often improving their structuring and standardisation, ... Hence, algorithms were perceived as fostering standardisation and professionalization. ... Algorithmic software could help to externally justify the assessment. ... If the algorithm confirmed the assessment of the user, it would serve as internal and external legitimation. ... Algorithms can create transparency provided that they are comprehensible; this is in contrast to human decision-making, which largely remains inscrutable.*"[48] "*Rather than relying on a single agent's personal assessments of whether a particular suspect is likely to reoffend, we might hope ... to yield some objective measures, insulated from individual irrationality or animus.*"[49] "*Objective statistical assessments are, in fact, superior to human judgment.*"[50]

The use of algorithm has great potential value for the criminal proceedings also in Slovak Republic, mainly in the scope of restorative justice. "*Restorative justice has great potential to be the justice of the future, to contribute to the elimination of crime and curing the shortcomings of the de lege lata status and positively influencing the resocialization of offenders.*"[51] The algorithms could help to indicate cases, where the application of restorative justice is most suitable.

The algorithms have been used in criminal proceedings already for decades in couple of countries and they show the positive aspects for accused, convicts and also for the work of prosecutors and judges. To introduce such methods also into Slovak legal order, couple of steps need to be done, from legislative changes to personal educational activities. Together with those steps also huge material and financial resources need to be accumulated for managing such new project. And also, it takes time to make such legislative changes, to create the software and databases, to learn the people how to use the new tools. Even when we see great potential for using of the algorithms in criminal proceedings in Slovak Republic, there will be the question of far future to prepare the society for such huge change in the traditional criminal proceedings in Slovak Republic.

Notes

1 This work was supported by the scientific project of Visegrad Fund N. 22210121.

2 JORGENSEN, Renée. Algorithms and the Individual in Criminal Law. Canadian Journal of Philosophy. Volume 52, 1/2022, 61.

3 CARVALHO, Henrique. The Preventive Turn in Criminal Law. Oxford: Oxford University Press, 2017.

4 SIMMLER, Monika, BRUNNER, Simona, CANOVA, Giulia, SCHEDLER, Kuno. Smart criminal justice: exploring the use of algorithms in the Swiss criminal justice system. Artificial Intelligence and Law, N. 31 (2023), p. 215.

5 SIMMLER, BRUNNER, CANOVA, SCHEDLER, Smart criminal justice, p. 234.

6 MIRÓ-LLINARES, Fernando. Predictive policing: Utopia or dystopia? On attitudes towards the use of big data algorithms for law enforcement. IDP-Internet, Law and Politics. Volume 30, p. 11.

7 SIMMLER, BRUNNER, CANOVA, SCHEDLER, Smart criminal justice, p. 213.

8 SIMMLER, BRUNNER, CANOVA, SCHEDLER, Smart criminal justice, p. 227.

9 PRUSS, Dasha. Mechanical Jurisprudence and Domain Distortion: How Predictive Algorithms Warp the Law, History and Philosophy of Science. University of Pittsburgh PSA 2021 Proceedings Preprint, pp. 11–12.

10 KHARCHENKO, Tatyana Yu, VORONINA, Irina E. The model of the decision-making support procedure on the example of criminal proceedings, Journal of Physics: Conference Series, 1203/2019, 012054, p. 1.

11 MURATOVA, Nadezhda, SOLOVYEVA, Natalya, SHINKARUK, Vladimir, RUDKOVSKIY, Victor, FANTROV, Pavel. Digitalization of the decision-making process in criminal proceedings. SHS Web of Conferences, 109/2021, 01026, p. 5.

12 SIMMLER, BRUNNER, CANOVA, SCHEDLER, Smart criminal justice, p. 215.

13 See also MIRÓ-LLINARES, Predictive policing: Utopia or dystopia?, pp. 5–6.

14 See, e.g., XU, Yaqiong, FENG, Tao. Analysis of Legal Issues of the Crime of Endangering Public Safety Based on Data Mining Algorithm. Hindawi. Security and Communication Networks, Volume 2022, Article ID 4794752, pp. 1–12. https://doi.org/10.1155/2022/4794752.

15 Actually, this part of algorithms using is close to deciding about the "guilt" by the computer. "Algorithms can be deployed to support legal assessments and decision-making in criminal proceedings. This field has not yet been developed to any great extent." In: SIMMLER, BRUNNER, CANOVA, SCHEDLER, Smart criminal justice, p. 216.

16 "Algorithms are mainly used to evaluate offender profiles and recidivism forecasts, eventually affecting sentencing." In: SIMMLER, BRUNNER, CANOVA, SCHEDLER, Smart criminal justice, p. 216.

17 "Determine the need for further examination of a convicted offender or decide on execution mode, probation, and early release." In: SIMMLER, BRUNNER, CANOVA, SCHEDLER, Smart criminal justice, p. 217.

18 Act No. 301/2005 Coll. on Criminal Procedure Code, as amended (hereinafter referred to as "Slovak Criminal Procedure Code" or "SCPC").

19 ČENTÉŠ, Jozef. Trestné právo procesné. Osobitná časť. Bratislava: Heuréka, 2016, p. 41.

20 ČENTÉŠ, Trestné právo procesné. Osobitná časť, p. 41.

21 ČENTÉŠ, Trestné právo procesné. Osobitná časť, pp. 56, 60–61.

22 ŽOFČÁK, Michal. Mediácia – proces medzi páchateľom a obeťou trestného činu. Bratislava Legal Forum 2018: Constitutional, Statutory and Criminological Attributes for Crime Victims. Proceedings from the scientific conference organized by Comenius University Bratislava, Faculty of Law, February 22–23, 2018, Bratislava: Faculty of Law, Comenius University, 2018, p. 245.

23 ŽOFČÁK, Mediácia – proces medzi páchateľom a obeťou trestného činu. Bratislava Legal Forum 2018

24 ČENTÉŠ, Trestné právo procesné, pp. 92–97, ŠTRKOLEC, Miroslav. Alternatívne spôsoby výkonu trestov – trestnoprocesné aspekty v kontexte náhrady škody poškodenému. Milestones of law in the Central Europe 2018. Proceedings from the scientific conference organized by Comenius University Bratislava, Faculty of Law, April 12–14, 2018, Bratislava: Comenius University, Faculty of Law, 2018, p. 450.

25 ŠTRKOLEC, Alternatívne spôsoby výkonu trestovp. 452.

26 STRÉMY, Tomáš, KLÁTIK, Jaroslav. Alternatívne tresty. Bratislava: C. H. Beck, 2018, pp. 25–26; see also MADLIAK, Jozef. Úvahy o pojme a účele trestu. Aktuálne otázky trestného zákonodarstva. Proceedings from international conference held on January 19, 2012. Bratislava: Paneuropean university, 2012, p. 132.

27 JURISOVÁ, Michaela. Vybrané fenomenologické ukazovatele verzus alternatívne tresty optikou verejnej mienky v podmienkach Slovenskej republiky. In: STRÉMY, Tomáš (ed.). Restoratívna justícia a systém alternatívnych trestov. Proceedings from international conference. Praha: Leges, 2017, p. 440.

28 Law no. 300/2005 Coll. The Criminal Code, as amended (hereinafter referred to as "Slovak Criminal Code" or "SCC").

29 GRIGER, Jozef, KRAMARČÍKOVÁ, Lenka, ĽORKO, Jakub. Metodika určovanie penitenciárnej recidívy. In: GRIGER, Jozef, TURAY, Lukáš (eds.). Resocializácia odsúdených a jej perspektívy. Proceedings from international conference, Omšenie, November 11–13, 2019, Bratislava: Generálne riaditeľstvo Zboru väzenskej a justičnej stráže, 2020, p. 54.

30 § 1 of Act No. 4/2001 Coll. on Prison and Judicial Guard, as amended.

31 § 4(1)(e)(f) of Act No. 4/2001 Coll. on Prison and Judicial Guard, as amended.

32 JURISOVÁ, Michaela. Špecializácia ZVJS v podmienkach Akadémie Policajného zboru v Bratislave. In: GRIGER, Jozef, TURAY, Lukáš (eds.). Resocializácia odsúdených a jej perspektívy. Proceedings from international conference, Omšenie, November 11–13, 2019, Bratislava: Generálne riaditeľstvo Zboru väzenskej a justičnej stráže, 2020, p. 148.

33 JURISOVÁ, Špecializácia ZVJS v podmienkach Akadémie Policajného zboru v Bratislave.

34 § 11 of Act No. 475/2005 Coll. on Execution of Prison Sentence, as amended.

35 § 15(3) of Act No. 475/2005 Coll. on Execution of Prison Sentence, as amended.

36 § 16 of Act No. 475/2005 Coll. on Execution of Prison Sentence, as amended.

37 § 64(2) of Decree No. 368/2008 Coll. on Prison Order, as amended.

38 § 2(2) of Slovak Constitution No. 460/1992 Coll., as amended.

39 Správa Národného kontrolného úradu o výsledku kontroly využívania Elektronického systému monitoringu obvinených a odsúdených osôb (Report of the National Control Office on the result of the control of the use of the Electronic Monitoring System of accused and convicted persons), 2023, p. 4.

40 YANG, Xiaolong. Automatic Decision Algorithm of Interpretation Power in Criminal Justice Based on Data Activity Consultant. Hindawi. Mobile

Information Systems. Volume 2021, Article ID 3922660, p. 2. https://doi.org/10.1155/2021/3922660.

41 § 3 of Act No. 171/1993 Coll. on Police Force, as amended.

42 § 2(12) SCPC.

43 § 418(1) SCPC.

44 SANDHU, Ayay, FUSSEY, Peter. The "uberization of policing"? How police negotiate and operationalise predictive policing technology. Policy and Society. Volume 31, 1/2021, 66.

45 SIMMLER, BRUNNER, CANOVA, SCHEDLER, Smart criminal justice, pp. 227, 231.

46 The ESMO project integrating the technology of trustworthy and reliable monitoring was supposed to bring more extensive the use of alternative sentences of house arrest, which should have been ensured by the planned capacity project with the possibility to simultaneously monitor up to 2,000 accused or convicted persons per year, as a result of which public finances were to be saved. ... all the technical devices purchased for monitoring people were used on average only less than 10 percent of the person-days of their total possible capacity. In: Správa Národného kontrolného úradu o výsledku kontroly využívania Elektronického systému monitoringu obvinených a odsúdených osôb (Report of the National Control Office on the result of the control of the use of the Electronic Monitoring System of accused and convicted persons), 2023, pp. 1, 5.

47 HOPKOVÁ, Denisa. Sudcom chýbajú úradníci, väzenské náramky za milióny ležia v skladoch. Available at: https://www.aktuality.sk/clanok/660144/naramky-pre-vaeznov-prachniveju-v-skladoch-a-sudcom-chybaju-uradnici-aby-naramky-pridelili/, published on February 2, 2019, last visit: June 30, 2023.

48 SIMMLER, BRUNNER, CANOVA, SCHEDLER, Smart criminal justice, pp. 229, 231.

49 JORGENSEN, Algorithms and the Individual in Criminal Law, p. 61.

50 PRUSS. Mechanical Jurisprudence and Domain Distortion, p. 2.

51 STRÉMY, Tomáš, TURAY, Lukáš. Resocializácia odsúdených a restoratívna justícia. In: GRIGER, Jozef, TURAY, Lukáš (eds.). Resocializácia odsúdených a jej perspektívy. Proceedings from international conference, Omšenie, November 11–13, 2019, Bratislava: Generálne riaditeľstvo Zboru väzenskej a justičnej stráže, 2020, p. 143.

Chapter 12

Using artificial intelligence in combatting cyber harassment and cyber bullying

Lenka Miklóssyová

12.1 Introduction

The phenomenon of cyber harassment has emerged as a pressing concern in the modern digital age, transcending borders and affecting individuals in numerous ways. Cyberstalking and cyberbullying have become a serious social problem because they happen in an anonymous and often difficult to monitor environment. These forms of electronic harassment use the anonymity and availability of technology to continuously monitor, threaten, or ridicule individuals. Victims often face prolonged psychological pressure, feelings of fear and isolation, which can lead to anxiety, depression, and, in extreme cases, self-harm or suicide. Research indicates that the emotional toll on victims can be comparable to that of physical harassment, causing profound disruptions in their daily lives and well-being.[1]

The danger of cyberstalking and cyberbullying is that the perpetrators can harass the victims at any time and in any place, thereby violating their safe space. In 2021, recognizing the growing threat posed by cyber harassment, the Slovak republic enacted a crucial amendment to the Act No. 300/2005 Coll., the Criminal Code (hereinafter referred to as the "**Criminal Code**"), marking a significant step in addressing this issue within the country.

This amendment introduced a comprehensive legal definition of **cyber harassment**, categorizing it as a *series of actions executed through electronic communication services, computer systems, or computer networks that result in a substantial degradation of the victim's quality of life*. New provision of § 360b of Criminal Code, which was incorporated into the Criminal Code by the aforementioned amendment, defines **cyber harassment** as:

- a humiliating, intimidating, improperly acting on behalf of, or otherwise harassing the victim on a prolonged basis; or
- b unlawfully disclosing or making available to a third party a visual, audio, or visual-audio recording of the victim's speech of a personal

DOI: 10.4324/9781003531500-20

nature, obtained with his or her consent, which is capable of significantly undermining his or her reputation or causing him or her other serious harm to his or her rights.[2]

The distinction between these types of behavior falling under the offence of cyber harassment suggests that in the first case this can be referred to as **cyberbullying**, while in the second case the behavior is more of a **violation of the victim's privacy** on the internet.

In this day and age, when we feel that cyber harassment is **much more prevalent** and **pervasive** on the internet than it was a few years ago, and despite the introduction of this legislation, the conviction rate for the crime of cyber harassment has remained quite low, with only **12 persons convicted** of this offense and **one of them actively serving a prison sentence.** This raises important questions about the effectiveness of the legal framework in combating cyber harassment and the broader challenges associated with addressing this issue in general. To address this persistent problem, a couple of Slovak scientists created an AI solution called "Troll Wall." This tool aims to combat hate comments and spam effectively, with a primary focus on moderating the comments section on various websites. By doing so, it helps to create a safer and more respectful online environment for the audience.

In this chapter, we will explore the complex landscape of cyber harassment in the Slovak republic, examining the legal framework, the challenges faced in prosecuting the perpetrators, and the potential impact of AI tools like Troll Wall in mitigating this issue. By shedding light on these aspects, we hope to contribute to a deeper understanding of cyber harassment and the measures that can be taken to address it effectively.

12.2 Cybercrimes

In general, cybercrime can be defined as any criminal activity involving a **computer** or a **network.** It encompasses a wide range of illegal activities that exploit the vulnerabilities of the digital world. When we delve deeper into the issue of cybercrimes, we can categorize them in three elementary categories – criminal activities that are *enhanced* by internet (e.g. credit card fraud), criminal activities that are *generalized* by the internet (e.g. bullying), and criminal activities that are *created* by the internet (e.g. hacking).[3] Cybercrimes therefore include a wide range of illegal activities, some of them being for example hacking, phishing, identity theft, cyberstalking, ransomware attacks, online fraud, and many more. In this chapter, however, we aim to specifically bring attention to **cyber harassment.**

Cyber harassment is a form of cybercrime that can be listed in the second category – a criminal activity that is generalized by the internet. Cyber harassment utilizes digital technologies, particularly social media and messaging platforms. This particular form of cybercrime has become a prevalent issue in today's society. It manifests in various forms, such as *threatening, scaring, shaming* by sharing or disseminating embarrassing or private information with the intent to humiliate or harm the victim's reputation, or even *stalking*, which means that the cybercriminal is monitoring, tracking, or obsessively following someone's online activities, often leading to a persistent invasion of privacy and emotional distress.[4]

Research shows that a significant number of adolescents come into contact with cyber harassment during their teenage years. According to a systematic review article that reviewed a total of 63 studies focusing on cyberbullying prevalence and risk factors during a five-year period, "*the prevalence rates of cyberbullying preparation ranged from 6.0 to 46.3%, while the rates of cyberbullying victimization ranged from 13.99 to 57.5%.*"[5]

Cyber harassment poses a multitude of dangers that extend far beyond the digital realm, impacting individuals and society as a whole. Firstly, it inflicts **significant emotional and psychological harm** on its victims, eroding their mental well-being and self-esteem. The constant barrage of abusive messages, threats, and harmful content can lead to severe **anxiety, depression,** and even **post-traumatic stress disorder**, affecting one's ability to lead a healthy and productive life. Moreover, cyber harassment often targets **vulnerable individuals**, including minors and marginalized communities, worsening the harm and perpetuating **systemic inequalities**. This conclusion was also proved by a study carried out by Slovak Research Institute of Child Psychology and Pathopsychology, which stated that: "*We also find differences between rural and urban adolescent respondents. Those from rural areas are more likely to experience name-calling and mocking (rural – 58.3%, urban – 38.6%), meeting someone pretending to be someone else (rural – 21.1%, urban – 9.4%), sexual innuendos and comments (rural – 40.0%, urban – 16.5%), and coming across pornography that they were not interested in (rural – 19.4%, urban – 9.4%). These differences are statistically significant. We ask what accounts for these differences.*"[6]

Beyond its immediate victims, cyber harassment can also lead to a toxic online environment, stifling free expression, and discouraging individuals from participating in digital spaces. In extreme cases, it can escalate to **physical harm** or even **loss of life**, making it a huge societal problem that requires proactive measures to combat and prevent it.[7]

12.2.1 Dangerous electronic harassment

In Slovak republic, the terms of "cyberbullying" or "cyber harassment" were not defined or known by criminal law until 2021. Such actions of the perpetrator depending on the facts of the case could be classified as either stalking, extortion, coercion, sexual abuse, etc. In July 2021, an offence of **dangerous electronic harassment (cyber harassment)** was added to the Slovak Criminal Code. Act No. 236/2021 Coll. supplementing Act No. 300/2005 Coll. on the Criminal Code as amended (hereinafter referred to as the "**Criminal Code Amendment**") defined cyber harassment as a series of actions conducted through electronic communication services, computer systems, or computer networks that cause a substantial degradation of the quality of life for the victim. These actions can take various forms, including continuous **humiliation, intimidation**, improper **impersonation**, or any other type of harassment that aims to harm the targeted individual.[8]

Furthermore, the legislation explicitly addresses the **unlawful disclosure of a recording** obtained **with consent**. This provision underscores the significance of consent in maintaining privacy and preventing the misuse of personal recordings in a digital context. For this type of offence, the law prescribes a maximum sentence of up to **three years of imprisonment.**[9]

Regarding the limit of the criminal rate, one could argue that, given the disparity between the criminal rates for offences such as dangerous threats under § 360 of the Criminal Code or dangerous stalking under § 360a of the Criminal Code (up to one year of imprisonment) and the offence of cyber harassment (up to three years of imprisonment), it would be "worth it" in terms of the scope of possible punishment not to move into cyberspace and to stick to the "classic" physical contact with the victim instead. However, the legislator's justification for the relatively high upper limit of the criminal rate lies in the fact that the use of **law enforcement access to data** constituting **telecommunications secrets** requires a **minimum** upper limit of **three years' imprisonment**, or the inclusion of the offence among the enumerated offences. And while the explicit inclusion of this offence among the enumerated offences would be problematic, as it might not meet the requirement of "seriousness" from the point of view of the jurisprudence of the Court of Justice of the European Union, if the upper limit of the criminal rate would be lower, it would make it more difficult for law enforcement to investigate this crime. The legislator therefore claims that, since there is no minimum lower limit of the criminal rate in this case and it is an offence in which the *material corrective*[10] is also taken into account in cases of conduct which is not dangerous to society, **there should be no disproportionately severe punishment of offenders.**[11]

The explanatory memorandum to the Criminal Code Amendment states that the reason for its adoption was "a particularly acute problem of cyberbullying in cyberspace – the so-called cyberbullying, or cyber harassment," which "started to occur especially in times of the COVID-19 pandemic when there was a broad-spectrum transfer of work and private activities of the inhabitants of the Slovak Republic to the digital space."[12] The explanatory memorandum also stated, that: "*Research to date shows that cyberbullying is one of the most common negative phenomena on the Internet. Aggressors find it easier to hurt someone they don't have to look directly in the eye, they are less aware of the emotions and hurt of the victim, and they are less aware of the seriousness of their actions and their responsibility for them – because the aggressor is protected from direct exposure by his or her apparent anonymity. For the victim, however, cyber harassment or bullying is even more serious – they cannot escape it anywhere, not even to the safety of their home. Aggressors can reach the victim at any time and in any place.*"[13] This growing problem of cyberbullying and cyber harassment was also confirmed by statistical data, as according to the aforementioned research conducted by the Research Institute of Child Psychology and Pathopsychology, the most frequent online experiences among young people are name-calling and ridicule (stated by 49.8% of respondents), the second most common negative phenomenon they encounter is slander, spreading false information (stated by 42.6% of respondents), followed by sexual innuendo and comments (stated by 30.0% of respondents).[14]

Nevertheless, as of today, there is only one person serving a prison sentence for this offence in the Slovak republic and total of 12 persons convicted.[15] We could argue that this low number of persons convicted of dangerous electronic harassment occurs precisely because of the fact that convicting offenders for cyber harassment presents numerous challenges for law enforcement agencies. On the other hand, a question arises, in which cases is cyber harassment such a serious act that it should be punished by means of criminal law, which should rightly be used in accordance with the principle of **ultima ratio.**

The ineffectiveness of the investigation of this crime lies in the **anonymous nature** of the internet, which often allows perpetrators to hide behind pseudonyms or false identities, making it challenging to identify them. This anonymity can extend across national borders, complicating jurisdictional issues and requiring international cooperation, which can be time-consuming and resource intensive.[16] Moreover, the fast-paced and constantly evolving environment of the digital world means that law enforcement agencies have to cope with new technologies, platforms, and tactics used by cyber harassers, which requires **constant training and adaptation.** Furthermore, the vast volume of online content and communication makes it difficult to prioritize and investigate each case effectively, leading to **limited resources** being allocated to these cases. Finally, **proving intent** and the

harm inflicted in cyberspace can be complex, as digital evidence may not always be available or easy to interpret. All these factors combine to create a significant hurdle for law enforcement in effectively combating and punishing cyber harassment.

In regard to the **ultima ratio** principle, we can argue that criminal law is/ought to be a means of punishing the **most serious manifestations of anti-social activity** that cannot be punished in any other effective way. On the other hand, when it comes to cyber space, the only entity that has the **proper means** at its disposal for the possibility of a proper investigation and clarification of such an act, are the **law enforcement authorities**. Although this is also a major challenge for them, as we have already stated in the preceding paragraphs, no other entity has the **capabilities** (for example in relation to invasion of privacy of offenders) to be able to effectively investigate such an act.

However, as technology advances, we are discovering new and new ways to combat this growing problem. There are now new **technological solutions** that may help to streamline the battle against this issue. And one of them is the use of AI and algorithms.

12.3 The role of artificial intelligence in combatting cyber harassment

In general, AI algorithms can be used in various ways to moderate cyberbullying, offering both **reactive** and **proactive** solutions. **Reactive moderation** involves users reporting harmful content, which AI algorithms can then review for accuracy. **Proactive moderation**, on the other hand, leverages AI tools like *natural language processing* (NLP), *machine learning* (ML), and *deep learning* (DL) to automatically detect and flag potentially harmful behavior in real time, even before it is reported by users. AI can scan large volumes of text, images, or videos to identify patterns of abusive language or behavior, helping platforms to identify and remove harmful content.

Typically, cyberbullying is prohibited on social media, with companies outlining this in their policy documents. Nevertheless, there are large volumes of cyberbullying content on these platforms, and social media companies face challenges in moderating or addressing such incidents. As a result, they are increasingly turning to aforementioned artificial intelligence (AI) and algorithmic tools to automate moderation tasks. While users can still report cyberbullying to platforms (reactive moderation), AI is also being progressively employed to scan and review content before it is flagged, as part of proactive moderation efforts.[17]

One of the models intended for combatting cyberbullying was also invented in Slovak republic. In March 2023, a couple of Slovak IT specialists invented an AI tool called **Troll Wall.**[18] This AI tool performs automated comment moderation and deals with hate comments or spam. TrollWall is trained on **human moderation of real comments** and **hides** comments based on the analysis of comments' meaning, context, and tone. If there's any mistake when determining the content of a comment, the moderator can always override and hide or unhide comments manually. Hidden comments can always be seen by the author and his friends or contacts to minimize the risk of worsening the situation, the author of the hidden comment therefore never knows about the fact that his comment was hidden.[19]

Denník N, a popular news platform in the Slovak republic started testing this tool a while ago, and during a period of a few months Troll Wall checked more than *108 thousand comments* on their Facebook page. Of this number of comments, it hid more than *14 thousand posts*, which is roughly *13 percent*. That means that approximately 13 percent of comments contained some form of hate speech, cyber harassment, or dangerous false information.[20]

The **advantages** of this leap forward are that the use of AI technology has revolutionized our ability to respond faster and more efficiently to cyber harassment. With solutions like Troll Wall, toxic content can be hidden within seconds, even during live video streaming. On the other hand, it **doesn't address the main issue** behind the origin of these posts and **doesn't** in any way **prevent** the perpetrator from continuing this behavior.

The biggest challenge for Troll Wall still lies with platforms like Facebook, where even reported death threats often go unaddressed due to insufficient tools and resources. It is crucial for social media platforms and technology companies to invest in advanced AI algorithms and robust moderation tools. **Collaboration** between platforms, policymakers, and the community is essential to develop strategies that effectively combat cyber harassment.[21]

12.3.1 The challenges of using artificial intelligence in combatting cyber harassment

While using AI algorithms may be of big help when combatting cyber harassment and cyber bullying, we still face various challenges while using them. **Proactive moderation** raises concerns about **users' privacy**, as content is proactively scanned, including direct messages, and it also affects users' freedom of expression when mistakes occur, such as the removal of non-bullying content. Only a few companies provide transparency on how this moderation works, whether direct messages are included in the process, or whether children's views have been sought regarding the desirability, perceived effectiveness, and design of such interventions. And it is children and young people who are the most at-risk group affected by this problem.[22]

With the adoption of the United Nations General Comment No. 25, children's rights under the United Nations Convention on the Rights of the Child (hereinafter referred to as the "**UNCRC**") extend to the digital realm. This means children have the right not only to protection (e.g., online safety and protection from cyberbullying) but also to privacy (in relation to AI-based monitoring), as well as the right to participation—the right to be consulted on issues that affect them, as outlined in Article 12 of the UNCRC. The design of online safety measures on platforms is thus highly relevant to young people. Researchers have consistently emphasized the need for online safety designs to strike a **balance** between **children's rights to protection** and **participation.**[23]

Using AI algorithms in this area may be met with other challenges as well, some of them for example being:

- **Over-blocking:** automatic moderation algorithms can be excessive in flagging and removing content, leading to the **unintentional censorship** of legitimate comments that do not violate the community guidelines. This can stifle free speech and limit constructive discussion. Moderation algorithms may struggle with **nuanced content**, **sarcasm**, **humor**, or **cultural references**, often resulting in false positives where some comments may be mistakenly flagged as violations. Moreover, automated moderation may not consider the context in which a comment is made, potentially **misinterpreting** the intent behind a statement, and removing it inappropriately.[24]
- **False negatives:** on the other hand, some harmful or offensive comments can slip through the automated filters, especially if they use coded language or new methods to evade detection, allowing cyber harassment to persist. Persistent cyber harassers may even adapt to automated moderation tactics, finding new ways to harass their targets that bypass existing filters.[25]
- **Bias and discrimination:** moderation algorithms can inherit biases present in their training data, potentially leading to unfair censorship or favoritism. This can disproportionately affect certain groups or viewpoints. Automated systems may even struggle to adapt to rapidly changing online discourse and cultural shifts, requiring frequent updates and adjustments to remain effective.

After all, the "thinking process" of an AI tool of any kind is very different from the thinking process of a human being. "*Human beings when making a decision might be guided by a set of explicit rules, or by their feelings. Also, humans are also selective about which information is relevant for them, in making a decision. Lacking this ability for "feel" or the one of selectivity, machines may consider factors that humans deem not important in making that decision.*"[26] Therefore, it is very important to carefully consider all the advantages and disadvantages of using AI tools. Balancing the advantages and disadvantages of automatic comment moderation requires careful consideration to reach a suitable middle ground that fosters a healthy online environment while **preserving free speech** and **avoiding undue censorship** at the same time.[27]

12.4 Conclusion

So, the question we can ask ourselves is, can AI be the most effective helper in combatting or even investigating cyber harassment? With its ability to analyze vast amounts of data, identify patterns, and detect toxic content, AI can greatly enhance the efficiency and effectiveness of investigations. It can help automate the process of flagging and reviewing abusive or harassing content, enabling faster response times, and reducing the burden on human moderators. Furthermore, AI can aid in the identification of fake accounts, bot networks, or coordinated harassment campaigns, which are often used by cyber harassers to evade detection.

By focusing on all of these possibilities that the use of AI algorithms brough to us, we can gain valuable insights into the nature of cybercrimes and the strategies to combat them. But, automated comment moderation stands as a **double-edged sword** in the battle against cyber harassment. On the one hand, it offers a robust and efficient means to tackle harmful online behaviors, providing a safer space for internet users to interact and share ideas. Its ability to swiftly identify and remove offensive content has undoubtedly contributed to a safer digital world.

However, we must not overlook the potential pitfalls. The automated systems are not infallible and can sometimes censor legitimate comments, stifling free expression and inhibiting constructive dialogue. Moreover, cyber harassers are persistent and resourceful, constantly evolving their tactics to evade detection, rendering moderation algorithms an imperfect solution, but still a better solution than human comment moderation, which proves to be inefficient and slow.

There are a number of studies that examine the impact of AI moderation on cyber harassment or cyber bullying, also targeting the viewpoint of young people, while they are the most affected group by this behavior. There are many pros of using AI-based tools such as NLP and ML, when they are used for proactive detection and removal of harmful content before it is reported by users. However, there is still tension between the benefits of such AI interventions and **concerns about privacy and freedom of expression**, especially when private messages or facial recognition are involved. In a study carried out by a group of Irish scientists, where they studied the effectiveness of AI-based cyberbullying interventions from youth perspective, one of the conclusions were that AI interventions could be more effective when **combined with peer support**. For instance, children could designate a trusted person (such as a friend or family member) as a support contact who could be alerted if cyberbullying is detected. The study also investigated bystander interventions, where witnesses to bullying could offer support to the victim and then collected feedback from youth (ages 12–17) through focus groups and interviews, asking for their opinions on the effectiveness of AI-based moderation, the potential privacy concerns, and how these interventions might affect their rights. And while many children acknowledged the importance of AI in tackling cyberbullying, they also **expressed concerns** about false positives, where friendly banter might be **mistakenly flagged** as harmful content.[28]

The key therefore lies in striking a **delicate balance** between harnessing the benefits of automated moderation while addressing its limitations. To effectively combat cyber harassment, we must **combine the power of technology with human oversight**, ensuring that context and nuance are considered in content moderation decisions. As technology advances, our strategies for handling online harassment must evolve in tandem, fostering a digital environment where freedom of expression is safeguarded, and individuals can participate without fear of abuse. Achieving this balance is crucial in creating a more respectful and secure online world.

Notes

1 HAREWELL, J.L., PINA, A., STOREY, J.E. (2021). *Cyberstalking: Prevalence, Characteristics, and Impact*. In: Powell, A., Flynn, A., Sugiura, L. (eds) The Palgrave Handbook of Gendered Violence and Technology. Palgrave Macmillan, Cham. https://doi.org/10.1007/978-3-030-83734-1_11.
2 Act No. 300/2005 Coll. the Criminal Code, § 360b.
3 GILLESPIE, A. A. *Cybercrime: Key Issues and Debates*. Abingdon: Routledge, 2016. ISBN 978-1-315-88420-2. p. 1928. Available at: https://www.google.sk/books/edition/Cybercrime/Gt8sCgAAQBAJ.
4 Act No. 300/2005 Coll. the Criminal Code, § 360b.
5 ZHU, C., HUANG, S., EVANS, R., ZHANG, W. *Cyberbullying among Adolescents and Children: A Comprehensive Review of the Global Situation, Risk Factors, and Preventive Measures*. In: Frontiers in Public Health, 2021, vol. 9. DOI: 10.3389/fpubh.2021.634909. ISSN 2296-2565.
6 GREGUSSOVÁ, M., TOMKOVÁ, J. a BALÁŽOVÁ, M. *Dospievajúci vo virtuálnom priestore: Záverečná správa z výskumu*. Bratislava: Výskumný ústav detskej psychológie a patopsychológie (Research Institute of Child Psychology and Pathopsychology), 2011. Available at: https://vudpap.sk/wp-content/uploads/2019/01/vudpap-vyskumne-ulohy-Dospievaj%C3%BAci-vo-virtu%C3%A1lnom-priestore.pdf.

7 BERAN, T., RINALDI, C., BICKHAM, D., RICH, M. (2012). *Evidence for the need to support adolescents dealing with harassment and cyber-harassment: Prevalence, progression, and impact.* School Psychology International. https://doi.org/10.1177/0143034312446976. pp. 562–576.
8 Act No. 300/2005 Coll. the Criminal Code, § 360b.
9 Act No. 300/2005 Coll. the Criminal Code, § 360b.
10 *The material corrective is used in the case of misdemeanours and reads as follows: "It is not a misdemeanour if, having regard to the manner in which the act was carried out and its consequences, the circumstances in which the act was committed, the degree of culpability and the motive of the perpetrator, its severity is insignificant"* (Act No. 300/2005 Coll. the Criminal Code, § 10 (2)).
11 Explanatory memorandum to the Act No. 236/2021 Coll. supplementing Act No. 300/2005 Coll. on the Criminal Code as amended. Available at: https://www.najpravo.sk/dovodove-spravy/rok-2021/dovodova-sprava-k-zakonu-c-236-2021-z-z.html.
12 Explanatory memorandum to the Act No. 236/2021 Coll. supplementing Act No. 300/2005 Coll. on the Criminal Code as amended. Available at: https://www.najpravo.sk/dovodove-spravy/rok-2021/dovodova-sprava-k-zakonu-c-236-2021-z-z.html.
13 Explanatory memorandum to the Act No. 236/2021 Coll. supplementing Act No. 300/2005 Coll. on the Criminal Code as amended. Available at: https://www.najpravo.sk/dovodove-spravy/rok-2021/dovodova-sprava-k-zakonu-c-236-2021-z-z.html.
14 GREGUSSOVÁ, TOMKOVÁ, BALÁŽOVÁ, M. *Dospievajúci vo virtuálnom priestore.*
15 *Internal database of the Prison and Judicial Guard of the Slovak republic & Statistical Yearbooks of the Ministry of Justice of the Slovak Republic.*
16 GŘIVNA, T., POLČÁK, R. *Kyberkriminalita a právo.* Vyd. 1. Praha: Auditorium, 2008. ISBN 978-80-903786-7-4. pp 220.
17 MILOSEVIC, T. et al. *Effectiveness of Artificial Intelligence-Based Cyberbullying Interventions from Youth Perspective.* In: Social Media + Society, 2023, 9(1). ISSN 2056-3051. p. 2. Available at: https://journals.sagepub.com/doi/pdf/10.1177/20563051221147325.
18 https://trollwall.ai/.
19 STRUHÁRIK, F. *Umelá inteligencia moderuje diskusie na facebookovej stránke Denníka N, darí sa jej skrývať nenávisť.* In: Denník N, 2023. [online]. Available at: https://dennikn.sk/3314628/umela-inteligencia-moderuje-diskusie-na-facebookovej-stranke-dennika-n-dari-sa-jej-skryvat-nenavist/.
20 STRUHÁRIK, F. *Umelá inteligencia moderuje diskusie na facebookovej stránke Denníka N, darí sa jej skrývať nenávisť.*
21 ELSAFOURY, F., KATSIGIANNIS, S., PERVEZ, Z., RAMZAN, N. *When the Timeline Meets the Pipeline: A Survey on Automated Cyberbullying Detection.* In: IEEE Access, vol. 9, 2021. https://doi.org/10.1109/ACCESS.2021.3098979. pp. 103541–103563.
22 MILOSEVIC et al. *Effectiveness of Artificial Intelligence-Based Cyberbullying Interventions from Youth Perspective*, p. 2.
23 MILOSEVIC et al. *Effectiveness of Artificial Intelligence-Based Cyberbullying Interventions from Youth Perspective*, p. 2.
24 ELSAFOURY et al. *When the Timeline Meets the Pipeline*, pp. 103541–103563.
25 ELSAFOURY et al. *When the Timeline Meets the Pipeline*, pp. 103541–103563.

26 GYURÁSZ, Z. *Ethics in the age of AI*. Bratislava legal forum 2020 [electronic document]: Disruptive technologies: regulatory and ethical challenges.: 1. vyd. ISBN 978-80-7160-567-6. Bratislava: Právnická fakulta UK, 2020. pp. 63-68.
27 GOLBECK, J. *Online Harassment*. Springer Cham: 2018. ISBN: 978-3-319-78582-0. https://doi.org/10.1007/978-3-319-78583-7_1. p. 268.
28 MILOSEVIC et al. *Effectiveness of Artificial Intelligence-Based Cyberbullying Interventions from Youth Perspective*, p. 2.

Chapter 13

Perspectives of using algorithms in assessing violent behaviour and recidivism in convicts

Current state and future in Slovak prisons

Lucia Vasilik

13.1 Introduction

Artificial intelligence (AI) has currently penetrated practically every industry, even our everyday economic and private activities. A proper distinction needs to be made between what AI is and what an algorithm is. In general, an algorithm is a narrower term than AI. An algorithm could be defined as a certain sequence of steps, a defined procedure aimed at solving a particular problem or achieving a particular goal. It is a finite sequence of clearly defined and unambiguous instructions that can be executed by a computer or any other computing device. Algorithms can be written in a variety of programming languages and are designed to provide a solution or output based on a specified input. Algorithms are widely used in computer science and programming to solve problems efficiently and predictably. AI itself uses algorithms as part of its underlying mechanisms, e.g. to process and manipulate data or perform specific tasks. Artificial intelligence (hereinafter also referred to as "AI"), on the other hand, expresses the ability of machines or computer systems to perform tasks that would typically require human intelligence. It is a kind of simulation of human cognitive abilities, in particular the ability to perceive, listen, reason, learn, and make decisions, based on the data provided. Various technical systems use AI to sense and scan the environment around them, usually through sensors, which are then processed by a computer, autonomously solving problems as they arise and adapting its behaviour based on the situation. AI bases its decisions on the analysis of previous actions, phenomena, and data provided in advance on which AI learns. According to the Proposal for a Regulation of the European Parliament and of the Council Laying Down Harmonised Rules on AI (AI Act) and Amending Certain Union Legislative Acts (hereinafter referred to as "AIA"). Title 1, art. 3, we can characterise an AI system as a "*software that is developed with one or more of the techniques and*

DOI: 10.4324/9781003531500-21

approaches listed in Annex I and can, for a given set of human-defined objectives, generate outputs such as content, predictions, recommendations, or decisions influencing the environments they interact with"[1].

The increasingly widespread use of AI brings significant benefits to society as a whole – it is particularly worth mentioning the use of AI in medicine (e.g. the detection of eye and skin cancer, preventive analysis that can predict health problems), in banking and finance (client risk management – risk assessment and scoring, recommendation of individually "tailored" products, client profiling, streamlining processes in accounting, etc.), in manufacturing and industry (in this context, there is often talk of so called 'fourth industrial revolution', i.e. Industry 4.0, which envisages the automation and exchange of data in manufacturing through the involvement of cyber-physical systems, the internet of things, cloud storage, and recognition systems).[2] On the other hand, there is a growing pressure for increased regulation of and control over AI, which is directly linked to the issue of compensation for damage caused by AI. The potential of AI is enormous, not only for the benefit of humanity but also to facilitate or create new ways of committing crime. Law enforcement agencies must adapt to these new trends. For them, AI not only poses challenges in crime detection but also opens new possibilities for prevention and fighting crime. Already today, AI is used across all stages of criminal proceedings (pinpointing high-crime locations, creating geospatial imagery, natural language processing, facial recognition, etc.). At the stage of execution of criminal sanctions in general, AI can be used in several areas. Firstly, (i) in the area of providing *security of prison buildings* and preserving the order and safety within them, (ii) in the area of *connecting the electronic systems and databases* of various state authorities and state institutions involved in the enforcement procedure, and for the automation of processes, (iii) in the area of *resocialisation, education and treatment* of the convicts, and (iv) in the area of *predictive and assessment tools*, e.g. to predict recidivism. In this chapter, we will focus on the last group – the predictive and assessment tools and the perspectives of the use of AI in risk assessment and needs identification.

13.2 Use of AI in predictive tools – Current state, perspectives, and risks

Predictive tools[3] are now commonly used around the world in the process of crime prevention and suppression, as well as in the process of working with offenders and victims of crime. Depending on the subject focus, we distinguish between general tools, e.g. tools developed for predicting general recidivism,[4] and specific tools, e.g. tools for assessing the risk of violent behaviour in custody or violent extremism,[5] tools for assessing the risk of violent recidivism,[6] tools for assessing the risk of sexual recidivism,[7] tools for assessing the risk of victimisation,[8] etc., several of which use a combined approach, i.e. assessing the risk of general recidivism as well as specific risks.[9] The development of predictive and assessment tools began in the US and the UK as a response to the intolerable situation caused by the alarming number of incarcerated persons with an upward trend. The first risk assessment tools – *the first generation of risk assessment*[10] – were used in England in the first half of the twentieth century (1900–1970). They involved unstructured judgement of the offender by a human assessor, with poor predictive value, elements of bias, unpredictability and inconsistency of approach by assessors. Risk assessment constructed in this way may have led to poor planning of interventions for a particular offender, without appropriate individualisation. In the second generation of risk assessment (1970–1990), the use of actuarial methods, i.e. the creation of a list of factors that are statistically related to crime, was introduced. Compared to the first generation, these tools generally had higher predictive value, but did not take into account the nature, severity, and immediacy of the threat of reoffending and the risk of reoffending after treatment or rehabilitation programme. They consisted mainly of static factors (e.g. Salient Factor Score – SFS[11]). *The third generation of risk assessment* (1990-early twenty-first century) already includes dynamic risk assessment, i.e. it takes into account dynamic predictors that may change, such as lifestyle, occupation, accommodation, personal attitudes, cognitive deficits, self-regulatory abilities, and personal behaviour. The third generation of tools represents a holistic, personalised, and analytical approach to risk assessment and, together with actuarial predictors, helps in determining the type of punishment and interventions (e.g. the Level of Service Inventory Revised – LSI-R tool). *The fourth generation* of tools (present) represents a more systematic and comprehensive approach to risk assessment. It is based on the principle of *risk-need-responsivity* (hereinafter referred to as "RNR"), i.e. risk assessment and needs identification, according to which the assessment of the convicted person is to be based on an evaluation of the risk he/she poses to society and the needs represented by criminogenic needs that have a direct relevance to reducing recidivism, e.g. targeted interventions and rehabilitation programmes aimed at identified needs (alcohol addiction, impulsivity and tendencies to aggression, weak social and family relationships, etc.). Andrews, Bonta, and Wormith include among the main criminogenic factors ("central 8"):

1 History of antisocial behaviour (early and continuing involvement in a number and variety of antisocial acts in a variety of settings)
2 Antisocial personality patterns (e.g. restlessly aggressive, weak self-control)
3 Antisocial cognition (e.g. attitudes, values, beliefs, rationalisations supportive of crime, criminal identity)

4 Antisocial associates (close association with criminal others and relative isolation from anticriminal others, immediate social support of crime)
5 Family and/or marital (nurturance and/or caring; monitoring and/or supervision)
6 School and/or work (low levels of performance and satisfaction in school or work)
7 Leisure and/or recreation (low levels of performance and satisfaction in anticriminal leisure pursuits)
8 Substance Abuse.[12]

Of these, the first four represent the "big four" most serious criminogenic factors. The criminogenic factors determine the offender's level of risk and need, which in a well-functioning criminal justice system should be followed up with individualised services and interventions to reform, treat, and resocialise the offender and reduce the risk of reoffending.

Thus, in an RNR assessment, "risk" determines *who to target* based on the level of identified risk (e.g. risk of recidivism, risk of violent behaviour while incarcerated, etc.). "Needs" determine *what should be done* (according to specific criminogenic needs). "Responsiveness" (sensitivity) determines *how the work* with the convict *should be carried out* in the most effective way, taking into account his/her personal or personality specificities. Thus, responsivity takes into account the unique characteristics of the individual in order to select appropriate interventions aimed at reforming, possibly treating the offender and reducing the risk of reoffending. The responsivity factor has two basic components: *general responsivity*, in which cognitive social learning methods are used for the purpose of influencing the offender's behaviour. These methods can be applied regardless of the type of offender (e.g. violent offender, juvenile offender, sex offender, etc.). *Specific responsivity* focuses on interventions that support an individual's specific strengths. It is a kind of "fine tuning" of general cognitive-behavioural interventions.[13] According to Lulei et al., risk and needs assessment tools are an essential part of the overall offender case management process. The higher the quality or predictive (risk) and identifying (needs) power of the tool, the higher the quality of the other processes potentially. This is because the results of the tools are followed up by specific interventions as well as subsequent evaluation.[14]

Predictive tools are currently applied by a human evaluator (e.g. probation officer, prison service employee, psychologist, etc.), by an AI evaluator based on machine learning, or by a combined approach, where predictive activity is performed using algorithms and then supplemented by a human evaluator who fills in specific items (usually pedagogical, psychological, or psychiatric evaluation of the evaluated person). It should be added that the main decision for the purpose of which the risk assessment and the determination of needs is made is always up to the human being (judge, director of the prison, commission, probation and mediation officer, etc.). AI itself does not make the decisions, it only informs them.

Each of these approaches has its pros and cons and carries risks and challenges that need to be anticipated in the development of the tool and then regularly assessed for validity and reliability. The application of predictive tools has important implications in relation to the persons being assessed. Predictive tools are used in a wide range of decisions in penitentiary and post-penitentiary care, determine the possibility of parole, prison security classifications, resocialisation and rehabilitation programmes, and are used in decisions on the sentences and in decisions on custody substitution and bail – according to which legal system.[15] Regardless of whether the evaluator is a human being, an algorithm, or both, the development and scaling of predictive tools is generally protected by copyright law or similar legislation of that state and is not publicly available. The developers of digital predictive tools using AI tend to be either private companies (especially in the US) contracted by state institutions and authorities, or less often state institutions and authorities directly. On the one hand, limiting access to predictive tools and the details of their operation seems obvious; making the scaling and specific items of this-or-that tool available would open up opportunities for those being assessed to thoroughly prepare for risk and needs assessments, especially if the psychological evaluation of the person being assessed is included, and the items are not only determined by static, hard-to-change data, such as social background, criminal history, education, but also by items that the assessed person can manipulate to some extent. On the other hand, the low level of transparency of predictive tools, especially those based on machine learning, is often criticised and possesses big risks as to the reliability and trustworthiness of the tool.[16]

Risk assessment at the stage of decision-making on the type and amount of punishment, regardless of the artificial or human nature of the assessor, is subject to frequent criticism. According to Van Ginneken,[17] risk assessment for this purpose violates the principle of proportionality of punishment, which should correspond with the seriousness of the offence. According to Von Hirsch, the seriousness of the offence must be judged according to the degree of culpability and the harm caused.[18] It is common for previous criminal activity to be considered in this process, usually as an aggravating factor. In this case, however, it is appropriate to take into account the time that has elapsed since the previous offence and the type of previous offence and its relationship to the current offence,[19] particularly in order to ensure that criminal history is taken into account only in the case of repeat offenders who show a continuous pattern of criminal behaviour despite prior warnings and attempts by the State to resocialise the offender. However, assessing the risk of recidivism in relation to possible future criminal activity (as opposed to considering only past criminal activity) is a different matter. Replacing the consideration of previous criminal activity in determining the type and level of punishment with a prediction of the risk of future recidivism could lead to a situation where, e.g. two first-time offenders who have committed similar offences of the same gravity under similar conditions could receive different sentences based on different estimates of potential future recidivism, which we consider *unacceptable*.

A frequent argument for the use of AI in predicting possible recidivism is the removal of subjectivism from the decision-making of individuals, who, in addition to their experience, may also introduce bias or explicitly racist and discriminatory attitudes into the assessment. The US is an infamous country in this regard, where an algorithm can decide a person's future in a criminal trial. The prison population index[20] in the US (in 2023) is the fifth highest in the world[21] after El Salvador, Cuba, Rwanda, Turkmenistan, and American Samoa, at 531 incarcerated persons per 100,000 inhabitants.[22] The pressure to reduce the prison population without risking an increase in crime has caused a turn in the US criminal justice system towards automated tools, leading to the massive development of AI-based predictive tools. These tools are used at many stages of the criminal justice process, from crime prevention to sentencing, often with very controversial results. Predictive risk assessment tools give a recidivism score based on details from an offender's profile. This score is taken into account by the judge in a large number of decisions that influence the selection of rehabilitation programmes, the custody of the defendant, and the severity of the sentence.[23] Modern algorithms use a machine learning system – they are trained on historical crime data to look for certain patterns related to criminal activity. Once they find these patterns, they assign them a score. The problem is that the algorithms do not distinguish between causality and correlation. For example, when an algorithm evaluates that low income is related to high recidivism, it creates causality from the statistical correlation of low income and recidivism, and individuals who have historically been targeted by disproportionate law enforcement (particularly low-income communities and minorities) are at risk of high recidivism scores. In theory, predictive algorithms should reduce the biases inherent in human decision-making, but when trained on historical data, they replicate and amplify the previous human biases embedded in them.[24] Most predictive tools are proprietary, subject to intellectual property. For this reason, any revision of their evaluation is almost impossible. There is a similar problem with the use of algorithms in the UK, where OASys (Offender Assessment System) was introduced in 2001 and has gradually begun to replace some of the roles of probation officers. Low transparency is a problem with AI in general.[25] This is, among other things, due to the *complexity* of the decision-making processes of sophisticated algorithms, which are difficult to understand without proper technical knowledge, and *the protection of personal data.*[26] Another issue is how to proceed when there is doubt about the correctness of an algorithm's assessment of the risk of recidivism. Since the scaling and scoring of individual predictors is not publicly available, and in several US states the AI algorithms are quite autonomous and difficult to control, the assessed inmate has no opportunity to challenge the outcome of the assessment.

By contrast, in the European Union (hereinafter referred to as "EÚ") this situation is addressed by Regulation (EU) 2016/679 of the European Parliament and of the Council of 27 April 2016 on the protection of natural persons with regard to the processing of personal data and on the free movement of such data, and repealing Directive 95/46/EC (General Data Protection Regulation, hereinafter referred to as the "GDPR").[27] Pursuant to Article 22(1) of the GDPR "*The data subject shall have the right not to be subject to a decision based solely on automated processing, including profiling, which produces legal effects concerning him or her or similarly significantly affects him or her.*" Paragraph 2 of that Article provides for exceptions to paragraph 1. In the area of enforcement of criminal sanctions that are the topic of this contribution, the GDPR has the nature of a *lex generalis* towards the Directive (EU) 2016/680 of the European Parliament and of the Council of 27 April 2016 on the protection of natural persons with regard to the processing of personal data by competent authorities for the purposes of the prevention, investigation, detection, or prosecution of criminal offences or the execution of criminal penalties, and on the free movement of such data, and repealing Council Framework Decision 2008/977/JHA (hereinafter referred to as "the Police directive").[28] The issue of automated individual decision-making, corresponding to Article 22 of the GDPR, is regulated in the Police Directive by Article 11, the wording of which is more restrictive than Article 22 of the GDPR due to the punitive nature of criminal proceedings and the possibility of intensive interference with fundamental rights: "*Member States shall provide for a decision based solely on automated processing, including profiling, which produces an adverse legal effect concerning the data subject or significantly affects him or her, to be prohibited unless authorised by Union or Member State law to which the controller is subject and which provides appropriate safeguards for the rights and freedoms of the data subject, at least the right to obtain human intervention on the part of the controller.*" Recital 38 of the Police Directive (although non-binding in nature) provides as follows: "*(...)In any case, such processing should be subject to suitable safeguards, including the provision of specific information to the data subject and the right to obtain human intervention, in particular to express his or her point of view, to obtain an explanation of the decision reached after such assessment or to challenge the decision. Profiling that results in discrimination against natural persons on the basis of personal data which are by their nature particularly sensitive in relation to fundamental rights and freedoms should be prohibited under the conditions laid down in Articles 21 and 52 of the Charter.*" Here, the use of a remedy – the reassessment of risk by a human assessor – seems to be the appropriate solution. The question is how much this procedure would burden prison staff in making such requests for virtually every "negative" assessment with a high recidivism risk score. Another option is to provide an explanation (information) to the person concerned, this procedure could in turn jeopardise trade secrets and intellectual property rights relating to the algorithm,[29] an explanation given to the algorithm could even provide the person concerned with information about the strategies of the competent authorities and potentially jeopardise ongoing investigations or other proceedings and decisions carried out in the context of the imprisonment.

13.3 Use of assessment tools in the Slovak Republic in imprisonment

In the Slovak Republic, tools are also used to assess risks and needs, the evaluation of which for the time being (and in the foreseeable future) belongs to humans. The national project Chance for Reentry,[30] implemented by the General Directorate of the Corps of Prison and Court Guard Service since October 2018,[31] is aimed at reducing the risk of social exclusion and increasing competences in the labour market, in order to minimise the risk of re-offending and limit the emergence of possible crisis situations and emergencies. The main activities and priorities of the national project included the creation and practical implementation, pilot testing and evaluation of resocialisation and educational programmes, their standardisation and the creation of an accreditation mechanism, the creation of *reentry units*[32] in partner penitentiary institutions, the education of convicts, the linking of penitentiary and post-penitentiary care on the "Bridges" platform and, last but not least, the creation of assessment tools.

Risk assessment and needs identification tools are one of the innovative elements towards effective resocialisation of the convicts. Procedurally, they are the first step in the offender's case management and their outcome determines the focus (content) and intensity (scope) of subsequent professional interventions (not only in the context of penitentiary treatment).[33] The following tools have been developed in the framework of the national project Chance for Retry:

- IAPSZ (*eng.* Individual Action Plan for Social Inclusion)
- HRON (*eng.* – Risk of Serious Harm Assessment – RoSH)
- CRA (*eng.* Crime Risk Assessment)
- IN (*eng.* Indication Tool)
- Sorting Mechanism

The IAPSZ (Individual Action Plan for Social Inclusion) is a planning and evaluation tool used by the social worker, psychologist and social curator – methodologist in the context of work with the convicted person during the imprisonment. This digitised tool is key in linking penitentiary and post-penitentiary care policies and its main objective is to maintain the continuity of effective interventions provided in the prison environment to the specific convict with those provided after release. It is a key and dominant element of the national project towards effective resocialisation.[34] Because of the need to reduce recidivism and to improve the effective integration of the convict into society after release from imprisonment, it is important for the convict to be provided with assistance in the areas of need as soon as possible after entering prison and, in particular, that this assistance in the indicated areas in the form of specialist interventions is continued after release from prison. In practical terms, this is about linking up the prison with Offices of Labour, Social Affairs, and Family.[35]

The IAPZ tool replaced the original treatment programme effective October 1, 2019. As of that date, every inmate placed in a reentry unit has an IAPZ processed and updated on an ongoing basis. On the date of the convicted person's release from the reentry unit, an evaluation of the resocialisation assistance plan (final evaluation) is required to be prepared in the IAPSZ in order to reflect the results of resocialisation in the comprehensive evaluation of the treatment programme. According to the Output Analysis of the national project Chance for Reentry, the original tool (the first version of the IAPSZ), which was in the form of an MS Excel document, underwent a pilot validation during which revisions were made to the different versions of the documents. Three versions of the document were produced in succession, with the last third version being digitised, resulting in a web-based application. The digitisation of the IAPSZ has made it possible to link all the offices of labour, social affairs, and family in Slovakia (hereinafter referred to as "social offices") with the prison services through special accesses, which ultimately means that on the day of the client's release, the IAPSZ is automatically assigned (after the client's consent) to a specific social office so that it can start working with the released person as quickly as possible if necessary.

Thus, the IAPSZ records the inmate's data necessary for the successful implementation of interventions in penitentiary and post-penitentiary care. These data are:

1 General personal data
2 Analysis of strengths, weaknesses, opportunities and threats in seven areas:

    a Behaviour in prison
    b Family, relationships and community

   c Housing
   d Education
   e Employment
   f Finances
   g Leisure

3 Risks and supervision
4 Needs and Plan
5 Programmes [records of completed programmes, indication of appropriate programmes, e.g. Family and Relationships Programme, Employment, Financial Literacy, Restart (addictions), the Second Chance (partner violence), Community Life (at-risk groups from segregated communities), etc.]
6 Current status
7 Administration[36]

The HRON (Risk of Repeated Violence Assessment) is a screening tool that has been under development since October 2019. Compared to the CRA tool, it has a specialised focus on predicting the infliction of an outcome in which persons are at risk of serious harm to their physical and psychological integrity. It is a prediction of violent crime, with an aspect of dangerousness and seriousness, whereby the dangerousness of the offender can be defined as the potential to cause serious injury or harm to the other person(s).[37] In the first phase of the HRON development, key criminogenic factors in relation to the target group of convicted offenders were selected based on scientific studies, and then modifications to the instrument items (individual predictors) and calibration adjustments were made. This was followed by an evaluation of the reliability of the instrument through two pilot tests, which took place in the first round from December 2020 to February 2021 and in the second round from June 2021 to September 2021. The number of respondents in the first round of validation was narrowed down to 33 persons, from which nine were subsequently selected who fell under the following criteria: male, age ≤ 50, descriptor in the internal information system "violence," "violent," "violent tendencies." After assessing the prevalence of risk factors, respondents were "scored" in the areas corresponding to the severity of the predictors (max 28 points). A high frequency of the proposed criminogenic factors was identified on the above research set. The second pilot testing was a retrospective study of 30 male respondents convicted of a crime of a violent nature and sentenced to an unconditional prison term who, after release, committed within 12 months a deliberate crime of a violent nature in which the victim was killed or suffered other serious harm with irreparable or intractable consequences. Of the research sample, 28 respondents exhibited a level of high risk, a percentage of 93%.[38] Based on the validation, 15 items of a static (e.g., age of the person under consideration, criminal history, etc.) and dynamic nature (e.g., addictions, interpersonal conflicts, etc.) were selected through which the risk of serious harm to society for a particular convict at the time immediately after release from imprisonment is assessed. Twelve of these predictors are general in nature, and three specific predictors are oriented to the uniqueness of the person being assessed (e.g., the results of the CRA). Thus, this instrument is used primarily with persons who have been convicted of violent crime. Unlike the CRA tool (see below), the HRON is not aimed at assessing the risk of general recidivism, but at predicting actions likely to produce a serious consequence in the form of an interference with a person's physical and psychological integrity. Such conduct requires increased supervision or even treatment of the dangerous convict. On the other hand, careful prediction is important from the offender's perspective to preserve his or her rights, which should not be unduly restricted based on a faulty prediction that may result in the detention of individuals for longer periods than necessary and the associated economic, social, and civil consequences.[39] The HRON was developed with a focus on two groups of convicted offenders – sex offenders and violent offenders who pose a potential or actual danger to society.

The CRA, a tool for assessing the risk of criminal recidivism, identifies the resocialisation prognosis, or the risk that the assessed person will commit a new offence within two years of release from the reentry unit from imprisonment. Within the Prison and Court Guard Service, it is mainly used in the assessment of a convict in parole proceedings (conditional release from imprisonment) to demonstrate compliance with the conditions for parole and to determine the resocialisation prognosis.[40] The instrument has been piloted three times, contains 6 sections (38 items) and the assessment is produced by 4 assessors.[41] The CRA is not the first recidivism risk assessment tool used in Slovakia. Initially, since 2009, the "Social Failure Risk Assessment" tool (a Slovak abbr. HRSZ, 13 predictors) was used, which was based on the Canadian LSI – R tool (the original had 54 predictors). The HRSZ was used to determine the level of risk of social failure and the level of resocialisation prognosis (favourable, less favourable, unfavourable). In 2021, the HRSZ instrument was replaced by the CRA instrument, which was piloted three times and the research cohort consisted of 2047 persons in prison. It currently has two modifications: the CRA-CR (Crime Risk Assessment – Conditional Release), evaluated for the purpose of parole decision-making, and CRA-RU (Crime Risk Assessment – Reentry Unit), evaluated prior to the placement of the convicted person in the reentry unit before the completion of his/her imprisonment in order to determine his/her resocialisation prognosis. The assessment uses statistical, clinical, and intuitive methods of individual prognosis to predict the risk of general recidivism. Compared to the original HRSZ instrument, one of the specific features of the CRA tool (also from the point of view of its international comparison) was the item "verification of the truthfulness of autoanamnestic data", through which random verification was recorded of information provided by the convict during the execution of the sentence, which cannot be detected automatically from external information systems (education, housing after release, length of employment prior to the start of the sentence, etc.). The purpose of this item was that the assessment of the prediction of the potential risk of recidivism should also reflect the possible purposeful and manipulative behaviour of the convict while serving the sentence.[42] The CRA-CR contains 37 predictors and the CRA-RU contains 38 predictors focusing on criminogenic risk factors that have predictive value in relation to criminal recidivism.[43] Both modifications are evaluated by several assessors (a social worker, an educator, a psychologist, a preventive-security service worker and a social curator-methodologist of the social office) who administer the items of the sections, such as selected risk factors, penitentiary treatment, selected outcomes of psychological evaluation, etc. The administration of the CRA questionnaires was carried out during the development of the tool in the eCRA application, which was then linked to the data reported by the Prison and Court Guard Service information system, thus ensuring automated completion in most of the items of a particular questionnaire with the possibility of subsequent editing by the assessor.[44] The final output of the instrument gives the total score in a range of minimum and maximum scores, as well as its percentage value. The key output is the level of risk of reoffending (low, medium, high) and the corresponding prognosis for resocialisation (favourable, less favourable, unfavourable). This means that the final outcome of the convict's assessment predicts the potential recidivism of the convict after release from imprisonment, but not his/her danger to society (this is what the HRON tool is used for). Only the final result of the calibrated sum of the individual items shall be made available to the competent authority in the context of the assessment of the resocialisation prognosis of a particular convict. It is up to the competent authority whether to take into account the result determined by the diagnostic tool of the Prison and Court Guard Service.[45] Thus, the outcome of the CRA tool is not binding on the authorities making, e.g. parole decisions. The CRA tool has been in live operation since 1 January 2021 and is fully digitised with automated completion of most items, it can, however, be edited by the assessor afterwards.

IN (Needs Indication Tool) is a screening tool created for the purpose of assigning convicts to specialised resocialisation and educational programmes. The IN prioritises a key criminogenic factor associated with identifying the need of the convict to attend a particular resocialisation programme.[46] The IN contains six sections with eponymous names of key criminogenic factors assigned to the relevant specialised resocialisation and educational programme, e.g. employment, addictions, financial literacy, etc. Each section has a maximum of five separate items, e.g. one of the items in the 'Employment' section is an item titled 'length of employment one year prior to entering imprisonment'.[47] Seventy-five inmates participated in the pilot validation of the IN (15 for each specialised resocialisation and education programme), of which 16 were included in the reentry unit. Since May 2021, the IN is part of the digitised Individual Action Plan for Social Inclusion (in its separate section/section "Programs").[48] According to the output analysis, it is still necessary to adjust the items and reconsider the calibration for this instrument, and to repeat the pilot validation on a larger sample of respondents.

The Sorting Mechanism – the aim of setting up the basic framework of the Sorting Mechanism tool is to place convicts in the reentry unit in terms of their abilities and opportunities for social inclusion, in terms of their application in the labour market, and in terms of the prediction of social failure and the identification of risks and the determination of needs. The framework of the Sorting Mechanism is an essential element in the procedure for the placement of convicts in reentry units, which is assessed by the relevant placement committee and approved by the director of the institution concerned. One of the consequences of the newly established "Basic framework of the Sorting Mechanism for the placement of convicted persons in the reentry unit" (and also of the progressively implemented philosophy and vision) is the placement of convicts in the reentry units in accordance with the accommodation capacity to the maximum extent possible. In particular, priority is given to the placement of those at medium and/or high risk of re-offending and social failure.[49]

All of the above-mentioned tools used in the Slovak Republic are in digitised form, however they are not yet supported by any kind of AI.

13.4 Conclusion

There are several types of risk assessment and needs identification tools, both in relation to (i) different target groups (e.g. the general prison population, those who have been placed on probation supervision by the court, delinquent youth, victims of crime – in terms of assessing the risk of victimisation, etc.), (ii) to different users or assessors (e.g. probation services, prison services, non-profit organisations, etc.), (iii) to different time phases in relation to the criminal justice system (sentencing, charging, etc.), and (iv) in terms of the development and content of the instrument into one of four generations.[50] Currently, AI-assisted predictive tools are already being used in criminal proceedings in several countries. In the use of AI in this particularly risky area, several key factors need to be taken into account, which we consider to be, in particular, transparency, fairness and respect for the rights of individuals in order to ensure auditable, unbiased and accurate prediction. In addition, ethical issues need to be taken into account, potential biases eliminated and adequate human control and oversight of the decision-making process ensured. Last but not least, the Member States of the European Union have to deal with ensuring adequate safeguards for data subjects on the reviewability of decisions based on automated systems within the meaning of Article 22 of the GDPR and Article 11 of the Police Directive.

The assessment tools developed within the Slovak Republic by the Prison and Judicial Guard Corps have been digitised, but are not yet supported by AI systems. This situation persists for a number of reasons. The first is the lack of technological support in the conditions of the ZVJS. The second is the problematic provisions of the GDPR and the Police Directive, which we discussed in the second section of this chapter in the area of the protection of the fundamental rights of data subjects in relation to the use of automated systems for individual decisions and the protection of personal data. However, this topic remains open for the future, especially in the context of increasing the efficiency and accuracy of individual predictions generated by the tools. However, any introduction of AI must only take place after due consideration, testing and verification of the credibility and impartiality of the AI system. We are of the opinion that even in such a case, individual predictions in the field of imprisonment should not be left to AI alone, but must be under the control and interaction of human evaluators.

Notes

1 Available at: https://eur-lex.europa.eu/resource.html?uri=cellar:e0649735-a372-11eb-9585-01aa75ed71a1.0001.02/DOC_1&format=PDF, p. 39.
2 See KOLAŘÍKOVÁ, L. HORÁK, F.: *Umělá intelligence & právo [eng. Artificial Intelligence & Law]*. Prague: Wolters Kluwer 2020, p. 35.
3 For example, COMPAS, LSI-R, LSCF – R, OASys (OGP, OVP, OSP), CAT-SR, VRAG, HCR-20, PLC-R, OGRS, RISc, RM2000V, PICTS, PBRS, Risk Matrix 2000, VERA-2R, etc.
4 For example, OGRS, COMPAS, OASys OGP (General Reoffending Predictor), etc.
5 For example, Custody Rating Scale, RASP, VERA-2R, LSCF – R, PCL–R, ERG 22+, SQAT, IR46, RRAP, the Radar, VAF, etc. See https://home-affairs.ec.europa.eu/system/files/2021-04/ran_cons_overv_pap_risk_assessment_in_prison_20210210_en.pdf.
6 For example, HCR-20, VRAG, etc.
7 For example, OASys OSP (Sexual Reoffending Predictor), Risk Matrix 2000, etc.
8 For example, Polyvictimization Assessment Tool. See also https://www.cdc.gov/violenceprevention/pdf/ipv/ipvandsvscreening.pdf.
9 For example, COMPAS, OASys, LSI-R, etc.

10 Available at: https://www.justiceinspectorates.gov.uk/hmiprobation/research/the-evidence-base-probation/supervision-of-service-users/assessment/.
11 See also HOFFMAN, P. J.: Recidivism among Released Federal Prisoners – Salient Factor Score and Five-Year Follow-Up. *Criminal Justice and Behavior*. Volume 12, Issue 4, 1985, pp. 501–507.
12 ANDREWS, D. A., BONTA, J., WORMITH J. S.: The Recent Past and Near Future of Risk and/or Need Assessment. *Crime & Delinquency*. Vol. 52, No. 1, 2006, p. 11. Available at: https://journals.sagepub.com/doi/epdf/10.1177/0011128705281756.
13 Available at: https://www.justiceinspectorates.gov.uk/hmiprobation/research/the-evidence-base-probation/models-and-principles/the-rnr-model/.
14 LULEI, M., TALLOVÁ B., ĽORKO, J.: Vývoj, obsah a výsledky pilotných testovaní nástrojov na hodnotenie rizík a určenie potrieb odsúdených osôb v zbore väzenskej a justičnej stráže na Slovensku [eng. Development, Content and Results of Pilot Testing of Risk Assessment and Needs Assessment Tools for Convicted Persons in the Prison and Court Guard Service in Slovakia]. *Collection of papers from the International scientific conference on forensic social work "Theoretical and practical basis of Social Work with perpetrators and victims of delinquent activities."* Bratislava: Comenius University Bratislava, 2021, p. 66.
15 Available at: https://theconversation.com/a-black-box-ai-system-has-been-influencing-criminal-justice-decisions-for-over-two-decades-its-time-to-open-it-up-200594.
16 See also https://www.technologyreview.com/2019/01/21/137783/algorithms-criminal-justice-ai/; https://www.ojp.gov/pdffiles1/nij/252038.pdf; https://www.technologyreview.com/2020/07/17/1005396/predictive-policing-algorithms-racist-dismantled-machine-learning-bias-criminal-justice/; https://news.harvard.edu/gazette/story/newsplus/how-social-change-brings-bias-to-predictive-models-used-in-criminal-justice-settings/; https://theconversation.com/a-black-box-ai-system-has-been-influencing-criminal-justice-decisions-for-over-two-decades-its-time-to-open-it-up-200594.
17 VAN GINNEKEN, E.F.J.C.: The use of risk assessment in sentencing. J.W. de Keijser, J.V. Roberts, & J. Ryberg (eds.): *Predictive sentencing: Normative and empirical perspectives*. Oxford: Hart Publishing, 2019, pp. 9–32. Available at: https://scholar.google.com/scholar_lookup?title=The%20use%20of%20risk%20assessment%20in%20sentencing&author=E.F.J.C.%20van%20Ginneken&publication_year=2019&pages=9-32, p. 6.
18 VON HIRSCH, A.: *Doing justice: The choice of punishments*. New York: Hill and Wang 1976. In VAN GINNEKEN: The use of risk assessment in sentencing.
19 ROBERTS, J. V., PINA-SÁNCHEZ, J.: Previous convictions at Sentencing: exploring empirical trends in the Crown court. *Criminal Law Review (London, England)*. Vol. 2014, Issue 8, 2014, p. 577-578.
20 Number of incarcerated persons per 100,000 inhabitants.
21 For comparison, the prison population rate of the Slovak Republic in 2023 is 185 (globally ranked 82nd), of Hungary 203 (globally ranked 70th), and of the Czech Republic 181 (globally ranked 89th).
22 See *World prison brief*: https://www.prisonstudies.org/highest-to-lowest/prison_population_rate?field_region_taxonomy_tid=All.
23 Available at: https://www.technologyreview.com/2019/01/21/137783/algorithms-criminal-justice-ai/.

24 Available at: https://www.technologyreview.com/2019/01/21/137783/algorithms-criminal-justice-ai/.
25 See also OSWALD, M. et al.: *The UK Algorithmic Transparency Standard: A Qualitative Analysis of Police Perspectives*. 2022. Available at: https://papers.ssrn.com/sol3/papers.cfm?abstract_id=4155549.
26 Available at: https://theconversation.com/a-black-box-ai-system-has-been-influencing-criminal-justice-decisions-for-over-two-decades-its-time-to-open-it-up-200594.
27 Available at: https://eur-lex.europa.eu/legal-content/EN/TXT/?uri=celex%3A32016R0679.
28 Available at: https://eur-lex.europa.eu/legal-content/EN/TXT/?uri=celex%3A32016L0680.
29 SAJFERT, J., QUINTEL, T.: *Data Protection Directive (EU) 2016/680 for Police and Criminal Justice Authorities*. 2019, p. 10. Available at: https://papers.ssrn.com/sol3/papers.cfm?abstract_id=3285873.
30 See https://sancananavrat.sk/.
31 The project was officially finished on September 30, 2023, and is continuously followed by the project Chance for Reentry 2, implemented from October 1, 2023 with an expected end date of June 2029.
32 Pursuant to Section 85 of the Slovak Act No. 475/2005 Coll. on the execution of imprisonment: "*A* ***reenter unit*** *shall be established in the institution, in which a convicted person who has been serving a sentence for more than three years as a rule, as well as a convicted person who needs to be assisted in creating favorable conditions for an independent way of life, shall be placed within a reasonable period of time prior to the expected termination of the execution of his/her sentence;*"
33 *Výstupná analýza – Šanca na návrat [eng. Exit Analysis –Chance for Reentry]*. Bratislava: General Directorate of the Corps of Prison and Court Guard Service, 2022, p. 58. Available at: https://sancananavrat.sk/wp-content/uploads/2023/04/Vystupna-analyza.pdf.
34 See https://sancananavrat.sk/wp-content/uploads/2023/05/Letak-SNN-SK_web_05_2023.pdf.
35 *Výstupná analýza – Šanca na návrat [Exit Analysis –Chance for Reentry]*, p. 59.
36 *Výstupná analýza – Šanca na návrat [Exit Analysis –Chance for Reentry]*, p. 58–59.
37 LULEI, M., TALLOVÁ B., ĽORKO, J.: Vývoj, obsah a výsledky pilotných testovaní nástrojov na hodnotenie rizík a určenie potrieb odsúdených osôb v zbore väzenskej a justičnej stráže na Slovensku, p. 72.
38 *Výstupná analýza – Šanca na návrat [Exit Analysis –Chance for Reentry]*, p. 64.
39 *Výstupná analýza – Šanca na návrat [Exit Analysis –Chance for Reentry]*, p. 63.
40 LULEI, M., TALLOVÁ B., ĽORKO, J.: Vývoj, obsah a výsledky pilotných testovaní nástrojov na hodnotenie rizík a určenie potrieb odsúdených osôb v zbore väzenskej a justičnej stráže na Slovensku, p. 68.
41 See https://sancananavrat.sk/wp-content/uploads/2023/05/Letak-SNN-SK_web_05_2023.pdf.
42 LULEI, M., TALLOVÁ B., ĽORKO, J.: Vývoj, obsah a výsledky pilotných testovaní nástrojov na hodnotenie rizík a určenie potrieb odsúdených osôb v zbore väzenskej a justičnej stráže na Slovensku, p. 70.
43 See https://sancananavrat.sk/wp-content/uploads/2023/04/Letak_CRA_web2.pdf.

44 LULEI, M., TALLOVÁ B., ĽORKO, J.: Vývoj, obsah a výsledky pilotných testovaní nástrojov na hodnotenie rizík a určenie potrieb odsúdených osôb v zbore väzenskej a justičnej stráže na Slovensku, p. 71.
45 See https://sancananavrat.sk/wp-content/uploads/2023/04/Letak_CRA_web2.pdf.
46 LULEI, M., TALLOVÁ B., ĽORKO, J.: Vývoj, obsah a výsledky pilotných testovaní nástrojov na hodnotenie rizík a určenie potrieb odsúdených osôb v zbore väzenskej a justičnej stráže na Slovensku, p. 67.
47 *Výstupná analýza – Šanca na návrat [Exit Analysis –Chance for Reentry]*, p. 65.
48 *Výstupná analýza – Šanca na návrat [Exit Analysis –Chance for Reentry]*, p. 74.
49 Available at: https://sancananavrat.sk/wp-content/uploads/2023/05/Letak-SNN-SK_web_05_2023.pdf, p. 5.
50 LULEI, M., TALLOVÁ B., ĽORKO, J.: Vývoj, obsah a výsledky pilotných testovaní nástrojov na hodnotenie rizík a určenie potrieb odsúdených osôb v zbore väzenskej a justičnej stráže na Slovensku, p. 67.

Bibliography

ANDREWS, D. A., BONTA, J., WORMITH J. S.: The recent past and near future of risk and/or need assessment. *Crime & Delinquency*. Volume 52, Issue 1, 2006, pp. 7–27

HOFFMAN, P. J.: Recidivism among released federal prisoners – Salient factor score and five-year follow-up. *Criminal Justice and Behavior*. Volume 12, Issue 4, 1985, pp. 501–507

KOLAŘÍKOVÁ, L., HORÁK, F.: *Umělá intelligence & právo [Artificial Intelligence & Law]*. Prague: Wolters Kluwer 2020, 216 pp., ISBN 978-80-7598-784-6.

LULEI, M., TALLOVÁ B., ĽORKO, J.: Vývoj, obsah a výsledky pilotných testovaní nástrojov na hodnotenie rizík a určenie potrieb odsúdených osôb v zbore väzenskej a justičnej stráže na Slovensku [eng. Development, Content and Results of Pilot Testing of Risk Assessment and Needs Assessment Tools for Convicted Persons in the Prison and Court Guard Service in Slovakia]. *Collection of papers from the International scientific conference on forensic social work "Theoretical and practical basis of Social Work with perpetrators and victims of delinquent activities."* Bratislava: Comenius University Bratislava, 2021, pp. 65–75.

OSWALD, M. et al.: *The UK Algorithmic Transparency Standard: A Qualitative Analysis of Police Perspectives*. 2022. Available at: https://papers.ssrn.com/sol3/papers.cfm?abstract_id=4155549.

ROBERTS, J. V., PINA-SÁNCHEZ, J.: Previous convictions at Sentencing: exploring empirical trends in the Crown court. *Criminal Law Review (London, England)*. Vol. 2014, Issue 8, 2014, pp. 575–588. Available at: https://www.researchgate.net/publication/292828321_Previous_convictions_at_sentencing_Exploring_Empirical_Trends_in_the_Crown_Court#fullTextFileContent

SAJFERT, J., QUINTEL, T.: *Data Protection Directive (EU) 2016/680 for Police and Criminal Justice Authorities*. 2019, 22 pp. Available at: https://papers.ssrn.com/sol3/papers.cfm?abstract_id=3285873

VAN GINNEKEN, E.F.J.C.: The use of risk assessment in sentencing. J.W. de Keijser, J.V. Roberts, & J. Ryberg (eds.), *Predictive sentencing: Normative and empirical perspectives*. Oxford: Hart Publishing 2019, pp. 9–32. Available at: https://scholar.google.com/scholar_lookup?title=The%20use%20of%20risk%20assessment%20in%20sentencing&author=E.F.J.C.%20van%20Ginneken&publication_year=2019&pages=9-32

VON HIRSCH, A.: *Doing justice: The choice of punishments*. New York: Hill and Wang 1976. In *Výstupná analýza – Šanca na návrat [eng. Exit Analysis –Chance for Reentry]*. Bratislava: General Directorate of the Corps of Prison and Court Guard Service, 2022, 132 pp. Available at: https://sancananavrat.sk/wp-content/uploads/2023/04/Vystupna-analyza.pdf

World prison brief: https://www.prisonstudies.org/highest-to-lowest/prison_population_rate?field_region_taxonomy_tid=All

Online sources

- https://theconversation.com/a-black-box-ai-system-has-been-influencing-criminal-justice-decisions-for-over-two-decades-its-time-to-open-it-up-200594
- https://www.technologyreview.com/2019/01/21/137783/algorithms-criminal-justice-ai/
- https://www.ojp.gov/pdffiles1/nij/252038.pdf
- https://www.technologyreview.com/2020/07/17/1005396/predictive-policing-algorithms-racist-dismantled-machine-learning-bias-criminal-justice/
- https://news.harvard.edu/gazette/story/newsplus/how-social-change-brings-bias-to-predictive-models-used-in-criminal-justice-settings/
- https://www.mdpi.com/2078-2489/14/8/426
- https://www.sciencedirect.com/science/article/pii/S0047235222000228
- https://www.justiceinspectorates.gov.uk/hmiprobation/research/the-evidence-base-probation/supervision-of-service-users/assessment/
- https://sancananavrat.sk/
- https://sancananavrat.sk/wp-content/uploads/2023/04/Letak_CRA_web2.pdf
- https://www.cdc.gov/violenceprevention/pdf/ipv/ipvandsvscreening.pdf
- https://home-affairs.ec.europa.eu/system/files/2021-04/ran_cons_overv_pap_risk_assessment_in_prison_20210210_en.pdf

Index

FSC
www.fsc.org
MIX
Papier | Fördert gute Waldnutzung
FSC® C083411

Kolibri 360 GmbH
Ferdinand-Jühlke-Straße 7
99095 Erfurt, Deutschland
produktsicherheit@kolibri360.de